# DAY HIKING OREGON COAST

3rd Edition

Bonnie Henderson

MOUNTAINEERS BOOKS

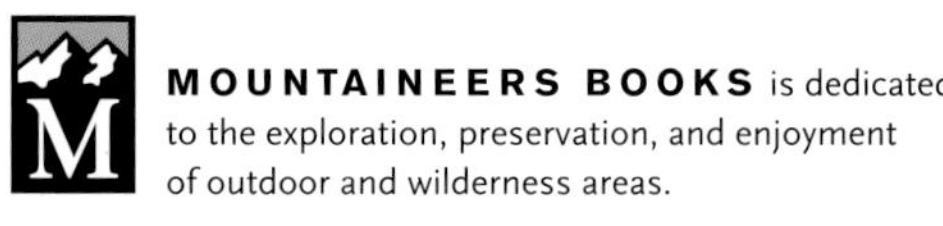

**MOUNTAINEERS BOOKS** is dedicated
to the exploration, preservation, and enjoyment
of outdoor and wilderness areas.

1001 SW Klickitat Way, Suite 201, Seattle, WA 98134
800-553-4453, www.mountaineersbooks.org



Printed in China
First edition, 2007. Second edition 2015. Third edition 2026.
Design: Jen Grable
Layout: McKenzie Long, Cardinal Innovative
Cartographer: Pease Press
All photographs by the author unless credited otherwise
Cover photograph: *Hikers can glimpse Short Sand Beach from the trail to Cape Falcon (Hike 19).*
Frontispiece: *Sunrise on Old Highway 101 Scenic Trail at Humbug Mountain State Park (Hike 95)* (Photo Vickie Skellcerf)
Final page: *The bouldery beach north of Seven Devils State Recreation Site is accessible only at low tide (Beach Walk 86).*

Leave No Trace Seven Principles © Leave No Trace, www.LNT.org

Library of Congress Cataloging-in-Publication Data is on file

Mountaineers Books titles may be purchased for corporate, educational, or other promotional sales, and our authors are available for a wide range of events. For information on special discounts or booking an author, contact our customer service at 800-553-4453 or mbooks@mountaineersbooks.org.

Printed on FSC®-certified materials

MIX
Paper | Supporting responsible forestry
FSC www.fsc.org FSC® C188448

ISBN (paperback): 978-1-68051-674-6
ISBN (ebook): 978-1-68051-675-3

*An independent nonprofit publisher since 1960*

# DAY HIKING
# OREGON COAST

# Contents

## Sand Lake to Pacific City



## Neskowin to Roads End, Lincoln City



## Lincoln City and Depoe Bay



## Newport to Beaver Creek



# THE CENTRAL COAST

## Seal Rock to Cape Perpetua



## Heceta Head to Florence

## Oregon Dunes North



## Oregon Dunes South



# THE SOUTH COAST

## Coos Bay to Bandon



## Bandon to Floras Lake



## Floras Lake to Humbug Mountain



## Humbug Mountain to Gold Beach

## Gold Beach to Crook Point



## Boardman to the Border



**OPPOSITE:** *Three Arch Rocks, in the ocean off Oceanside, is a haven for nesting seabirds.*

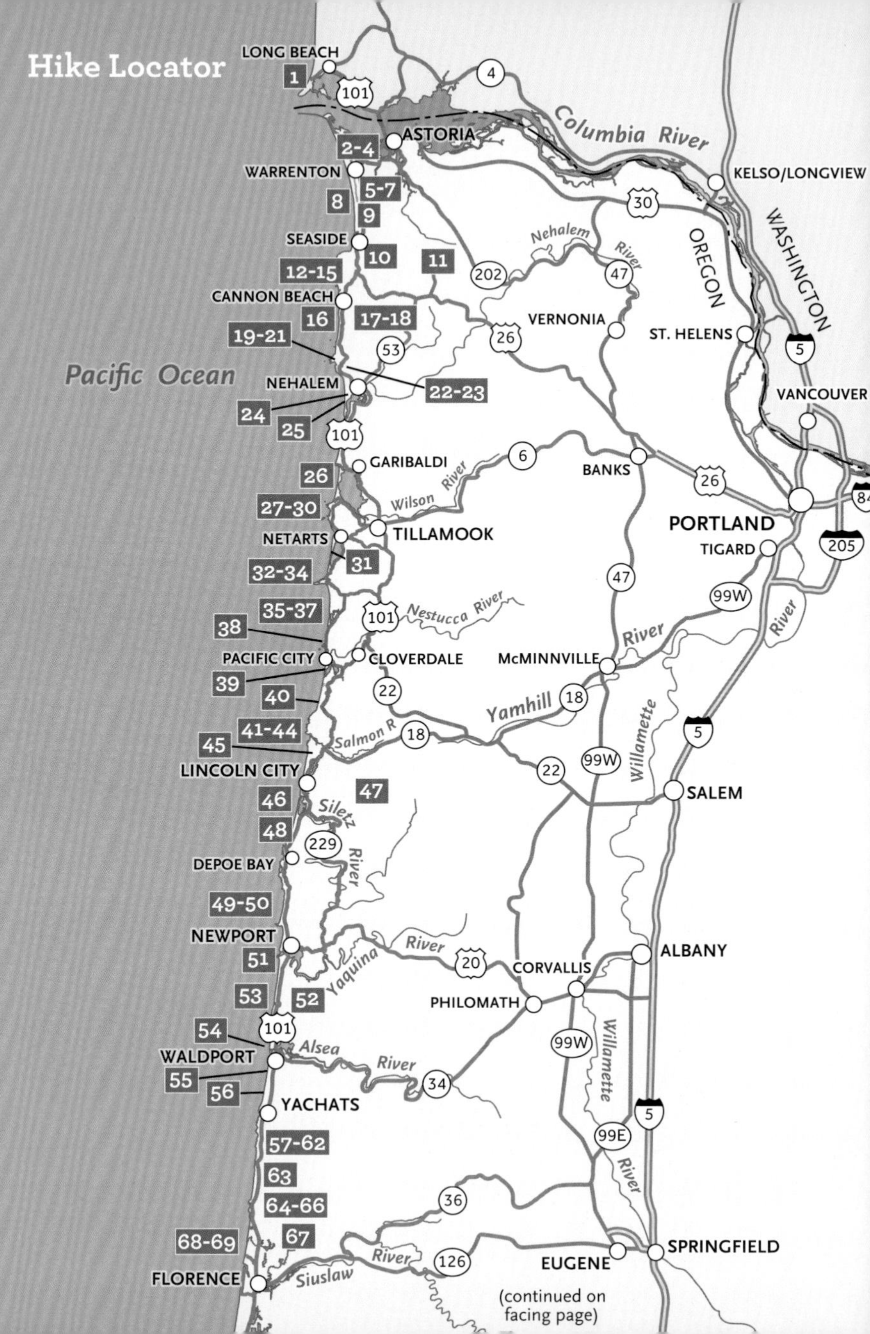

(continued on facing page)

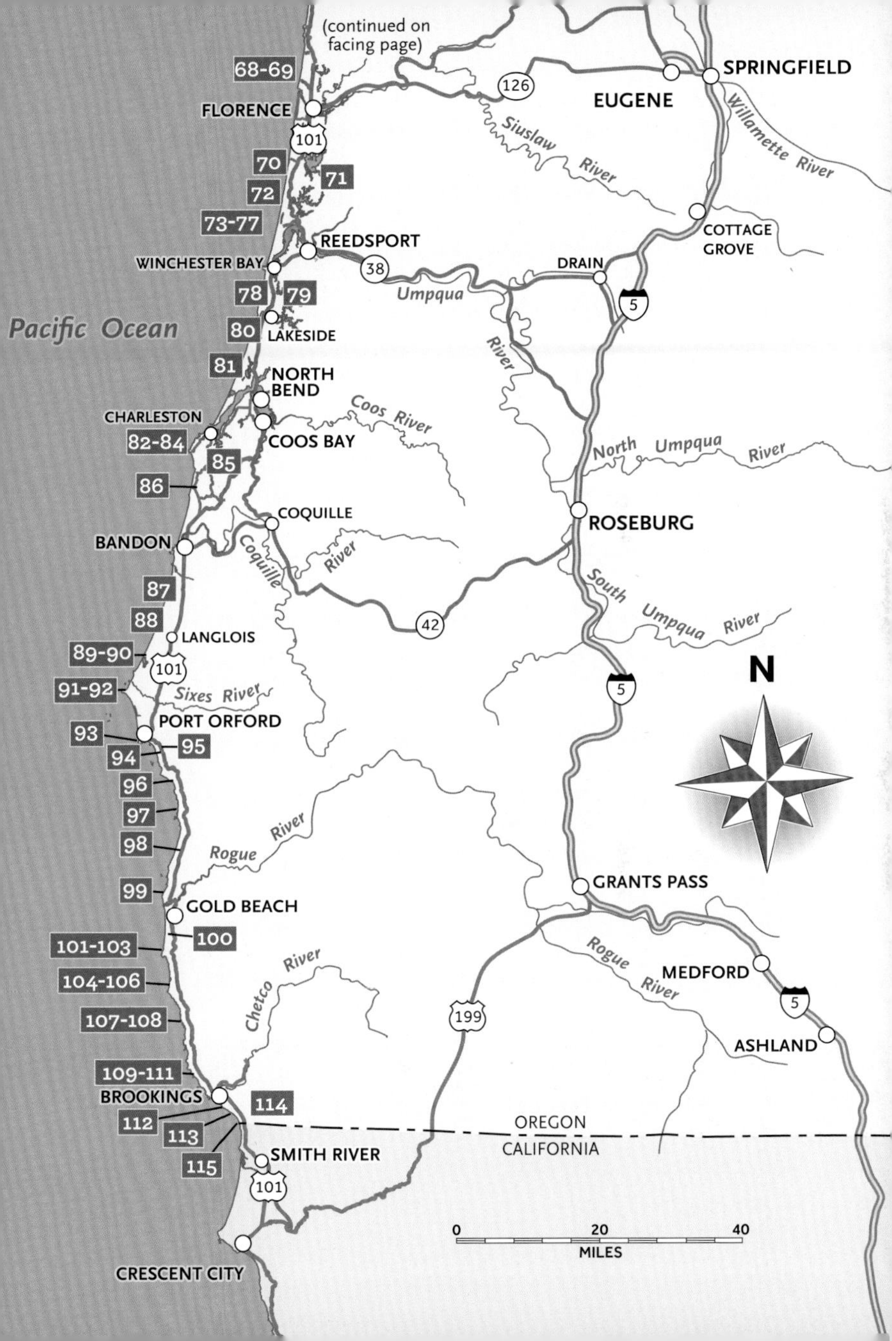
(continued on facing page)
68-69
FLORENCE
101
126
EUGENE
SPRINGFIELD
Siuslaw River
Willamette River
70
71
72
73-77
REEDSPORT
WINCHESTER BAY
38
COTTAGE GROVE
DRAIN
Umpqua River
5
78
79
Pacific Ocean
80
LAKESIDE
81
NORTH BEND
Coos River
CHARLESTON
82-84
COOS BAY
85
North Umpqua River
86
COQUILLE
ROSEBURG
BANDON
Coquille River
South Umpqua River
87
88
42
LANGLOIS
89-90
101
91-92
Sixes River
5
N
PORT ORFORD
93
95
94
96
97
Rogue River
98
99
GOLD BEACH
GRANTS PASS
100
101-103
Rogue River
MEDFORD
104-106
Chetco River
5
199
107-108
ASHLAND
109-111
BROOKINGS
114
112
113
OREGON
115
CALIFORNIA
SMITH RIVER
101
0
20
40
MILES
CRESCENT CITY

# Hikes at a Glance

| HIKE | ROUNDTRIP DISTANCE (IN MILES) | RATING |
|---|---|---|
| **THE NORTH COAST** | | |
| **Columbia River to Seaside** | | |
| 1. North Head and McKenzie Head | 4 | ** |
| 2. Beach Walk: Columbia River to Gearhart | 16 one way | |
| 3. Skipanon River Trail | 1.8 | ** |
| 4. Coffenbury–Swash Lake Loop | 6.8 | ** |
| 5. Fort to Sea—Kwis Kwis Trails, East Loop | 2.7 | *** |
| 6. Fort to Sea—Kwis Kwis Trails, West Loop | 4.2 | *** |
| 7. Fort Clatsop South Slough Loop | 3.3 | *** |
| 8. Sunset Beach via Fort to Sea Trail | 5 | ** |
| **Seaside to Arch Cape** | | |
| 9. Beach Walk: Seaside | 2.5 one way | |
| 10. Circle Creek Wetlands Walk | 2.4 | ** |
| 11. Saddle Mountain | 4.8 | *** |
| 12. Tillamook Head | 10 | *** |
| 13. Clatsop Loop Trail | 2.7 | ** |
| 14. Indian Point to Ecola Point | 4.5 | ** |
| 15. Crescent Beach | 2.4 | *** |
| 16. Beach Walk: Cannon Beach to Arch Cape | 7.4 one way | |
| 17. Cannon Beach Trail Loop | 2.3 | ** |
| 18. Ecola Creek Forest Reserve | 3.2 | ** |
| **Cape Falcon to Tillamook Bay** | | |
| 19. Cape Falcon | 4 | *** |
| 20. Short Sand Beach | 1 | ** |
| 21. Elk Flats to Short Sand Beach | 2.5 | ** |
| 22. Neahkahnie Mountain North Trail | 4.4 | *** |
| 23. Neahkahnie Mountain South Trail | 2.8 | *** |
| 24. Beach Walk: Manzanita | 5.2 one way | |
| 25. Beach Walk: Rockaway Beach | 6 one way | |
| **Cape Meares to Cape Lookout** | | |
| 26. Bayocean Spit | 5.2 | ** |
| 27. Beach Walk: Cape Meares | 5.4 one way | |

DOG-FRIENDLY WILDFLOWERS OLD GROWTH HISTORICAL
WHALE WATCHING TIDEPOOLS ESTUARY VIEWS SAND DUNES

| DIFFICULTY | Dog-friendly | Wildflowers | Old growth | Historical | Whale watching | Tidepools | Estuary views | Sand dunes |
|---|---|---|---|---|---|---|---|---|
| | | | | | | | | |
| | | | | | | | | |
| 2 | • | | | • | • | | • | |
| flat | • | | | | | | | |
| 1 | • | | | • | | | | |
| 3 | • | | | • | | | | |
| 2 | • | | • | • | | | | |
| 3 | • | | • | • | | | | |
| 2 | • | • | | • | | | | |
| 2 | • | | | • | | | | |
| | | | | | | | | |
| flat | • | | | | | | | |
| 2 | | | • | | | | | |
| 3 | | • | • | | | | | |
| 3 | • | | • | • | | | | |
| 2 | • | | • | • | | | | |
| 2 | • | | • | | | | | |
| 2 | • | | • | | | | | |
| flat | • | | | | | • | | |
| 2 | • | | | | | | | |
| 2 | • | | • | | | | | |
| | | | | | | | | |
| 3 | • | | • | | • | | | |
| 1 | • | | • | | | • | | |
| 2 | • | | | | • | • | | |
| 3 | • | • | • | | • | | | |
| 2 | • | • | • | | • | | | |
| flat | | | | | | | | |
| flat | • | | | | | | | |
| | | | | | | | | |
| 3 | • | | | • | | | • | |
| flat | • | | | | | | | |

| HIKE | ROUNDTRIP DISTANCE (IN MILES) | RATING |
|---|---|---|
| 28. Cape Meares Summit | 4 | ** |
| 29. Beach Walk: Short Beach | 0.7 one way | |
| 30. Beach Walk: Oceanside | 2.7 one way | |
| 31. Beach Walk: Netarts Spit | 5.8 one way | |
| 32. Cape Lookout North Trail | 4.6 | ** |
| 33. Cape Lookout Trail | 4.7 | *** |
| 34. Cape Lookout South Trail | 3.6 | ** |
| **Sand Lake to Pacific City** | | |
| 35. Beach Walk: Cape Lookout to Sand Lake Estuary | 4 one way | |
| 36. Whalen Island | 1.4 | * |
| 37. Sitka Sedge Loop | 3.5 | ** |
| 38. Beach Walk: Sand Lake Estuary to Nestucca Spit | 8.5 one way | |
| 39. Two Rivers Peninsula Loop | 2.5 | ** |
| **Neskowin to Roads End, Lincoln City** | | |
| 40. Beach Walk: Nestucca Bay to Neskowin | 4.8 one way | |
| 41. Cascade Head North Rainforest Trail | 5 | * |
| 42. Harts Cove | 13.4 | *** |
| 43. Cascade Head South Rainforest Trail | 7 | ** |
| 44. Cascade Head Preserve | 4.8 | *** |
| 45. The Knoll | 3.1 | ** |
| **Lincoln City and Depoe Bay** | | |
| 46. Beach Walk: Lincoln City | 7.5 one way | |
| 47. Drift Creek Falls | 3.5 | ** |
| 48. Beach Walk: Gleneden Beach | 5.7 one way | |
| **Newport to Beaver Creek** | | |
| 49. Beach Walk: North of Newport | 6 one way | |
| 50. Beach Walk: Between the Newport Lighthouses | 3.9 one way | |
| 51. Beach Walk: South Beach to Seal Rock | 8 one way | |
| 52. Beaver Creek Loop | 3.6 | ** |
| **THE CENTRAL COAST** | | |
| **Seal Rock to Cape Perpetua** | | |
| 53. Beach Walk: Seal Rock | 0.6 one way | |
| 54. Beach Walk: North of Alsea Bay | 3.2 one way | |
| 55. Beach Walk: Alsea Bay to Yachats | 6.4 one way | |
| 56. Yachats 804 Trail | 1.4 | ** |

| | DIFFICULTY | | | | | | | | |
|---|---|---|---|---|---|---|---|---|---|
| | 2 | • | | • | • | • | | | |
| | flat | • | | | | | • | | |
| | flat | • | | | | | • | | |
| | flat | • | | | | | | | |
| | 3 | • | | • | | | | | |
| | 3 | • | | • | | • | | | |
| | 2 | • | | • | | | • | | |
| | | | | | | | | | |
| | flat | • | | | | | • | | |
| | 1 | • | | | | | | • | |
| | 1 | • | | | | | | • | |
| | flat | • | | | | | | | |
| | 2 | | • | | | | | • | |
| | | | | | | | | | |
| | flat | • | | | | | • | | |
| | 2 | • | | • | | | | | |
| | 3 | • | • | • | | • | | | |
| | 3 | • | | • | | | | | |
| | 2–3 | | • | • | | • | | • | |
| | 2 | • | | • | | • | | | |
| | | | | | | | | | |
| | flat | • | | | | | | | |
| | 2 | • | | • | | | | | |
| | flat | • | | | | | | | |
| | | | | | | | | | |
| | flat | • | | | | | • | | |
| | flat | • | | | | | • | | |
| | flat | • | | | | | | | |
| | 2 | • | | | | | | • | |
| | | | | | | | | | |
| | | | | | | | | | |
| | flat | • | | | | | • | | |
| | flat | • | | | | | | | |
| | flat | • | | | | | | | |
| | 1 | • | | | | | | | |

| HIKE | ROUNDTRIP DISTANCE (IN MILES) | RATING |
|---|---|---|
| 57. Amanda Trail | 5.4 | ** |
| 58. Cape Perpetua: Four Short Hikes | 0.9 to 2.2 | ** |
| 59. St. Perpetua Trail | 3.2 | ** |
| 60. Cooks Ridge | 7.2 | ** |
| 61. Gwynn Creek–Cooks Ridge Loop | 6.3 | *** |
| 62. Cummins Creek Loop | 6.2 | *** |
| 63. Cummins Ridge | 11.6 | ** |
| **Heceta Head to Florence** | | |
| 64. Beach Walk: Rock Creek to Hobbit Beach | 3 one way | |
| 65. China Creek Loop | 3.9 | *** |
| 66. Heceta Head Lighthouse | 2.4 | ** |
| 67. Cape Mountain Loop | 7.5 | ** |
| 68. Beach Walk: Baker Beach to the Siuslaw River | 6.4 one way | |
| 69. Sutton Creek Trail | 5.4 | *** |
| **Oregon Dunes North** | | |
| 70. Beach Walk: Siuslaw River to Siltcoos River | 9.7 one way | |
| 71. Siltcoos Lake | 5 | ** |
| 72. Beach Walk: Siltcoos River to Umpqua River | 14.1 one way | |
| 73. Waxmyrtle Trail | 2.4 | ** |
| 74. Taylor and Carter Dunes | 2.7 | ** |
| 75. Oregon Dunes Loop | 4.5 | ** |
| 76. Tahkenitch Creek Loop | 5.1 | ** |
| 77. Tahkenitch–Threemile Lake Loop | 6.6 | *** |
| **Oregon Dunes South** | | |
| 78. Beach Walk: Umpqua River to Tenmile Creek | 8.6 one way | |
| 79. Eel Lake | 4 | ** |
| 80. John Dellenback Dunes Trail | 5.2 | *** |
| 81. Beach Walk: Tenmile Creek to North Spit Coos Bay | 15.6 one way | |
| **THE SOUTH COAST** | | |
| **Coos Bay to Bandon** | | |
| 82. Beach Walk: Bastendorff | 1 one way | |
| 83. Sunset Bay to Simpson Reef Overlook | 6.6 | ** |
| 84. Cape Arago Pack Trail Loop | 3.6 | ** |
| 85. Coos Bay South Slough Loop | 3 | *** |
| 86. Beach Walk: Seven Devils to Coquille Spit | 10.5 one way | |

| | DIFFICULTY | | | | | | | | |
|---|---|---|---|---|---|---|---|---|---|
| | 3 | • | | • | • | • | | | |
| | 1 | • | | • | | | • | | |
| | 3 | • | • | • | | • | | | |
| | 3 | • | | • | | | | | |
| | 3 | • | | • | | | | | |
| | 3 | • | | • | | | | | |
| | 3 | • | | • | | | | | |
| | | | | | | | | | |
| | flat | • | | | | | | | |
| | 2 | • | | • | | | | | |
| | 2 | • | | • | • | • | | | |
| | 3 | • | | | • | | | | |
| | flat | | | | | | | | |
| | 3 | • | | | | | | | |
| | | | | | | | | | |
| | flat | • | | | | | | | |
| | 2 | • | | • | | | | | |
| | flat | | | | | | | | |
| | 2 | | | | | | | • | |
| | 2 | | | | | | | | • |
| | 2 | | | | | | | | • |
| | 3 | | | | | | | • | • |
| | 3 | | | | | | | | • |
| | | | | | | | | | |
| | flat | | | | | | | | |
| | 2 | • | | • | | | | | |
| | 3 | | | | | | | | • |
| | flat | | | | | | | | |
| | | | | | | | | | |
| | | | | | | | | | |
| | flat | • | | | | | | | |
| | 3 | • | | | | • | | | |
| | 2 | • | | • | | | | | |
| | 2 | • | | | | | | • | |
| | flat | • | | | | | • | | |

| HIKE | ROUNDTRIP DISTANCE (IN MILES) | RATING |
|---|---|---|
| **Bandon to Floras Lake** | | |
| 87. Beach Walk: Bandon to Floras Lake | 17.5 one way | |
| 88. Lost Lake | 2.6 | * |
| **Floras Lake to Humbug Mountain** | | |
| 89. Floras Lake and Blacklock Point Loop | 7.3 to 8.5 | ** |
| 90. Blacklock Point Loop | 4 to 5.2 | ** |
| 91. Beach Walk: North of Cape Blanco | 2.8 one way | |
| 92. Beach Walk: Cape Blanco to Port Orford Heads | 7 one way | |
| 93. Port Orford Heads | 1.2 | ** |
| 94. Beach Walk: Port Orford to Rocky Point | 2.4 one way | |
| 95. Humbug Old Highway 101 Loop | 1.7 | * |
| 96. Humbug Mountain | 5.3 | *** |
| **Humbug Mountain to Gold Beach** | | |
| 97. Beach Walk: Arizona Beach to Sisters Rocks | 1.8 one way | |
| 98. Beach Walk: Ophir to Neskia Beach | 5.8 one way | |
| 99. Beach Walk: Otter Point to the Rogue River | 3 one way | |
| **Gold Beach to Crook Point** | | |
| 100. Beach Walk: Gold Beach | 5.5 one way | |
| 101. Cape Sebastian 333 Trail Loop | 4.2 | ** |
| 102. Cape Sebastian Waterfall Trail | 3.8 | ** |
| 103. Cape Sebastian | 3.4 | ** |
| 104. Beach Walk: Cape Sebastian to Pistol River | 2.2 one way | |
| 105. Beach Walk: Pistol River to Crook Point | 2.3 one way | |
| 106. Lola Lake Loop | 5.8 | ** |
| **Boardman to the Border** | | |
| 107. Secret Beach | 1 to 2.9 | *** |
| 108. China Beach | 1.5 | *** |
| 109. Indian Sands | 2.5 | ** |
| 110. Whaleshead Beach Loop | 3.6 | ** |
| 111. House Rock Viewpoint to Lone Ranch Beach | 4 | *** |
| 112. Beach Walks: Brookings Beaches | 0.4 to 0.8 one way | |
| 113. Beach Walk: McVay Beach to Winchuck River | 2.5 one way | |
| 114. Oregon Redwoods Trail | 2.2 | ** |
| 115. Beach Walk: Winchuck River to Pelican State Park | 0.7 one way | |

| | DIFFICULTY | | | | | | | | |
|---|---|---|---|---|---|---|---|---|---|
| | | | | | | | | | |
| | flat | | | | | | • | | |
| | 2 | • | | | | | | | • |
| | | | | | | | | | |
| | 3 | • | | | | • | | | |
| | 2 | • | | | | • | | | |
| | flat | • | | | | | • | | |
| | flat | • | | | | | | | |
| | 1 | • | • | | • | • | | | |
| | flat | • | | | | | | | |
| | 2 | • | | | | | | | |
| | 3 | • | | • | | | | | |
| | | | | | | | | | |
| | flat | • | | | | | • | | |
| | flat | • | | | | | | | |
| | flat | • | | | | | | | |
| | | | | | | | | | |
| | flat | • | | | | | | | |
| | 2 | • | | • | | | | | |
| | 2 | • | | • | | • | | | |
| | 3 | • | | • | | • | | | |
| | flat | • | | | | | | | |
| | flat | • | | | | | | | |
| | 3 | • | | | | | | | |
| | | | | | | | | | |
| | 1–2 | • | | • | | | • | | |
| | 1 | • | | • | | | • | | |
| | 2 | • | | • | • | | | | |
| | 2 | • | | • | | | | | |
| | 3 | • | | • | | • | | | |
| | flat | • | | | | | • | | |
| | flat | • | | | | | • | | |
| | 2 | • | | • | | | | | |
| | flat | | | | | | | | |

# Introduction: Oregon's Hikeable Coastline

The Oregon coast you glimpse from your car window while traveling down US Highway 101, with its busy towns—its motels and outlet malls and casinos and golf courses—is one Oregon coast. But there's another Oregon coast, a timeless realm of primeval forests and undulating sand dunes, of wide beaches, hidden coves, and towering headlands, elk, and eagles. The Oregon coast has not been spared development. But there remain long and short stretches of wildness, where the ocean's roar drowns out all other sounds and the views haven't changed much in thousands of years. That Oregon coast is the subject of this guidebook.

Why hike the Oregon coast? The area's combination of accessibility and remoteness, walkable sandy beaches and hikeable forested headlands, is unique in the United States. Tidepools, secluded beaches, forests, shifting sand dunes: All are part of the Oregon coast hiking experience. And it's easy to reach. From Portland and other population centers in western Oregon, the beach is a bit more than an hour away by car. The weather is mild. It rarely snows at the coast in winter, so trails are accessible year-round. Even in the stormy winter months there are always opportunities to sneak in a beach walk during a sun break or, with raingear, a hike in the coastal forest during a drizzle.

Generations of Oregonians have preserved, and continue to preserve, large stretches of beachfront and nearby land for public use and secured beach access at frequent intervals along their coastline. Since humans first arrived here and continuing into the early automobile era, the beaches have served as the coast's primary north–south highway. Oregon's landmark 1967 Beach Bill formalized that tradition, granting the public access to all of the state's beaches, not just to the high-tide line but all the way to the vegetation line. Construction of US 101 in the 1930s moved thru traffic off the beach; most beaches in Oregon are now vehicle-free.

In addition to beachfront land, large portions of headlands and estuaries have been conserved, some primarily for the benefit of wildlife but most of it accessible to humans on foot. These trails have been linked with the beaches to create the border-to-border Oregon Coast Trail, unique in the nation.

This book is a comprehensive guide to day hikes and beach walks on Oregon's shoreline and adjacent public lands. Its scope is the entire coastline—the beaches and headlands—immediately accessible from US 101 (plus a few in the western foothills of the Coast Range that I couldn't resist including, and one across the Columbia River in Washington).

Bear in mind that hikes on the Oregon coast are, generally speaking, not on wilderness trails. Some trails feel quite remote

**OPPOSITE:** *All of Oregon's sandy beach is public land up to the vegetation line.*

## THE FIRST PEOPLE ON THE OREGON COAST

A walk today down the beaches and through the dunes and forests of the Oregon coast is a walk through the traditional lands of dozens of different tribes. Though all are influenced by the marine environment, their languages and cultures are in some cases vastly different from those of their neighbors, as their ancestors arrived on the Oregon coast thousands of years ago at different times and via different routes.

People have been living on the Oregon coast for a long time. For decades archaeologists thought that the first migrants from Asia arrived about 13,500 years ago, traveling overland across the Bering Land Bridge (better known as the Beringia subcontinent) to the middle of the continent and spreading south (and east and west) from there. But the latest archaeological evidence suggests that the first people probably came at least 16,000 to 17,000 years ago—maybe as much as 20,000 to 30,000 years ago. And they likely came not on foot but by boat, sustained in large part by the resource-rich kelp beds in the nearshore ocean of the North Pacific.

But it was not the same Oregon coast we know today. By the height of the Last Glacial Maximum about 20,000 years ago, sea levels worldwide were more than 400 feet lower than they are today. That put Oregon's shoreline far to the west—in some places more than 20 miles west. Not until about 6,000 years ago did the sea off Oregon rise to reach about where it is today. That sea level rise has complicated archaeology on the Oregon coast. Much of the evidence of the first people's daily lives—the middens, the charcoal from fires, the dwellings and tools they used—has since drowned or been destroyed by waves. And with huge tsunamis striking the Oregon coast from offshore earthquakes every 300 to 700 years or so, whole communities may have disappeared in an instant, to later be replaced by new arrivals.

To date, the earliest known evidence of people on the Oregon coast comes from Indian Sands, north of Brookings, where ancient stone tools and chips from tool-making operations have been found. Remnants of a stone hearth, pieces of charcoal and flakes of stone 7 feet below ground, found on a bluff south of Bandon, indicate that the area was inhabited as much as 10,000 years ago. More evidence in the form of large middens has been found in the Oregon Dunes, near Tahkenitch Lake and at other sites. Middens are ancient refuse heaps where people piled shells, fish bones, and other waste from meals. Middens also reveal everyday objects and evidence of isolated houses and burials.

We know more about coastal dwellers from the past 1500 years. During most of this period, people lived in rectangular houses built of split cedar or redwood planks. Some houses on the north coast were very large—up to 100 feet long and 40 feet wide—and were home to several families or even an entire village. On the south coast, each family in a village tended to have its own small plank house. These homes were clustered at the mouths of rivers and bays, where food was most plentiful.

Despite the brutality of colonialization, including devastation from the introduction of new diseases, descendants of survivors still live here and know this land as their traditional homelands. They're improving life in their own communities (and making charitable gifts to improve life for others in Oregon) with funds from casinos in such towns as Florence, Lincoln City, Coos Bay, and Grande Ronde. Some honor their culture and celebrate their heritage with newly built community plank houses modeled after those that sheltered their ancestors.

*If the wind's up, be sure to bring a kite to the beach at Oceanside.*

and aren't particularly well traveled, granting hikers a degree of solitude. Some beaches may not be visited by humans for days at a time; others are popular, even crowded on summer weekends. But part of what's so appealing about the Oregon coast is its variety. It's quite easy in summer to find a popular beach abuzz with vacation energy: kites flying, children building sand castles, dogs and their people, friends huddled around beach fires into the evening. It's just as easy, if you know where to go, to find a remote beach where there are few, if any, other people with whom to share miles of open sand or an orange-and-rose sunset. This book is designed to help you pick and choose the kind of coastal experience you want.

## TAKE THE KIDS

With so many relatively easy, appealing, and varied trails, the Oregon coast is a great place to take children hiking. Pick a trail with a special destination, such as a waterfall or cape-top view, or one that leads to a hidden beach. After all, the beach itself is the main attraction for kids. Opportunities to fly kites or build sand castles add interest to a beach walk. But try going empty-handed and let the kids make their own fun: gently nudging the tentacles of a sea urchin in a tidepool; prowling the beach for agates or fossil shells; poking around in the driftline after high tide for piles of ropy kelp, feathers, seaweed, or flotsam spilled from container ships; or finding long-at-sea lumber hosting colonies of gooseneck barnacles, plastic bottles labeled in foreign languages, and other "treasures."

Keep an eye on children. Every winter in particular, bad things happen on the Oregon coast to people of all ages who turn their back on the ocean, or who jump onto drift logs that get lifted and rolled by incoming waves, or who clamber on slippery shoreline rocks (see Hazards). The ocean here is cold, the currents strong, and the surf often rough. Take the kids to the beach, by all means! Just take reasonable precautions and plan to wade, not swim.

## WHAT TO TAKE

For longer coastal trail hikes or beach walks, carry the same gear you would on any hike or backpacking trip (see Ten Essentials). A few suggestions specific to the Oregon coast:

**Raingear.** Most of the year it's a good idea to at least carry it.

**Mosquito repellent.** Not a problem most places, but mosquitoes can appear in boggy areas in spring and summer.

**Sunscreen.**

**Water.** Potable water is sometimes, but not always, available at trailheads; you'd be wise to bring your own.

**A tide table.** Little booklets with a year's worth of tides for a specific area are widely available on the coast and often given out for free, or you can use an online app such as Tide Alert from the National Oceanic and Atmospheric Administration (NOAA). Make sure you check for your specific location, as high and low tides vary widely from south to north (by as much as one and a half hours). Most beaches can be walked at any tide in summer, but some rocky points can only be rounded at low tide, and some beaches disappear during winter's highest tides.

## THE TEN ESSENTIALS

The following list of Ten Essentials developed by The Mountaineers is a good baseline for backpacking and for day hiking on the more remote trails and beaches in this book. The point of the Ten Essentials has always been to answer two basic questions: Can you prevent emergencies and respond positively should one occur (items 1–5)? And can you safely spend a night—or more—outside (items 6–10)? Use this list as a guide and tailor it to the needs of your outing.

1. Navigation (map and compass)
2. Headlamp (or flashlight)
3. Sun protection (sunglasses and sunscreen)
4. First-aid supplies
5. Knife (and repair kit or multitool)
6. Fire
7. Emergency shelter
8. Extra food
9. Extra water
10. Extra clothes

## OREGON BEACH DOS AND DON'TS

Oregon's beaches and headlands have some rules, and challenges, that may be unfamiliar even to experienced hikers.

**Beach fires.** Allowed on open sand, west of the vegetation line, using small wood. Fires are not allowed in or near piles of driftwood or against drift logs.

**Dogs on the beach.** On most Oregon beaches and some forest trails, dogs are allowed off-leash as long as they are under voice control. Dogs must be leashed on trails in state parks and other special areas such as South Slough National Estuarine Research Reserve. Some wildlife refuges prohibit dogs to avoid disturbing native wildlife. From March 15 to September 15, dogs are not allowed at all (on- or off-leash) on the beach on much of the central Oregon coast, including Oregon Dunes National Recreation Area (and some parts of the north and south coast), to protect nesting snowy plovers, a threatened species of shorebird; these areas are well signed. In those areas, dogs are allowed on access trails through the forest or dunes, just not on the beach itself. For more information about why and how snowy plovers are being protected in Oregon, see sidebar "Sharing the Beach with Western Snowy Plovers" in Oregon Dunes North.

**Kites.** Yes! But not everywhere. Kite-flying (and dogs and camping) are not allowed spring

## WEATHER ON THE OREGON COAST

The Oregon coast is a year-round hiking destination. Summer has by far the best weather, but winter has its charms too. With raingear, there is almost never a day when you can't enjoy a hike or a beach walk.

July through October are the warmest, driest months on the Oregon coast, but rarely is it really hot; average highs are 65°F to 70°F in summer, tempered by nearly constant north breezes that are strongest at midday. These are also the months when rivers and streams are lowest and easiest to wade and when the lowest daytime tides occur. At times in July and August, when it gets very hot inland, the coast can get socked in with fog—Fogust, some call it—accompanied by a fierce north wind for a few days at a time. October is a transitional month and can be pleasant or fiercely stormy.

November through January is the rainiest season here in the southern end of the temperate rainforest. Oregon's rainiest place is the Coast Range, where just 10 miles inland from the coast annual precipitation can reach 200 inches. On the coast, 80 to 100 inches is normal in the north, 60 inches in the Bandon–Coos Bay area, and 80 inches from Port Orford south. Seventy percent of that rain falls from November to March. What's also true is that winter on the coast, while often cloudy and sometimes drizzly, is generally mild. It rarely snows, though now and then an east wind brings a string of days with clear skies and frozen dunes.

Most years a serious winter storm or two will rip through the coast, snapping off treetops or pushing trees over, roots and all, blocking trails with blowdown. (You can still see evidence of the gale of 2007, the Labor Day 2020 windstorm, the freak snowstorm of March 2023, and others on some of these trails.) Before making a long drive to a trailhead, it's prudent to check with the relevant national forest or state park to make sure the trail you're aiming for is open.

*The Oregon coast's most dramatic weather comes in the winter, but hikers should carry raingear year-round.*

## OREGON BEACH BILL: BEACHES FOR THE PEOPLE

In most coastal states, including California and Washington, it's perfectly legal to own and fence off stretches of ocean beach from public access. In Oregon, however, all 262 miles of beaches and 64 miles of headlands are public lands and open to the public, thanks to a remarkable piece of legislation signed by a remarkable governor, Tom McCall, in 1967. But the story of Oregon's Beach Bill really begins at the turn of the twentieth century with another visionary Oregon governor, Oswald West.

Elected in 1911, Governor West was an early and forceful advocate of preservation of public lands. He convinced the state legislature to designate all Oregon beaches as public highways, since there was, in fact, no other route along the coast. "I pointed out that thus we would come into miles and miles of highway without cost to the taxpayer," he later told a reporter. "The legislature and the public took the bait—hook, line, and sinker."

West's legislation protected beaches only up to the high-tide line, however. As real estate interests began focusing more attention on the coast in the 1960s, clearly more action was needed to establish public ownership of the entire dry-sand beach. After several citizens complained to the state in July 1966 about being denied access to a portion of the beach in front of a Cannon Beach motel, a state parks committee began examining the issue. Seven months later the committee approved the Beach Bill and presented it to the legislature; within five months it was passed and was signed into law by Governor McCall. It still stands, despite appeals to the Oregon Supreme Court. For many years the beaches were administered by the state highway department; today they're overseen by the Oregon Parks and Recreation Department (OPRD).

through summer in snowy plover conservation zones; see Dogs on the Beach above.

### Leave No Trace

As outdoor enthusiasts, we have an ethical responsibility to respect the natural environment. The Leave No Trace Center for Outdoor Ethics is a nonprofit organization dedicated to using science, education, and stewardship to ensure a sustainable future for the natural world. As part of its mission, the organization has developed seven principles of Leave No Trace—a framework for us to minimize our impact on the environment. Here's how they might apply today hiking on the Oregon Coast.

**Plan ahead and prepare.** This can include avoiding peak visitation times at your intended hiking location, seeking out less-popular areas, avoiding posting about already-overused trails on social media, and always following the Leave No Trace adage of "Pack it in, Pack it out."

**Travel and camp on durable surfaces.** Stick to walking on the main trail rather than wandering off-trail, especially in sensitive habitat preserves. Avoid taking shortcuts through switchbacks or along any part of the trail, even if others have already done so. Dispose of waste properly. There are plenty of toilets at parks and waysides along the Oregon coast: look for notes in the beach walks and hike descriptions in this book and plan to use these toilets before you set out. That way you won't have to worry about how to properly handle your waste in the woods. If you do get stuck, dig a scat (or cat) hole at least 6 inches deep well off the trail (and not in the dunes in front of someone's house) and at least 200 feet from any water source, and refill the hole with soil (feces don't break down in sand). Carry a resealable plastic bag to carry out your used toilet paper and any other waste, from food wrappers to cigarette butts—even if it's not yours.

**Leave what you find.** Hunting for shells, fossils, and agates is part of the fun on a beach walk but be thoughtful about how much you carry away; other critters may want to use that shell themselves. Do not remove any historic or prehistoric relics you might find.

**Minimize the effects of campfires.** In Oregon, you are allowed to build fires with small pieces of driftwood you find on the beach, as long as they are on the open sand west of the vegetation line. But keep your bonfire's size within reason and not so huge that it's still burning when you're ready to leave. Beach fires are not allowed in piles of driftwood or against drift logs. If you purchase firewood, buy it locally to avoid introducing non-native insects that may be hiding in the wood.

**Respect wildlife.** Observe wildlife from a distance, and be especially aware during sensitive times, such as mating, calving, and nesting seasons. This applies to critters ranging from elk—a frequent sight on parts of the coast—as well as seals and their young and tiny shorebirds such as snowy plovers. If your dog tends to chase wildlife, be especially careful by keeping your dog on a leash (or leave it at home, especially during snowy plover nesting season.) Never feed wild animals.

**Be considerate of others.** People have different ways of enjoying themselves outdoors. Respect others by being considerate of the quality of their experience. Be courteous and yield to others on the trail.

*Cars are allowed on Oregon beaches in very limited locations, notably between Fort Stevens State Park and Gearhart on the northernmost coast.*

## TSUNAMIS: BE PREPARED, NOT SCARED

*Signs posted at beach access sites indicate how far local and distant tsunamis are likely to flood and remind beachgoers to move quickly to high ground after an earthquake.*

Tsunamis are an infrequent phenomenon on the Oregon coast but a possibility hikers should be aware of. Most tsunamis worldwide are triggered by earthquakes on the ocean floor. To understand the risk and how to minimize it, it's essential to understand the two very different types of tsunamis that occasionally strike the Oregon coast.

A *distant* tsunami is one caused by a very large earthquake hundreds or thousands of miles away, for instance, the coast of Japan or Alaska. These tsunamis take hours to cross the ocean to Oregon, and by the time they arrive, they typically have diminished greatly. Many towns on the Oregon coast have a system of tsunami warning sirens. If you are not near a town, be aware that arriving distant tsunamis are preceded by a sudden, significant withdrawal of water at the shore. If you notice the ocean suddenly receding far more than normal, simply move farther up or off the beach. Distant tsunamis are rare and typically are only dangerous in bays and harbors or near the waterline on the beach. Other than the tsunami following the 2011 Japan earthquake (which, by the time it reached Oregon, was perceptible only in a few harbors), the last distant tsunami large enough to do even minor damage here was in 1964, and prior to that possibly in 1899, both from earthquakes off Alaska.

A *local* tsunami is an even rarer but far more dangerous phenomenon, and the warning sign is unmistakable: It is preceded by a huge earthquake. An underwater fault line called the Cascadia Subduction Zone runs just off the Pacific Northwest coast from Vancouver Island south to Cape Mendocino, California (south of Eureka), and now and then (at intervals of about 200 to 1000 years) it generates a very large earthquake that, in turn, triggers a tsunami that strikes the coast in 12 to 30 minutes (quicker on the southern Oregon coast). If you happen to be on the beach when a large earthquake strikes (4 to 6 minutes of severe shaking), head as fast as you can to the highest ground you can reach and stay there. The last such Cascadia earthquake, a magnitude 9, struck on January 26, 1700, at about nine o'clock in the evening; the tsunami it generated devastated coastal villages and caused destruction as far away as Japan. Read my 2014 book *The Next Tsunami: Living on a Restless Coast* to learn more.

## HAZARDS

Weather, waves, tides, and the landforms they create produce particular hazards for those exploring in the coast environment. Take precautions to avoid getting into trouble with the following potential dangers.

**Sneaker waves.** These are unusually large waves that surge up the beach from an otherwise calm ocean, catching beachgoers off guard with sometimes deadly results. They used to be considered random occurrences, but researchers at Oregon State University have found that they are generated by far-off storms, and they nearly always occur from October through April on the US West Coast. In addition to actual sneaker waves, you can always be surprised by an unusually high "rogue" wave in any season. If you're knocked down near where a creek is emptying into the ocean, it's even more difficult to drag yourself out of the surf. The rule of thumb: Don't turn your back on the ocean and be particularly careful during winter beach visits.

**Ocean hazards.** If the Pacific Ocean along Oregon weren't an uninviting 47°F to 52°F year-round, even more swimmers would be caught by the rip currents (undertows) common along this coast. The danger is twofold: A swimmer fighting a rip current may be unable to swim to shore and may drown, or may perish from hypothermia, simply from excessive exposure to the cold water. If you do get caught in a current that's pulling you away from the shore, don't try to swim against it directly. It's best to work at staying afloat in a horizontal position and remaining calm. Swim or drift parallel to the shore until you get out of the current; then attempt to swim in to shore at a different spot. Better yet, wade but don't swim in the ocean off the Oregon coast (unless you're wearing a wetsuit and holding on to a surfboard).

**Rolling logs.** Stay off drift logs at or anywhere near the surf line. Not infrequently, children (and adults) playing on such logs are crushed after an unexpectedly high wave lifts and rolls the log.

**Rock shelves at the shoreline.** They're slippery, and waves can rush in and knock you off your feet; in the tumult of cold water, you may be unable to climb back out. A memorial monument on the Yachats 804 Trail attests to how quickly tragedy can strike.

**Tsunami.** Very unlikely on any given day, but something to be aware of; inform yourself. Read details in sidebar "Tsunamis: Be Prepared, Not Scared."

**Falling trees.** Stay out of headland forests during major winter storms.

**Cars.** They're allowed on the beach in a few places, mainly on the far northern coast between the *Peter Iredale* shipwreck and Gearhart. In such areas, keep your eyes open, especially near beach access points where drivers tend to speed up to get through the soft sand.

**Cliffs and jetties.** Not only does free-climbing on steep cliff faces pose obvious, inherent risks, but much of the rock at the shore is crumbly sandstone, which only increases the danger of falling. Some popular trails follow right along the tops of steep seaside cliffs—safe only if you stick to the trail. Informal spur trails leading from marked trails down to hidden beaches or coves are to be taken at your own risk. Walk out onto a bay-mouth jetty only with great caution. It may look (and be) safe at low tide, but when the tide rises, large waves may wash onto the jetty, particularly during storms.

**Poison oak.** You may encounter patches of poison oak along the trails on the southern Oregon coast (I have seen it only south of Port Orford). If you're unfamiliar with it, look it up. It's extremely annoying if you're sensitive to it; figure on two weeks of itching, weeping skin.

## LESS-WORRISOME HAZARDS

**Bears.** There are black bears on the Oregon coast, but they're small (females are 5 to 6 feet long, 125 to 200 pounds, so probably

## HIKING THE OREGON COAST TRAIL

*Backpackers on the Oregon Coast Trail traverse beaches, forested headlands, rivers and creeks, and open sand dunes.*

The Oregon coast offers long-distance hikers the opportunity to walk the state's coast border to border, from the Columbia River to California, almost entirely on beaches and trails. It's possible thanks to the still-evolving Oregon Coast Trail (OCT), which began as the brainchild of University of Oregon geography professor Sam Dicken in 1959. Trail-building by the Oregon Parks and Recreation Department (OPRD) began in earnest in the early 1970s.

A long-distance coastwide trail is a hiking opportunity unique to Oregon. Nearly half of the trail's roughly 400 miles are on sandy beach (accessible to the public, thanks to the Oregon Beach Bill). Existing trails in state parks and national forests, plus links built specifically for the OCT, make up about one-fifth of the route, and the rest is on road shoulder—quiet backroads and, where unavoidable, the shoulder of US Highway 101. Boat ferries are available at some bay mouths.

Backpacking on the OCT is a bit different from most backpacking trips in, say, the mountains. Some stretches are quite remote, but you're often passing by towns, so it's easy to resupply. Drinking from surface streams (even filtered) is not a good idea, but there are plenty of tap water sources along the way. There are (limited) opportunities for dispersed camping, but more often hikers camp in campgrounds (and relieve themselves in toilets). All these and other details are included in my guidebook *Hiking the Oregon Coast Trail*. Additional information and updates are available at trailkeepersoforegon.org/oct.

about your size), shy, and mostly vegetarian; if you're lucky, you might catch a glimpse of one, but probably not. Dogs, especially those that are off-leash and confrontational, can trigger a defensive response in these bears, which otherwise tend to be shy and not aggressive.

**Cougars, coyotes, and elk.** There are cougars in the Coast Range, but they rarely venture down to the coast. According to wildlife managers, there is no record of a fatal cougar attack on a human on the Oregon coast; should you encounter one, make yourself look large and don't run. Coyotes are plentiful but usually shy; keep your distance and they'll do the same. If you're lucky, you might spot browsing elk; again, keep a respectful distance. Elk can be very aggressive toward dogs and their humans, especially if they have calves with them.

**Poisonous snakes.** There are none here.

# How to Use This Guide

This book describes seventy-four trail hikes and forty-one accessible beaches along the Oregon coast divided into parts along the north, central, and south Oregon coast. Parts are further organized into subsections roughly 20 miles long, each featuring an introduction, overview map, and highlights. To enrich your journey, throughout the book sidebars describe natural phenomena and evidence of human history you are likely to encounter on the Oregon coast.

## DAY-USE FEES

Most trailheads and beach access sites on the Oregon coast do not require day-use fees. However, sixteen do charge fees, including several state parks plus trailheads in Oregon Dunes National Recreation Area and Cape Perpetua Scenic Area. If you plan to be out and about on the coast for more than a day or two, consider getting an Oregon Pacific Coast Passport, a multi-agency vehicle pass that covers entry or day-use fees at all fee-required state parks as well as federal fee sites (Forest Service, National Parks Service, and Bureau of Land Management). Annual and five-day passports are available at many visitor centers or online; no fee if you arrive by bike, bus, or on foot.

## TRAIL HIKES

All the hikes in this book are described as roundtrip outings. But with so many access points, many trails and beach walks can be

*Backpackers and day hikers enjoy the North Coast's wide, hard-sand beaches.*

*Neon yellow emergency beach access signs meant to help find you in an emergency also help with wayfinding on the Oregon coast.*

tackled as one-way hikes if you have a second (shuttle) vehicle.

**Overall ratings.** Each hike has a purely subjective rating that's depicted with one, two, or three asterisks. Those rated *** tend to be longer hikes with a lot of variety and interest, with great shoreline views or through magnificent forest; these are the hikes I mention when friends ask, "What are your favorite hikes on the Oregon coast?" Those rated * tend to be shorter and less interesting, but they may perfectly fit your needs on a given day and a given part of the coast. Nearly all of the hikes are kid-friendly but keep reading the descriptions to determine whether they may be right for your particular kids' tastes and abilities.

**Difficulty ratings.** These are on a 1 to 3 scale, with the more difficult hikes rated 3. These estimates take into account the length of the walk and the elevation gain (if any), but they can't account for the weather, your preparedness, or the fitness of the hikers. Beach Walk difficulty ratings are typically based not on length of the walk (most are open-ended, which is part of the charm) but on the walking surface; cobbles, very soft sand, or a challenging access trail may rate 3, while very firm sand rates 1 for easy.

**Distance figures.** The listed trail mileage is the total distance for an out-and-back or loop hike. You often don't need to hike the whole way to get a satisfying experience, and some hikes include suggestions for extending your trip or making it a one-way hike if you have a shuttle car available.

**Elevation gain.** This figure includes all the ups and downs of the hike, out and back, and not just the elevation of the trail's high point.

## BEACH WALKS

In this guidebook you will find descriptions of virtually every accessible beach, north to south, on the Oregon coast (all but the very shortest pocket beaches). Oregon has 262 miles of ocean beach in total. But headlands naturally divide beaches into what scientists call littoral cells—pockets of beach defined by the large headlands at either end. This book further divides beaches where rivers or large creeks cut across them, effectively ending the beach (at least in winter, and in summer except perhaps at low tide). The results are beach

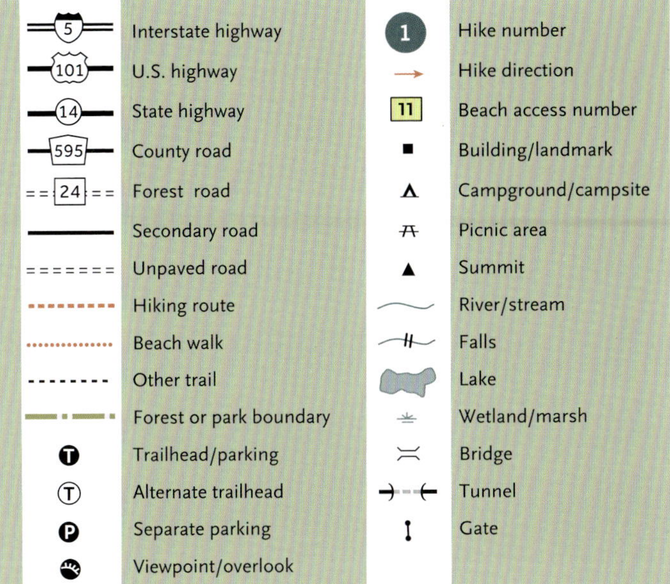


descriptions that range from less than 1 mile to about 16 miles one-way.

You get to choose how far you want to walk and where you want to start. Primary access points are listed north to south—at road ends, state parks and waysides, national forest day-use areas, or wide spots alongside US 101, though some beaches have many more informal access points besides those listed here. Many, but not all, are marked with emergency beach access signs that are indicated throughout the text as BA. These are numbered neon yellow signs, designed to help you identify your location to emergency responders in case of emergency. But they turn out to be very handy for wayfinding too, such as when you take a long beach walk, turn around, and can't quite remember where you started. Typically you'll find one sign in the dunes (visible from the beach) and a matching one at the access site, such as a parking area.

It is a point of pride in Oregon that not only are the beaches public (up to the vegetation line), but the public's access to those beaches is respected and defended. Oregon's beaches are managed by Oregon State Parks.

## MAPS

The maps in this book should suffice for a day hike. If you can find more detailed paper maps of the Oregon coast that include trails, great! They're helpful for planning, but they're becoming hard to find. You might be able to find a map of Oregon Dunes National Recreation Area, or of the entire

Siuslaw National Forest, at a ranger station along the coast (or online).

More and more people now depend on smartphone navigational apps, such as AllTrails, Gaia GPS, or FarOut Guide. The key here is to make sure your phone is charged (better yet, keep a small battery pack, charger, and cord in your pack), and put your phone on airplane mode to save battery while you're walking.

## ICONS

Symbols at the start of each hike provide key information and highlight some of the hike's special features. Notes and the hike description provide more detailed information. You might see a gray (or less commonly, an orca) whale from nearly any high point along the coast; the whale-watching icon indicates that either there is a high point with good ocean views or whale-watching volunteers trained by Oregon State Parks are posted at or near the trail for a week in late March and again in late December during gray whale northbound and southbound migration.

 Dog-friendly year-round

 Exceptional wildflowers in season

 Exceptional forest or trees

 Historical significance

 Good whale-watching

 Good tidepools at low tide

 Estuary views

 Open sand dunes

## A NOTE ABOUT SAFETY

Safety is an important concern in all outdoor activities. No guidebook can alert you to every hazard or anticipate the limitations of every reader. Therefore, the descriptions of roads, trails, routes, and natural features in this book are not representations that a particular place or excursion will be safe for your party. When you follow any of the routes described in this book, you assume responsibility for your own safety. Under normal conditions, such excursions require the usual attention to traffic, road and trail conditions, weather, terrain, tides, the capabilities of your party, and other factors. Keeping informed on current conditions and exercising common sense are the keys to a safe, enjoyable outing.

—Mountaineers Books

**OPPOSITE:** *Gulls flock at the mouth of Ecola Creek, just north of Haystack Rock at Cannon Beach (Beach Walk 16).*

# THE NORTH COAST

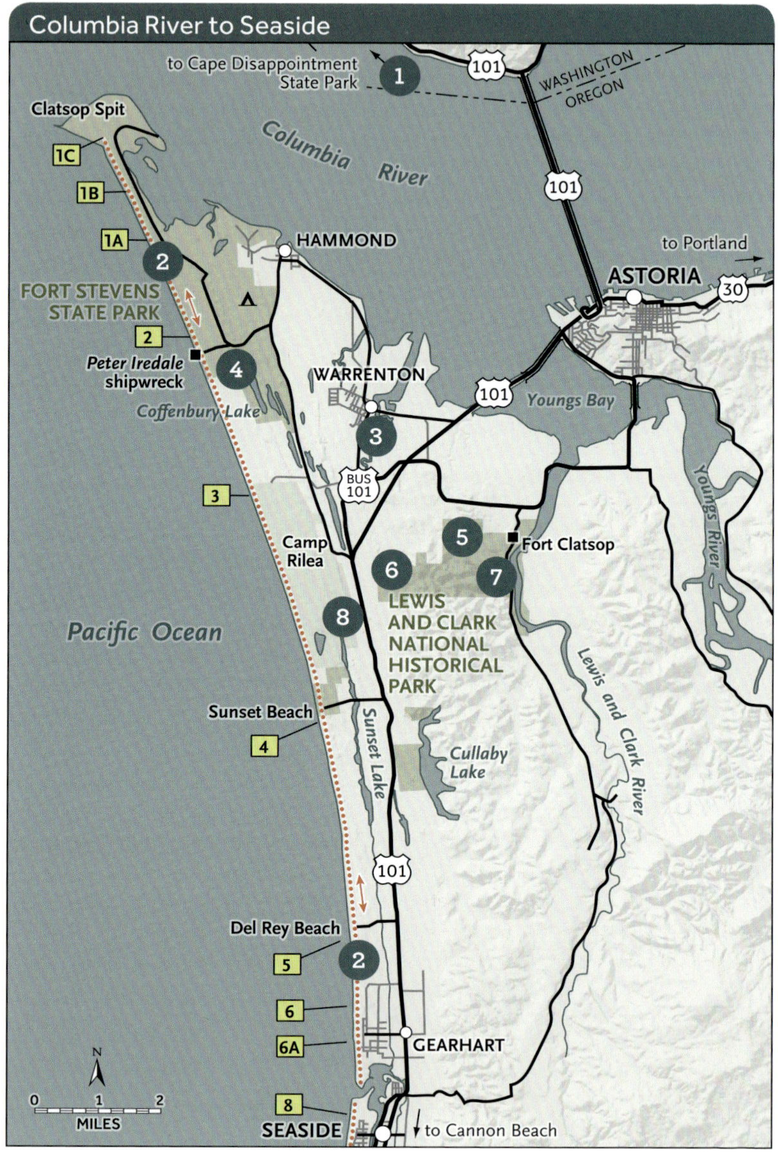
Columbia River to Seaside
to Cape Disappointment State Park
1
101
WASHINGTON
OREGON
Clatsop Spit
1C
1B
1A
Columbia River
101
HAMMOND
to Portland
ASTORIA
30
2
FORT STEVENS STATE PARK
2
Peter Iredale shipwreck
4
WARRENTON
101
Youngs Bay
Coffenbury Lake
3
BUS 101
3
Youngs River
5
Camp Rilea
Fort Clatsop
6
7
8
LEWIS AND CLARK NATIONAL HISTORICAL PARK
Pacific Ocean
Lewis and Clark River
Sunset Beach
Sunset Lake
4
Cullaby Lake
101
Del Rey Beach
2
5
6
GEARHART
6A
N
0 1 2
MILES
8
SEASIDE
to Cannon Beach

**HIKERS ON OREGON'S NORTH COAST** have access to the state's widest beaches, composed of sand that has been washing down the Columbia River for eons and settling on the continental shelf north and south of the river's mouth. The beaches of the north coast are broken up by a parade of hikeable capes and headlands—Tillamook, Arch, Falcon, Meares, Lookout, Kiwanda, Cascade, Yaquina—as well as coastal-fronting mountains—Neahkahnie and Saddle—protected as state parks. There are also national forests, national wildlife refuges, and in a couple of spots, privately owned but publicly accessible preserves. Trails at Sand Lake, Yaquina Bay, and lower Beaver Creek provide access to two estuaries and a freshwater marsh.

## COLUMBIA RIVER TO SEASIDE

The beach south of the Columbia River is the widest and one of the longest beaches in Oregon. It's so wide, hikers might not mind that they share most of this beach with cars. Other than the beach itself, the most interesting trail walking in the area is at Fort Clatsop, part of Lewis and Clark National Historical Park. The Fort to Sea Trail, between Fort Clatsop and Sunset Beach, approximates the route the Lewis and Clark Expedition took from Fort Clatsop—the winter quarters they built in December 1805 on what is now called the Lewis and Clark River—to the Pacific Ocean to hunt, trade, and make salt. This trail was built as part of the local 2005 bicentennial commemoration of the expedition; since then, a flurry of trail-building at the park has considerably expanded loop hiking options.

In addition to the walks described here, consider shorter or more developed paths in and around Astoria and Warrenton. The Cathedral Tree Trail (1.6 miles, 390 feet elevation gain roundtrip) starts in a wooded hillside neighborhood in Astoria and runs up Coxcomb Hill, site of the landmark Astoria Column. In Warrenton and Hammond, old levees on the Columbia River and its tributaries have been repurposed as walking paths, including the Waterfront Trail and the Airport Dike Trail, offering great river views and bird-watching in certain seasons. Astoria also has a paved 6.4-mile River Walk along the Columbia. Coffenbury Lake (at Fort Stevens State Park) has limits on boat speed, making it appealing for fishing, paddling, and hiking. Nearby Cullaby Lake (a county park, and like Coffenbury, a dune swale lake) offers easy, mostly level walking as well as paddling at the lake's quiet north end. More quiet paddling is possible on the Lewis and Clark River, and high-tide touring on Newanna Creek in Seaside.

### 1 North Head and McKenzie Head

RATING/DIFFICULTY: **/2

ROUNDTRIP: 4 miles

ELEV GAIN: 1,280 feet

**Contact:** Cape Disappointment State Park; **Notes:** Washington State Park day-use fee. Dogs on leash. Toilets; **GPS:** 46.298191°, –124.072545°

**Wait, isn't Cape Disappointment in Washington state? Yes! But it's so close to Oregon (just across the mouth of the Columbia River) and so full of geographical and historical points of interest (not one but two lighthouses overlooking the impossibly wide Columbia) that it seems**

*North Head Lighthouse is one of two lighthouses in Cape Disappointment State Park; it went into service in 1898, 42 years after Cape Disappointment Lighthouse.*

**to belong in this guidebook. This hike takes in one lighthouse and a dramatic high point. But don't leave the park without adding in a walk to the second lighthouse as well.**

## GETTING THERE

From Astoria, cross the Columbia River on the Astoria-Meglar Bridge, then turn left and continue on US Highway 101 following signs west to Ilwaco and, from there, up into Cape Disappointment State Park on North Head Road. Follow signs to parking for North Head Lighthouse.

## ON THE TRAIL

Start with a quick 0.6-mile walk out to North Head Lighthouse to the west, looping around the old assistant lighthouse keepers' residence (now a vacation rental). Back at the parking area, look for a trail heading south just west of the restrooms. Follow it as it descends south through the woods, rises to a high point, drops again to cross Fort Canby Road, then makes a final 0.3-mile climb to the top of McKenzie Head, 1.1 miles from the parking area where you began. To the east and nearly 100 feet below lies McKenzie Head Lagoon; to the west, the Pacific Ocean. Return as you came.

## EXTEND YOUR HIKE

Don't leave the park without checking out Cape Disappointment Lighthouse, with its dramatic views of the Columbia River bar. This lighthouse predates Oregon's first lighthouse; it went into service in 1856, a year before the first light at the mouth of the Umpqua River, making it the oldest functioning lighthouse on the US West Coast.

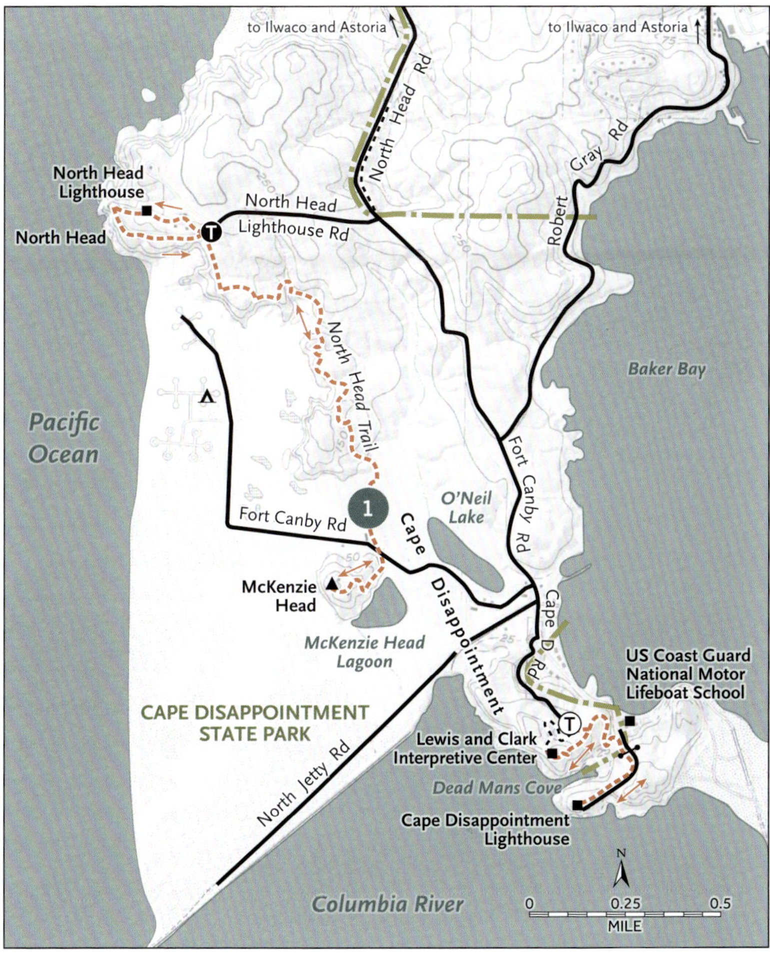


(The North Head Lighthouse was completed forty-two years later.) To take this additional 1.9-mile loop, hop back in the car and follow North Head Road south (becomes Fort Canby Road, then Cape D Road) to the road's end parking area. One trail switchbacks up the hillside; save that for your return and join the trail heading east out of the parking lot. Immediately pass a junction (bear left). In about 0.2 mile a spur to the right leads to a view into Dead Mans Cove; don't miss it! It loops back to the main road, which quickly crosses a paved road; below it is the US Coast Guard National Motor Lifeboat School, where Coast Guard personnel learn how to handle lifeboats in some of the most challenging conditions in the country, where the Columbia meets the Pacific. From here, walk up the road (closed to public vehicles) to the lighthouse at the top of the headland, 1 mile from where you started.

After taking in the view, walk back down, then turn left at the junction just above the parking area. The trail quickly leads to the back side of the Lewis and Clark Interpretive Center; a paved path takes you around to the front. It's open daily 10AM to 5PM year-round. Return to your car on the switchbacked, paved path leading down the hill.

## 2 Beach Walk: Columbia River to Gearhart

ONE-WAY DISTANCE: 16 miles

One of Oregon's two longest beaches is its northernmost, from the Columbia River south to the Necanicum Estuary at Gearhart. Sand has been washing down the Columbia River—whose watershed drains parts of seven Western states and one Canadian province—for eons. That sand settles on the continental shelf along southern Washington and south to Tillamook Head (and beyond). Construction of jetties has led even more sand to accumulate at the mouth of the river. The result for hikers: A very long, very wide, and very hard beach that is lovely for walking.

It's also mostly undeveloped. Most of the dunes here are protected by public agencies or a private land conservancy. Not until you head south, approaching "downtown" Gearhart, do you see any buildings. And even when you start passing neighborhoods, you won't see them, as they're set back far from the beach.

It's also one of few stretches of Oregon beach where vehicles are allowed, which takes some of the fun out of walking here. You'll need to stay alert for cars, especially near beach access points, where drivers tend to rev up to get through the soft sand; keep a close eye on kids and dogs. No driving is allowed north of the *Peter Iredale* (except in winter) or south of 10th Street in Gearhart.

One other caution: The Oregon Military Department runs a large training facility, Camp Rilea, that fronts the beach for 3-plus miles north of Sunset Beach access (roughly to Delaura Beach Road, Beach Access 3). It's a remote stretch of beach with few walkers most days. But the camp closes part or all of those 3 miles of beach to the public when it does live weapons training in the adjacent dunes, which occurs many days in summer and some days in winter. Operations are briefly suspended at the top of each hour to allow vehicles to transit the closure zone, which doesn't help hikers much. But soldiers patrol the beach and will let you walk out or possibly give you a ride to keep the coast clear. Visit oregon.gov/omd/rilea/pages/range-operations.aspx for a schedule indicating when the range will be in operation (and the beach closed to recreation), but note that the schedule sometimes changes at the last minute.

### BEACH ACCESS

BA 1C: beach parking lot C, Fort Stevens State Park, off Jetty Road. OPRD day-use fee. Vault toilet.

BA 1B: beach parking lot B, Fort Stevens State Park, off Jetty Road. OPRD day-use fee.

*The wreck of the iron-hulled* Peter Iredale *has been rusting on the sand adjacent to Fort Stevens State Park since 1906.*

BA 1A: beach parking lot A, Fort Stevens State Park, off Jetty Road. OPRD day-use fee.

BA 2: *Peter Iredale* shipwreck parking, Fort Stevens State Park, end of Peter Iredale Road. OPRD day-use fee. Restrooms.

BA 3: end of Delaura Beach Road, Warrenton. No formal parking; with soft sand and high water year-round, this access road is accessible only by very-high-clearance vehicles.

BA 4: Sunset Beach State Recreation Site, end of Sunset Beach Road, Warrenton. Vault toilet.

BA 5: Del Rey Beach State Recreation Site, end of Beach Road via Highlands Lane, Warrenton.

BA 6: end of 10th Street, Gearhart. Limited street parking.

BA 6A: end of Pacific Way, Gearhart. Limited street parking. Restrooms one block east at tennis courts.

## WHERE TO WALK

**South of the jetty.** Park at parking lot C, in Fort Stevens State Park, where a tall platform grants views of the Columbia and passing container ships. Look for the sign indicating the northern trailhead of the Oregon Coast Trail and follow the sand trail from there through the dunes about a quarter mile before it drops down to the beach. From here you have 3.5 miles of car-free walking (except possibly in winter) to the *Peter Iredale*. Or park at the *Peter Iredale* and walk north. Watch for paragliders flying low along the dune front.

## FOLLOWING THE KELP HIGHWAY

*Giant clumps of kelp are a frequent sight on the beach in winter.*

Mirroring the terrestrial forests growing along the shoreline, the nearshore ocean off Oregon harbors huge forests of giant kelp. Instead of roots, kelp use holdfasts to attach their long stems to rocks on the seafloor. From there, stems of kelp grow toward the light, lengthening by as much as 18 inches a day. Like terrestrial forests, kelp forests are places of great diversity: Many species of fish, invertebrates, birds, and marine mammals depend on them for food and shelter. Coastal storms sometimes rip clumps of kelp from the seafloor, holdfasts and all, and deposit them in piles on the beach, where they continue to serve an important role in the ecosystem, providing food and shelter to sand-dwelling critters that in turn become food for shorebirds such as snowy plovers and sanderlings.

Kelp is even believed to have played a major role in the peopling of the Western Hemisphere. Most archaeologists now believe that the first waves of people to migrate from Asia to North America likely traveled by boat, following what has been called the "kelp highway," sustaining themselves in part from fishing and hunting in the kelp beds just offshore.

**Along Camp Rilea.** If they're not shooting guns (see above), the walk north from Sunset Beach access is one of the quietest stretches of beach, unless you happen to head out early in the morning on a clam tide. Then you get to watch (or join) the frenzy of digging for elusive razor clams.

**South of 10th Street, Gearhart.** It's about 1.5 car-free miles from the end of the beach driving stretch south to the mouth of the Necanicum—longer at low tide, when more beach is exposed, and you can wander around the sand spit onto what's called Little Beach.

**Any direction from parking lot A or B, Fort Stevens State Park.** These huge parking areas usually have almost no cars. You'll have to watch out for drivers, but you'll see few other hikers.

**Anywhere at sunset.** Beach driving is mostly a daytime phenomenon; no one wants to get stuck on the sand after dark with a rising tide on the way. A sunset walk just about anywhere on this long beach can be heavenly.

**Bonus Walk: North of the jetty.** Not part of this 16-mile beach, as it is actually on the Columbia River, is what's known among locals as Social Security Beach, for the retirees (and others) who gather to fish when the salmon are running. Views of the river and passing ships are spectacular. Look for a road leading north off Jetty Road, between beach parking lots C and D, to a sandy pullout for a few vehicles. You can walk northwest, following the curve of sand, about 2 miles to where the beach ends at the North Jetty, or walk southeast toward parking lot D, if tide permits. Dogs on-leash; no dogs or kites on portions of the beach March 15–September 15 where the beach is signed for snowy plover protection.

## 3 Skipanon River Trail

RATING/DIFFICULTY: **/1
LOOP: 1.8 miles
ELEV GAIN: 70 feet

**Contact:** City of Warrenton; **Notes:** Dogs on-leash. Toilets; **GPS:** 46.16436°, –123.92074°

**This mowed path that follows the quiet Skipanon River's east bank is part of a network of trails built on the dikes that keep the Warrenton–Hammond community above water. In the late nineteenth century, Chinese laborers employed by city founder Daniel Knight Warren built the dikes that line the Skipanon. Warren's restored Victorian-era home, built in 1885, sits above the marina on the Skipanon's west bank; you might catch a glimpse of it across the water from the north end of the trail.**

### GETTING THERE

From US Highway 101 just south of the Youngs Bay Bridge to Astoria, turn west on East Harbor Street, then (in about 1 mile) left into the parking area for the Warrenton Boat Basin. Alternate starting points are the 8th Street Dam (park along street) and Skipanon River Park.

### ON THE TRAIL

To start a clockwise loop hike from the marina parking area, follow the mowed grass trail as it swings to the north and east along a bulge in the river before heading south along the east bank, offering views of the river and nearby neighborhoods. At 1 mile, walk around the gate to meet the 8th Street Dam that spans the river; cross it and walk one block west to South Main Avenue, then follow it north to Southeast 3rd Street, and take it east two blocks to Skipanon River Park. Head north on paved Warrenton Waterfront Trail to the Harbor Street Bridge; cross it and return to your starting point.

*The Skipanon River winds out of the dunes and rises and falls substantially with the tides.*

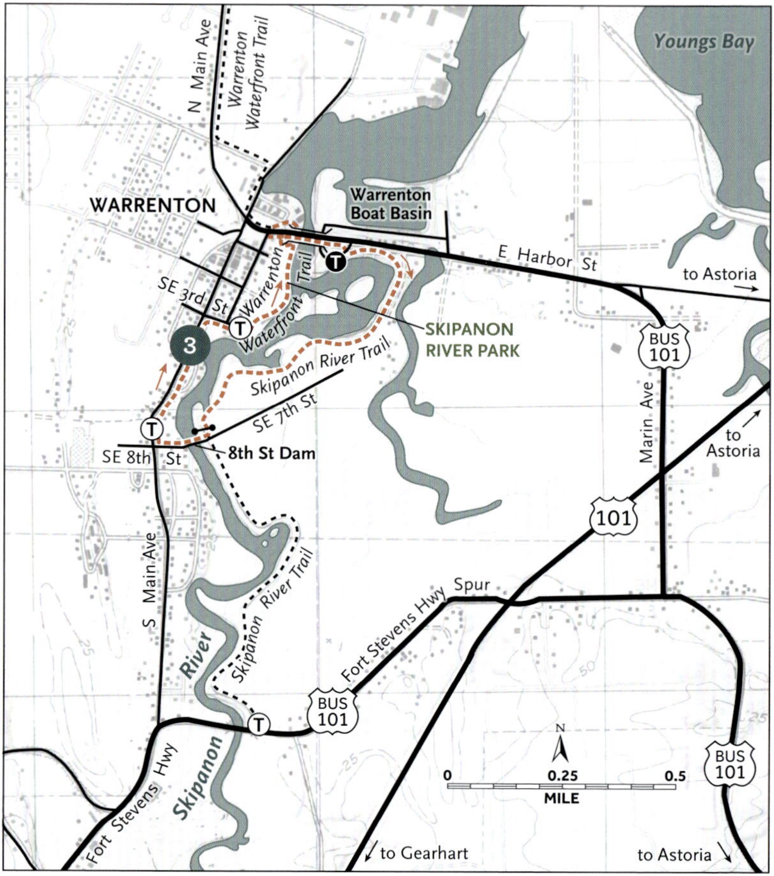

## EXTEND YOUR HIKE

From the 8th Street Dam, the trail continues south along the Skipanon River for 1 mile to the Business US 101 spur leading to US 101, giving you the option of a 3.8-mile roundtrip walk. Roadside parking is available at the highway spur.

## 4 Coffenbury–Swash Lake Loop

RATING/DIFFICULTY: **/3

LOOP: 6.8 miles

ELEV GAIN: 670 feet

**Contact:** Fort Stevens State Park; **Notes:** OPRD day-use fee. Dogs on-leash. Toilets; **GPS:** 46.17815°, –123.96592°

**Fort Stevens is a great park for hiking and cycling, whether you're camping in the large, forested campground or visiting for the day. You can make short or long hikes in several places, even combining them with a beach walk. This 6.8-mile loop includes dunes and beach walking and a visit to a World War II gun battery, among other points of interest. Add in circumnavigation of Coffenbury Lake to make it a 9-mile loop. Or shorten your hike to an easy, nearly level 2.2-mile walk just around the lake. On hot days Coffenbury Lake is appealing for swimming since it's out of the wind that blows on the beach most afternoons. There are two sandy swimming areas on the lake. Motorboats are allowed, but a speed limit of 10 miles per hour keeps the wakes down and the atmosphere relatively tranquil.**

## GETTING THERE

From US Highway 101 south of Astoria, follow signs to Fort Stevens State Park, heading south on NW Ridge Road and, once inside the park, following signs west on Peter Iredale Road to Coffenbury Lake. Alternately park at the *Peter Iredale* shipwreck site or at Beach Parking Lot A.

## ON THE TRAIL

From the vicinity of the restrooms at the north end of Coffenbury Lake, follow the paved bike path north. The trail soon leads through a pedestrian tunnel; immediately turn left onto a dirt footpath (Russell Ridge

*The loop hike from Coffenbury Lake to Swash Lake takes in a range of habitats and landmarks, from freshwater lakes and ocean beach to historical military installations and an early 20th century shipwreck.*

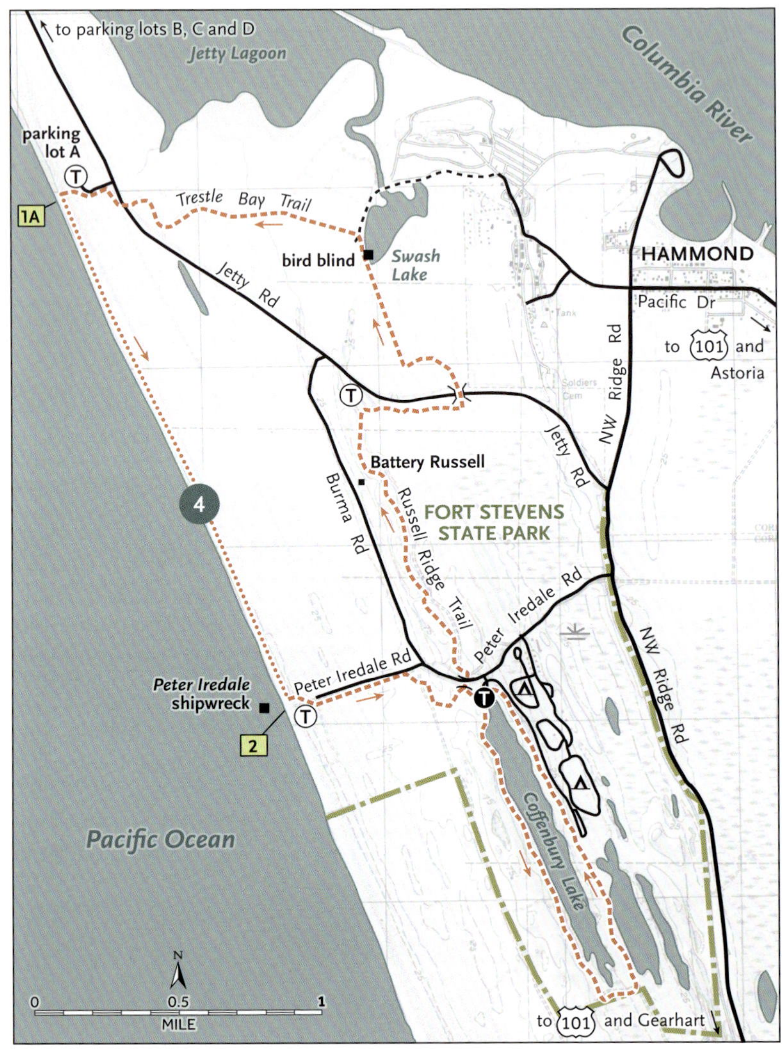


Trail). At 1.2 miles you'll skirt Battery Russell on your left. Fort Stevens was part of a "triangle of firepower" at the mouth of the Columbia from the Civil War through World War II. Completed in 1904, Battery Russell is the only site in the continental US that has been attacked by enemy forces since the War of 1812. During World War II, a Japanese submarine fired seventeen shells that landed nearby, severely rattling local residents but causing no injuries. Continuing, you'll pass toilets on your left; follow the now-paved route to the right around the parking area, then bear left to cross Jetty Road on a tall footbridge to head toward Swash Lake, where a bird blind invites you to peek at the waterfowl that sometimes stop by. Then make a sharp left onto paved Trestle Bay Trail to head toward Jetty Road and, across the road, Beach Parking Lot A at 3.6 miles.

Follow a sand trail out to the beach and head south for 2 miles until you reach the remains of the *Peter Iredale*, an English sailing ship that ran aground here in 1906; its iron hull has been rusting away on the beach ever since. Here, head inland to the parking lot and pick up the paved path on the south side of the access road; it leads back to your starting point at Coffenbury Lake.

To add in a counterclockwise lake walk, pick up the trail along the northern shoreline near the restrooms (on the rise west of the lake). The trail gradually ascends about 50 feet then returns to the lake's edge, following it closely the rest of the way. At the far end, your route meets an old road; take a left onto it to cross the lake's marshy south end and then veer left again where the footpath resumes. Walk through the grassy picnic and swimming area on the lake's east side to regain the trail at the lake's edge and return to the north parking area.

## 5 Fort to Sea—Kwis Kwis Trails, East Loop

RATING/DIFFICULTY: ***/2
LOOP: 2.7 miles
ELEV GAIN: 550 feet

**Contact:** Lewis and Clark National Historical Park; **Notes:** National Park Service day-use

*The view from the overlook on Clatsop Ridge stretches to the ocean when the weather cooperates.*

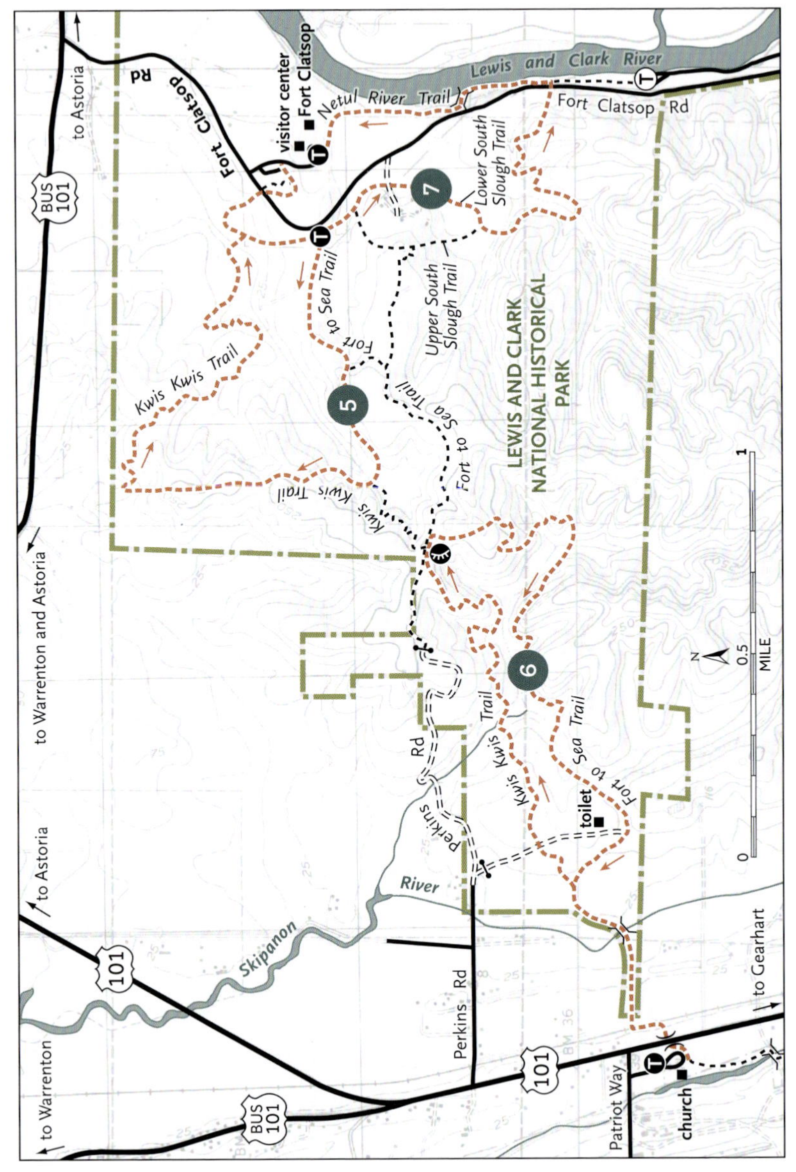

Lewis and Clark River
Fort Clatsop Rd
visitor center
Fort Clatsop
Netul River Trail
Lower South Slough Trail
Upper South Slough Trail
Fort to Sea Trail
Kwis Kwis Trail
LEWIS AND CLARK NATIONAL HISTORICAL PARK
to Astoria
to Warrenton and Astoria
to Warrenton
to Gearhart
BUS 101
101
Perkins Rd
Patriot Way
Skipanon River
toilet
church
0
0.5
1
MILE
N

fee. Dogs on-leash. Toilets; **GPS:** 46.13387°, –123.88526°

**The Fort to Sea Trail extends 5.7 miles from its eastern trailhead at Fort Clatsop to its western trailhead at Sunset Beach (see Hike 8). This hike combines the upper portion of the newer Kwis Kwis Trail with a section of the Fort to Sea to create a loop through the forested northern section of Lewis and Clark National Historical Park at Fort Clatsop. The trail name comes from the Chinook people's term for squirrel, mimicking the squirrels' own calls; listen for them as you follow this trail through the woods.**

## GETTING THERE

From US Highway 101 south of the Youngs Bay Bridge in Warrenton, turn east at the light on Ensign Lane (Business US 101) and follow signs to Fort Clatsop Road on the right. Take it south 1.2 miles (passing the entrance to Fort Clatsop/Lewis and Clark National Historical Park at 1 mile) to a spur road on your right; it leads to the small Fort to Sea trailhead parking area, with space for at least six cars. (Or park at the main Fort Clatsop parking area and take the access trail to trailhead.)

## ON THE TRAIL

Following signs for the Fort to Sea Trail, head west through the woods on a wide, compacted gravel road that is level at first and then ascends gently. At 0.3 mile, bear right to pick up the Kwis Kwis Connector trail, then right again at 0.6 mile at a second junction. The trail rolls up and down through the woods to about 1.2 miles, where it makes a sharp right and descends past a magnificent bigleaf maple tree on the left; sounds of traffic (and yells of people on a nearby zipline) reveal how close you are to the park's northern boundary. After a short descent, the trail resumes rolling gently through the forest, which is still recovering from the gale of December 2007. At the next junction (at 2.5 miles), turn right (a left leads to the fort) and follow a long wooden boardwalk for most of the final 0.2 mile back to the trailhead.

## EXTEND YOUR HIKE

Study the map and read the other Fort Clatsop trail descriptions to come up with longer (or shorter) day hikes, either out-and-back or one-way with a shuttle car.

# 6 Fort to Sea—Kwis Kwis Trails, West Loop

RATING/DIFFICULTY: ***/3
LOOP: 4.2 miles
ELEV GAIN: 400 feet

**Contact:** Lewis and Clark National Historical Park; **Notes:** Dogs on-leash. No toilets at trailhead, but vault toilet along trail; **GPS:** 46.12103°, –123.92723°

**The most appealing section of the Kwis Kwis Trail at Fort Clatsop is the long wooden boardwalk completed in 2014 that winds through a lush wetland near the lower (western) end of the trail—the same wetland glimpsed from above by hikers on the Fort to Sea Trail. It is part of this loop hike that begins just off US 101 and circles up to the overlook at the top of the Fort to Sea Trail. Quickest access is from the intermediate Fort to Sea trailhead at the church alongside US 101. Alternately, detour onto this stretch of the Kwis Kwis Trail on a 5.7-mile one-way hike from Fort**

*A long boardwalk allows you to walk through the lush wetland on the lower Kwis Kwis Trail.*

**Clatsop (National Park Service day-use fee) to Sunset Beach.**

## GETTING THERE

Southbound on US Highway 101 from Astoria, turn west off US 101 onto Patriot Way at about milepost 12; rather than continuing straight into the National Guard's Camp Rilea, bear left into the parking lot for Pioneer Presbyterian Church. Hikers are welcome to leave cars in this parking lot, just not on Sunday mornings.

## ON THE TRAIL

Walk southeast out of the parking area south of the church to pick up the Fort to Sea Trail. Follow the path east and north (becomes asphalt) through a tunnel under US 101. After 0.4 mile on the now unpaved path through the dunes, you'll cross the upper Skipanon River (more of a stream here). After a series of short boardwalks through the boggy woods, you'll reach a trail junction. Bear left to get onto the Kwis Kwis Trail, which crosses a gravel road, to follow the edge of a wetland. At 1.2 miles, cross a corner of the bog on a long wooden boardwalk. At the end of the boardwalk, the trail ascends the hillside, reenters the forest, and continues up and down, but mostly up, contouring around ravines before joining gravel Perkins Road briefly. Pass the continuation of Kwis Kwis Trail across the road and quickly turn right to pick up the Fort to Sea Trail westbound. In a short distance you will reach the trail's summit on Clatsop Ridge at an overlook to an ocean view at 2.2 miles.

Heading south, what was a wide road becomes a narrow path that plunges down the forested hillside. The trail descends on switchbacks and then contours along the hill, granting you glimpses of the wetlands you walked through on your way up. At 3.4 miles, you'll cross a gravel road (with a vault toilet on your right). Shortly you'll reach the junction with the Kwis Kwis Trail on your right, completing the loop. Continue west, crossing the Skipanon River, to the tunnel under US 101 and back to your starting point.

### EXTEND YOUR HIKE

Study the map and read the other Fort Clatsop trail descriptions to come up with longer (or shorter) day hikes, either out-and-back or one way with a shuttle car.

## 7 Fort Clatsop South Slough Loop

RATING/DIFFICULTY: ***/2

LOOP: 3.3 miles

ELEV GAIN: 250 feet

**Contact:** Lewis and Clark National Historical Park; **Notes:** National Park Service day-use fee. Dogs on-leash. Toilets. See map on page 48; **GPS:** 46.13387°, –123.88526°

**The South Slough Trail at Fort Clatsop circles around what used to be a diked pasture and is once again a wetland of the kind Lewis and Clark would have seen on their brief stay in this area in the winter of 1805–06. The wetland is particularly lovely in spring and summer, and this loop is just the right length for an interesting and invigorating walk.**

### GETTING THERE

From US Highway 101 south of the Youngs Bay Bridge in Warrenton, turn east at the light onto Ensign Lane (Business US 101) and follow signs to Fort Clatsop Road on the right. Take it south 1.2 miles (passing the entrance to Fort Clatsop/Lewis and Clark National Historical Park at 1 mile) to a spur road on your right; it leads to the small Fort to Sea trailhead parking area, with space for at least six cars. Alternately, you can park at the Netul River Landing trailhead (1.25 miles south of the park entrance by road; no parking fee) and walk the Netul River Trail north 0.2 mile to access the loop.

### ON THE TRAIL

Follow the trail out of the parking area and make an immediate left on the signed South Slough Trail. It drops for 0.1 mile and then rises to an opening in the forest; a sharp right heads onto a trampled grass path leading to a dirt path through the trees (the Upper South Slough Trail). Instead, stay on the main, Lower South Slough Trail. At 0.25 mile you'll glimpse Fort Clatsop Road and cross a gravel service road. From here the trail veers away from the road, following the edge of the broad wetland just inside the forest's edge. Trail gives way to boardwalk in particularly boggy spots. At 0.6 mile the trail switchbacks into the woods and shortly meets the Upper South Slough Trail. Bear left here, drop down to a creek crossing, then ascend again, briefly but steeply in places, before switchbacking down the other side of the hill to hit a particularly lovely stretch of boardwalk that snakes through a skunk cabbage bog at about 1 mile.

From here the trail ascends again, steadily but moderately with a couple of switchbacks, for 0.3 mile, then descends steeply to hit Fort Clatsop Road at 1.6 miles. Cross the road

*Cross a tidal slough as you follow the Netul River at Fort Clatsop.*

and pick up Netul River Trail heading north, reaching Fort Clatsop in about 0.7 mile. Follow signs to the Fort to Sea Trail, which takes off from the parking lot closest to the park entrance, crosses the park road, and veers left at a junction, leading back to the trailhead parking area.

You can shorten this loop to just 2.5 miles by bypassing Fort Clatsop itself. From the junction with the Netul River Trail, head north. But just after crossing a substantial footbridge over a slough at the edge of the Lewis and Clark River, leave the trail and follow the paved road shoulder north 0.2 mile to where the gravel service road (mentioned above) leads left a short distance to the trail crossing. Go right to follow the trail back to where you started.

## EXTEND YOUR HIKE

Study the map and read the other Fort Clatsop trail descriptions to come up with longer (or shorter) day hikes, either out-and-back or one-way with a shuttle car.

# 8 Sunset Beach via Fort to Sea Trail

RATING/DIFFICULTY: **/2
ROUNDTRIP: 5 miles
ELEV GAIN: 300 feet

**Contact:** Lewis and Clark National Historical Park; **Notes:** Dogs on-leash. Toilets at Sunset Beach trailhead; **GPS:** 46.12103°, –123.92723°

**The Fort to Sea Trail (total of 5.7 miles one-way) crosses US 101 near the Pioneer Presbyterian Church on its way to Sunset Beach. An out-and-back hike on just the western trail section takes you across a couple of hidden dune swale lakes on substantial footbridges and traverses terrain ranging from cow pastures to piney woods and wetlands. With trailheads at either end, a 2.5-mile one-way hike with a shuttle car is also possible.**

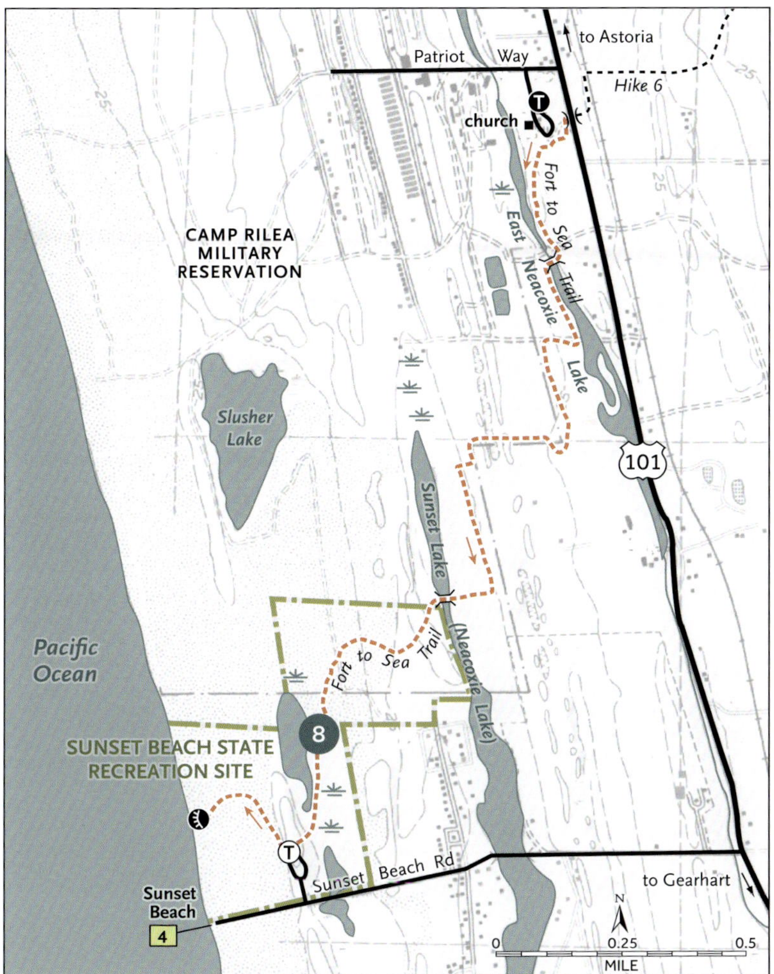


## GETTING THERE

Southbound on US Highway 101 from Astoria, turn west off US 101 onto Patriot Way at about milepost 12; rather than continuing straight into the National Guard's Camp Rilea, bear left into the parking lot for Pioneer Presbyterian Church. Hikers are welcome to leave cars in this parking lot, just not on Sunday mornings. The trail terminates at Sunset Beach State Recreation Site, an alternative starting point to make it an eastbound hike; to drive there, turn west off US 101 between mileposts 13 and 14 and continue 1 mile to trailhead parking on your right.

## ON THE TRAIL

Walk southeast out of the parking area south of the church to pick up the Fort to Sea Trail (a mown path here) westbound. It angles along a wooden fence up a field past the church, crests a low ridge, and drops down to East Neacoxie Lake at 0.2 mile, crossing it on a floating footbridge. For the next mile or so, the route zigzags over and along farmers' fields and right across a cow pasture, using stiles to get through fences. It cuts through an arm of Camp Rilea Armed Forces Training Camp, where you'll find the trail enclosed in cyclone fencing for a stretch. At 1.2 miles you reach the trail's longest footbridge, one crossing Sunset Lake (also called Neacoxie Lake). Head up and over a couple more ridges, then zigzag down sand dunes and pass a wetland at 1.7 miles. The trail drops down through a pine forest (substantially thinned by the gale of 2007) to emerge behind the restrooms at the Sunset Beach trailhead parking area at 2.2 miles.

Pick up the last 0.3 mile of the Fort to Sea Trail at the north end of the parking lot; it leads through pines, over a pair of footbridges, and out through dunes to the Pacific. It is in this vicinity that members of the Lewis and Clark party, wintering at Fort Clatsop in 1805–06, reached the beach on their treks between the fort and salt-making operations at the ocean. From here they continued south another 8 miles or so to present-day Seaside, where they found rocks to build a furnace, wood to burn, fresh water to drink, and game animals to hunt. Return as you came.

## EXTEND YOUR HIKE

Study the map and read the other Fort Clatsop trail descriptions to come up with longer (or shorter) day hikes, either out-and-back or one-way with a shuttle car.

*A floating bridge crosses Neacoxie Lake on the Fort to Sea Trail.*

## SEASIDE TO ARCH CAPE

South of the Necanicum Estuary that separates Seaside and Gearhart, the wide, flat beach continues a few miles to the base of 1225-foot Tillamook Head, a north coast landmark that rings with human history (Hike 12). Here Clatsop and Nehalem people have thrived for thousands of years, and they recently reacquired a portion of their traditional homelands on the estuary. Members of the Lewis and Clark party followed "a small Indian parth" over the headland to see and, they hoped, acquire (from Native people living at present-day Cannon Beach) blubber from a beached whale. Eighty years later, a lighthouse was built on Tillamook Rock, a mile offshore; it is no longer in service except to the seabirds that perch and nest on its ledges. The shoreline and seaside cliffs at Tillamook Head are protected as Ecola State Park. There is no campground at this park, but there is camping available nearby, at the RV Resort at Cannon Beach (RVs), The Retreat at Cannon Beach (RVs, cabins, and tents), and Wright's for Camping (tents).

South of Tillamook Head is a stretch of beach nearly nine miles long. It starts with little Indian and Crescent Beaches—followed by a long uninterrupted stretch of sand past the town of Cannon Beach, iconic Haystack Rock, and some secondary headlands—and ends at Arch Cape. Like several Oregon coastal towns, Cannon Beach has developed walking trails off the beach—a nice option when beach weather is less than optimal (Hike 17). With its ancient cedar trees—extremely rare on this coast after more than a century of intensive logging—Ecola Creek Forest Reserve in Cannon Beach is well worth a visit (Hike 18).

## 9 Beach Walk: Seaside

**ONE-WAY DISTANCE:** 2.5 miles

The beach at Seaside is a lively place on sunny summer days, full of people (but no cars), everyone almost elbow-to-elbow during beach volleyball tournaments and at the end of the Hood to Coast relay race (on the fourth weekend of August). Lifeguards are present all summer. In winter, of course, there is plenty of solitude despite the beach's proximity to the tourist shops on Broadway.

The paved Promenade, or "Prom," more than a century old, runs just above the dunes from 12th Avenue south to Avenue U. The most parking is at what's called The Cove, where the sandy beach turns to cobbles and where surfers stage their paddles out into the waves; it's also a great place for winter wave-watching. Most visitors seem to use street parking or walk from their lodgings to get to the beach. Many streets, not just those listed above, end with a sand trail to the beach (but limited street parking), including 5th Avenue (Beach Access 9A), Broadway (Beach Access 10), and Avenue G (Beach Access 10A). Other street ends are marked in the dunes with white signs (e.g., S for Avenue S).

### BEACH ACCESS

BA 8, N. Franklin Street at 8th Avenue, Seaside. Parking in wide gravel lot.

BA 9, west end of 12th Avenue, Seaside. Toilets.

BA 10B, end of Avenue U, Seaside. Parking for about a dozen vehicles.

BA 11, Seltzer Park off Sunset Boulevard, Seaside. Parking, toilets.

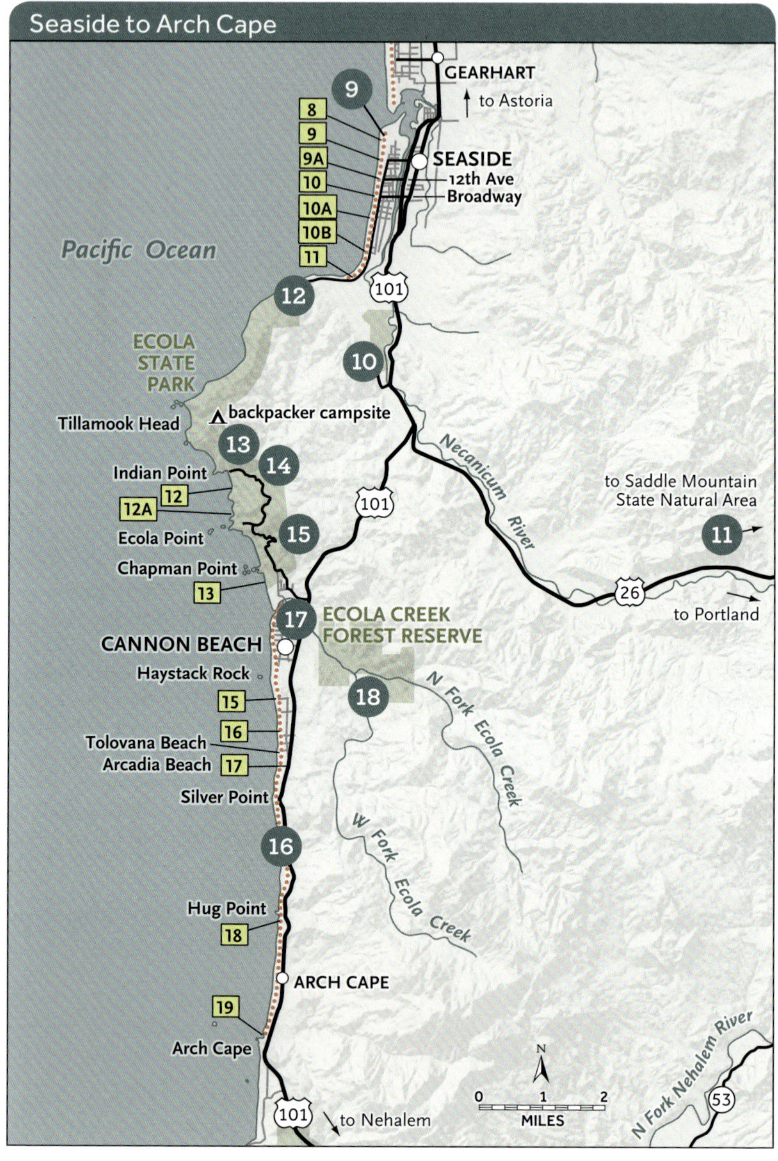
Seaside to Arch Cape
GEARHART
to Astoria
SEASIDE
12th Ave
Broadway
Pacific Ocean
101
ECOLA STATE PARK
Tillamook Head
backpacker campsite
Indian Point
Ecola Point
Chapman Point
CANNON BEACH
ECOLA CREEK FOREST RESERVE
Necanicum River
to Saddle Mountain State Natural Area
26
to Portland
Haystack Rock
Tolovana Beach
Arcadia Beach
Silver Point
N Fork Ecola Creek
W Fork Ecola Creek
Hug Point
ARCH CAPE
Arch Cape
to Nehalem
MILES
N Fork Nehalem River
53

*The Seaside Prom runs parallel to the beach for 1.5 miles.*

## WHERE TO WALK

**Bird-watchers.** Park at Beach Access 8 and follow a sand trail over the dunes to the Necanicum Estuary, where there is always something for nature-lovers to see. It's by far the quietest place on Seaside Beach.

**Catch the buzz.** Park at Beach Access 9 and head south, toward Tillamook Head. You may pass beach volleyball games, families flying kites, sandcastle builders, and even a swing set in the dunes. Walk south to Beach Access 10B, take the sand trail east a short distance to the end of the Promenade, and follow the Prom back north for a 2.8-mile loop walk.

**Big waves.** Park at Seltzer Park, along Sunset Boulevard, where surfers paddle out to the base of Tillamook Head, then follow the trail through the cobbles to get to the beach; walk north as far as you like. The parking area here is also a popular spot for winter storm watching.

## 10 Circle Creek Wetlands Walk

RATING/DIFFICULTY: **/2
LOOP: 2.4 miles
ELEV GAIN: 30 feet

**Contact:** North Coast Land Conservancy; **Notes:** Open daily dawn to dusk. No dogs allowed; **GPS:** 45.95458°, –123.93112°

**From high on Tillamook Head, Circle Creek drops down to the coastal plain and meanders north to join the Necanicum**

*A winding boardwalk at North Coast Land Conservancy's Circle Creek Habitat Reserve allows you to walk through a tidal swamp and keep your feet dry.*

**River south of downtown Seaside. In 2002 the nonprofit North Coast Land Conservancy purchased 364 acres here and began the process of turning cleared pasture back into the lush rainforest it once was. Together with the upland forest at its fringe, the floodplain hosts a variety of native wildlife: coastal coho salmon, red-legged frogs, salamanders, beaver, coyote, migratory songbirds, waterfowl, nesting bald eagles, and dozens of elk. Visitors are welcome to witness this large-scale restoration project by walking the Wetlands Walk and the little (0.3-mile) Legacy Loop, which winds through a lush Sitka spruce swamp brimming with skunk cabbage in early spring.**

## GETTING THERE

From the junction of US Highway 101 and US 26 south of Seaside, take US 101 north 0.7 mile and turn left on Rippet Lane (0.1 mile south of the bridge over the Necanicum River). Drive west and north 0.4 mile, past a gravel quarry, to Circle Creek Conservation Center, at the end of the road.

## ON THE TRAIL

Past the Circle Creek Conservation Center, follow an old farm road and wooden bridge across Circle Creek, then veer left and follow trail posts on the mowed path that curves along the creek through the floodplain. After the trail drops nearly to creek level at the "avulsion point"—where the Necanicum

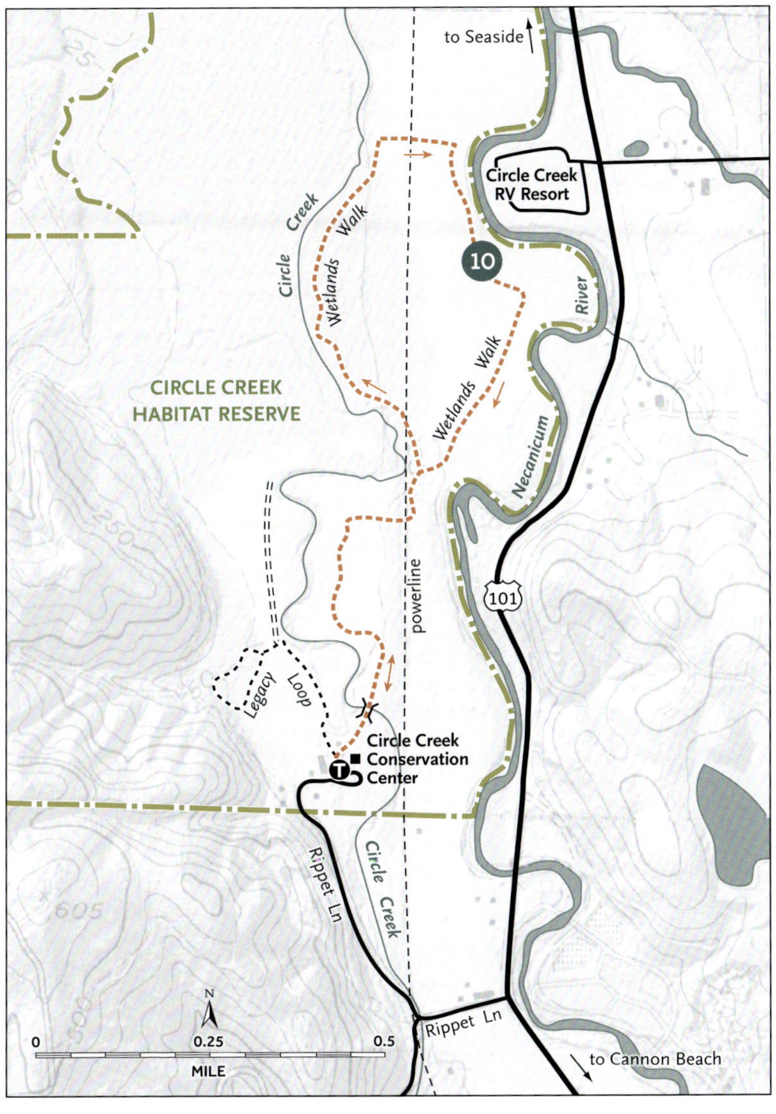

to Seaside
Circle Creek RV Resort
Circle Creek
Wetlands Walk
10
River
Wetlands Walk
CIRCLE CREEK HABITAT RESERVE
Necanicum
powerline
101
Legacy
Loop
Circle Creek Conservation Center
Rippet Ln
Circle Creek
Rippet Ln
to Cannon Beach
0
0.25
0.5
MILE
N

River and Circle Creek converge during periods of high water—follow the mowed path to the left to reach the first of a series of long boardwalks. These boardwalks fill gaps in a berm that was built decades ago to control flooding; these gaps now allow water to flow freely across the floodplain. At the end of the last section of boardwalk, either return as you came or follow a mowed route east and south to return to the avulsion point and the conservation center.

## 11 Saddle Mountain

RATING/DIFFICULTY: ***/3

ROUNDTRIP: 4.8 miles

ELEV GAIN: 1,630 feet

**Contact:** Saddle Mountain State Natural Area; **Notes:** Dogs on-leash but not recommended (see On the Trail). Vault toilets. Water available; **GPS:** 45.96301°, –123.68948°

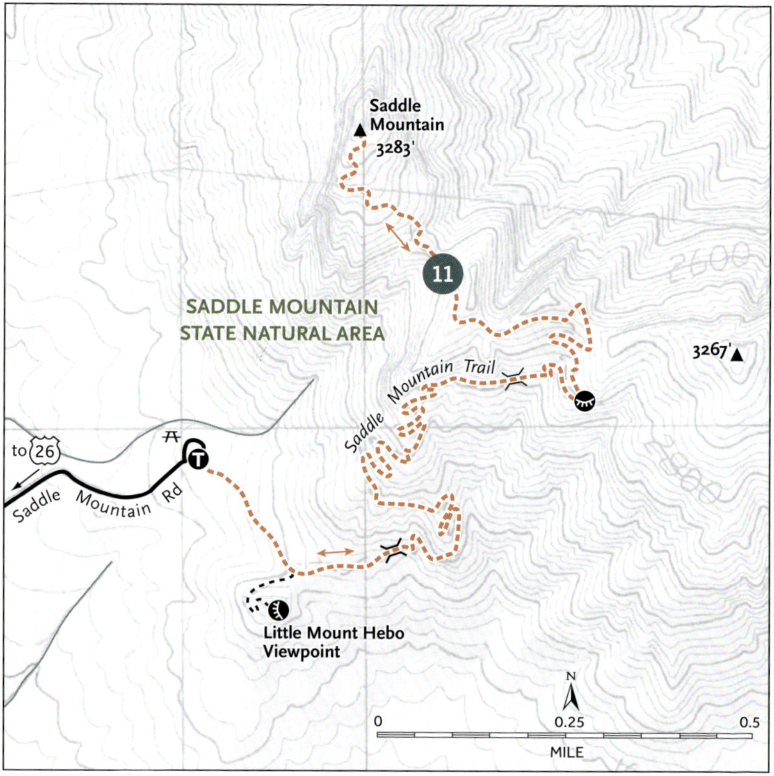

*Aptly named pillow basalt characterizes the terrain approaching the summit of Saddle Mountain.*

Saddle Mountain owes its prominence in the landscape to the pillow basalt it's made of. As with nearby Tillamook Head and offshore sea stacks, this basalt is sturdier and more erosion-resistant than the predominantly sandstone hills around it. It's the highest and most iconic point in the northern Coast Range: two humps (the tallest 3,283 feet high), treeless at the summit, stand well above the surrounding forested landscape. A hike to the top of Saddle Mountain rewards you, weather permitting, with an unbeatable view, including the lower Columbia River and Youngs Bay, the Pacific Ocean, a number of Coast Range peaks, and the snow-capped summits of (among others) Mount Hood, Mount St. Helens, Mount Rainier, and even the Olympic Mountains. Early fall is a good bet for clear weather and fall colors. May and June offer some of the best and most unusual wildflower displays in the Northwest, from fiery orange Chambers paintbrush to chocolate and pink fawn lilies. Note that snow and fallen trees may cause the park to be closed for parts of the winter.

### GETTING THERE

From the junction of US Highway 26 and US 101 south of Seaside, follow US 26 about 8 miles east and turn north at the sign for Saddle Mountain State Natural Area. Follow signs about 7 miles to the trailhead parking lot. (Camping is no longer allowed at the trailhead.)

### ON THE TRAIL

The 2.4-mile hike is, but for a dip just below the summit, a steady uphill climb. It begins in forest dominated by vine maple and alder; a short spur 0.25 mile past the trailhead leads to the Little Mount Hebo Viewpoint, with a great view of Saddle Mountain's two-hump summit to the north. The trail moves into Douglas-fir and western hemlock territory before breaking into open treeless meadows—known among botanists as balds—where you can see a wide array of plants, some of them classified as rare or endangered and some unique to this peak. The last pull to the summit is steep, even stair-stepped, in places. The state park has laid wire fencing atop many steep and gravelly sections in the upper half to stabilize the trail and prevent slipping, but take great care; the fencing underfoot creates a tripping hazard of its own when shoe tread or trekking poles catch in the wire.

It can also be difficult for dogs to walk. After carrying down a 160-pound Great Pyrenees dog with feet cut by trail's wire fencing, the Cannon Beach Rural Fire Protection District posted that Saddle Mountain Trail is "not very dog-friendly. Over the years we have had several calls for dogs that needed assistance off the mountain due to dehydration or cut/raw paw pads. The trail has copious amounts of welded wire fencing on the ground to provide traction and stability of the trail. Many of these sharp wires are sticking straight up. As well, walking on wiring and rocks for an extended amount of time can be very rough on your fur baby." Cable handrails offer hikers more support. After taking in the view, return as you came.

## 12 Tillamook Head

RATING/DIFFICULTY: ***/3
ROUNDTRIP: 10 miles
ELEV GAIN: 3,210 feet

**Contact:** Ecola State Park; **Notes:** Dogs on-leash; Toilets at south trailhead and along trail; **GPS:** 45.97364°, –123.95407°

**Tillamook Head dominates the skyline in Seaside, where it forms a brooding backdrop to the lively beach scene. Signage along the trail that ascends the head reminds hikers of the Lewis and Clark expedition's acquaintance with this landmark. In January 1806, members of the expedition used a rough approximation of this trail to hike over Tillamook Head to the mouth of Ecola Creek (present-day Cannon Beach) to barter for blubber from a beached whale. Most day hikers don't hike the entire trail out and back. Rather they might hike part way (such as to Clarks Mountain from the north trailhead and back, 3.6 miles and 1,350 feet roundtrip) or they might arrange an end-to-end one-way hike with a shuttle vehicle. The trail has been in poor condition for many years; unless that has changed, you can expect muddy stretches and places where boardwalk has broken down and needs to be navigated with care.**

*Three-sided shelters surround a fire ring at the backpackers campsite atop Tillamook Head.*

## GETTING THERE

To reach the north trailhead in Seaside, turn west off US Highway 101 at the traffic light at Avenue U, drive 0.2 mile, turn left onto South Edgewood Road, and follow the road 1.2 miles (it becomes Sunset Boulevard) until it ends at a trailhead parking area. (To access the south trailhead, drive to Cannon Beach and follow signs at the north end of town to Ecola State Park; follow Ecola Park Road 4 miles to the Indian Beach parking area at the end of the road. There are toilets here, and an OPRD day-use permit is required.)

## ON THE TRAIL

Starting from the north trailhead in Seaside, follow the signed trail up through the woods. After about 0.5 mile the trail steepens and begins switchbacking up the hillside, steeply in places, especially (at 1.2 miles) where the trail detours around an old landslide. The trail summit, at Clarks Mountain, is at 1.8 miles; from here the trail rolls through the forest, with occasional views west to the ocean, before coming to a trail junction at 3.8 miles. Here you'll find a vault toilet and, a short walk to the west, a backpackers campsite with a covered picnic table and three log shelters arranged around a fire ring, each with four bunks (but no water). A short spur trail leads west to the ruins of a once-secret World War II radar site. Back at the junction, bear right for a scenic route (called the Lighthouse Trail) along the shoreline, or bear left on the slightly shorter Clatsop Loop Trail (see Hike 13). The two trails rejoin near a footbridge over Indian Creek, just before the trail reaches the vault toilets at the end of the parking area at 5 miles. Return as you came.

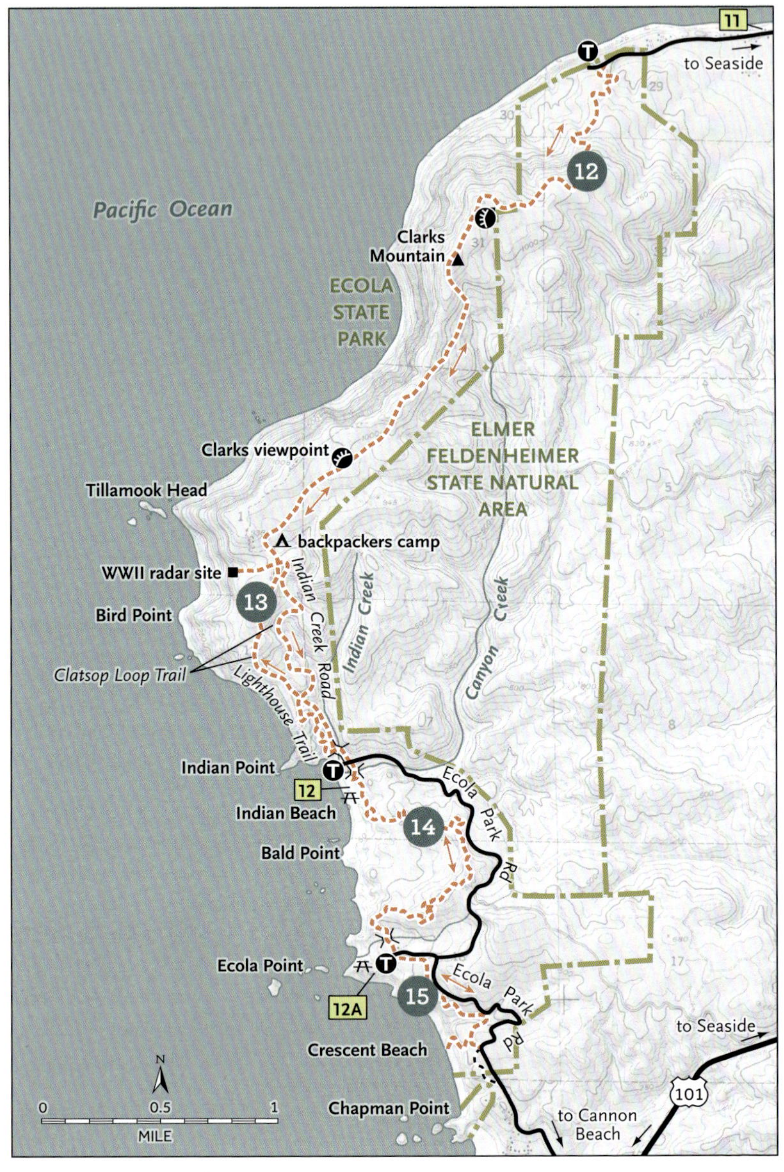

11
to Seaside
12
Pacific Ocean
Clarks Mountain
ECOLA STATE PARK
ELMER FELDENHEIMER STATE NATURAL AREA
Clarks viewpoint
Tillamook Head
backpackers camp
WWII radar site
13
Bird Point
Indian Creek Road
Indian Creek
Canyon Creek
Clatsop Loop Trail
Lighthouse Trail
Indian Point
12
Indian Beach
14
Ecola Park Rd
Bald Point
Ecola Point
12A
15
Crescent Beach
to Seaside
Chapman Point
101
to Cannon Beach
0
0.5
1
MILE
N

## 13 Clatsop Loop Trail

RATING/DIFFICULTY: **/2
LOOP: 2.7 miles
ELEV GAIN: 1,000 feet

**Contact:** Ecola State Park; **Notes:** OPRD day-use fee. Partially open to bikes. Dogs on-leash. Toilets; **GPS:** 45.93113°, –123.97844°

**The easiest way to hike onto Tillamook Head is via the Clatsop Loop Trail, which starts and ends at the Indian Beach parking area at the road's end in Ecola State Park, near Cannon Beach. It follows the main Tillamook Head trail near the bluffs above the ocean to a campsite atop the headland then loops back on an old forest road (still a park service road) alongside Indian Creek. Be prepared for mud on the trail up along the shoreline (or go both out and back on the road portion). Bicycles are allowed on the road portion of the trail only.**

### GETTING THERE

From US Highway 101 southbound, take the northernmost Cannon Beach exit at milepost 28, turn right at the first stop sign and right again at the sign to the park; from US 101 northbound, take the Sunset Boulevard exit to Cannon Beach (south of milepost 29), drive north through town, and after crossing Ecola Creek, turn left and then right into the park. The trailhead is at the end of the road in 4 miles, at the Indian Beach parking area.

### ON THE TRAIL

For a clockwise loop, head north out of the parking lot and immediately take a left to cross Indian Creek on a footbridge. Follow the narrow trail as it ascends steadily through the forest, passing some very large, old trees, before topping out and descending briefly to a junction at 1.4 miles. Before returning on the loop trail, continue north 0.2 mile to visit the backpackers campsite. A short walk west leads to the remains of what was, during World War II, a secret radar site charged with

*The view toward Indian Beach from the Lighthouse Trail*

detecting possible enemy aircraft; today it's mostly moss-covered and nearly obscured by vegetation. Return to the trail junction and bear left to descend 1.3 miles on the road along Indian Creek (drier, gentler grade) to the Indian Beach parking area.

## 14 Indian Point to Ecola Point

RATING/DIFFICULTY: **/2

ROUNDTRIP: 4.5 miles

ELEV GAIN: 900 feet

**Contact:** Ecola State Park; **Notes:** OPRD day-use fee. Dogs on-leash. Toilets at both trailheads. Water at Ecola Point only. See map on page 64; **GPS:** 45.93113°, –123.97844°

**Ecola Point and Indian Beach are joined by a 2.25-mile trail that starts and ends on a bluff above the shoreline but mostly travels through deep woods back from the cliffs. The trail's route used to follow close to the cliffs until chronic landslides caused it to be rerouted. The trail can be quite muddy in winter.**

### GETTING THERE

From US Highway 101 southbound, take the northernmost Cannon Beach exit at milepost 28, turn right at the first stop sign and right again at the sign to the park; from US 101 northbound, take the Sunset Boulevard exit to Cannon Beach (south of milepost 29), drive north through town, and after crossing

*Nurse logs and stumps proliferate where the trail from Indian Point to Ecola Point swings away from the sea cliffs and into the forest.*

*With a low tide and some luck, you can continue south on the sand from Crescent Beach past Chapman Point to Cannon Beach.*

Ecola Creek, turn left and then right into the park. The northern trailhead is at the end of the road in 4 miles, at the Indian Beach parking area.

## ON THE TRAIL

You could begin at either end, but for a north–south hike, drive to the end of the road at Indian Beach and pick up the trail heading toward the beach. After crossing Canyon Creek on a substantial footbridge, veer left where a right turn leads down to the beach. At 0.3 mile the trail makes a sharp turn to the left and climbs into the forest. It makes a mostly gradual climb to the trail's high point around 2 miles. It descends gradually, with a few switchbacks, to reconnect with the old trail at 1.9 miles. You'll cross a footbridge shortly before reaching the parking area at Ecola Point. Return as you came (unless you've arranged a one-way hike with a shuttle vehicle).

# 15 Crescent Beach

RATING/DIFFICULTY: ***/2

ROUNDTRIP: 2.4 miles

ELEV GAIN: 250 feet

**Contact:** Ecola State Park; **Notes:** OPRD day-use fee. Dogs on-leash. Toilets. See map on page 64; **GPS:** 45.919441°, –123.97305°

**This remote-ish pocket beach can be reached via a sometimes slick 1.2-mile trail through the woods and down a steep hillside.**

## GETTING THERE

From US Highway 101 southbound, take the northernmost Cannon Beach exit at milepost 28, turn right at the first stop sign and right again at the sign to the park; from US 101 northbound, take the Sunset Boulevard exit to Cannon Beach (south of milepost 29), drive north through town, and after crossing Ecola Creek, turn left and then right into the park. The trailhead is 2 miles ahead, at the Ecola Point parking area.

### ON THE TRAIL

The trail begins near the restrooms at the top of the parking area. After climbing some stairs you'll reach the park road; follow it for a few paces until the trail resumes, heading down the bank. It rolls through the forest (muddy in places), crossing a creek on a footbridge at about 0.5 mile. At 1 mile you'll reach a junction; turn right, switchback down the steep forested hillside, cross another little bridge, and you'll hit Crescent Beach just north of a slowly eroding sandstone spire. Not many people take the trouble to walk to this lovely, half-mile-long pocket beach, lending it an appealing remoteness. Return as you came. (Don't use the trail that leads off the beach south of the sandstone spire and hits the park road just outside the park entrance sign; it runs through private property.)

## 16 Beach Walk: Cannon Beach to Arch Cape

ONE-WAY DISTANCE: 7.4 miles

This may be the be the best-known, most-photographed beach in Oregon. There are always people on the beach near town, walking dogs or just walking or, in summer, building sandcastles (for fun or as part of the town's annual and wildly popular sandcastle contest); it's much quieter at the northern and southern ends of this long beach. Headlands north and south of Cannon Beach can shorten the beach for walkers at mid- or high tide. There are many more access points than those listed here; all have parking areas (which can fill up quickly in summer).

### BEACH ACCESS

Les Shirley Park, off E. 5th Street north of Ecola Creek. Small parking area, toilets.

BA 15, Haystack Rock/Ecola Court, midtown Cannon Beach. Public parking two blocks east at S. Hemlock Street and E. Gower Avenue. Public restrooms on west side of Hemlock at edge of hotel parking area.

BA 16, Tolovana Beach State Recreation Site. OPRD day-use fee. Large parking area, restrooms.

BA 17, Arcadia Beach State Recreation Site. Small parking area, vault toilet.

BA 18, Hug Point State Recreation Site. Small parking area, vault toilet.

### WHERE TO WALK

**Chapman Point.** From Les Shirley Park, walk along Ecola Creek and veer north toward Chapman Point. Typically walkers can round the point at low tide and reach Crescent Beach, at least in summer, but even then deep "crab holes" can develop, requiring serious wading even at low tide.

**North or south from Haystack Rock.** Haystack is perhaps the best-known natural landmark on the Oregon coast and part of Oregon Islands National Wildlife Refuge. Park in the public parking area at Hemlock and E. Gower Avenue (fills quickly in summer) and walk between the hotel buildings to the paved access path at Beach Access 15. The rock is just to the north; staff and volunteers with Haystack Rock Awareness Program are on duty at daytime low tides in summer, teaching visitors about how to tidepool without hurting the inhabitants and training spotting scopes on the rock, where

*Hug Point is a highlight of the beach walk south of Cannon Beach, but you must hit it at low tide.*

orange-beaked tufted puffins tend to arrive in April to start nesting. Heading north it is 0.5 mile to Ecola Creek, where you can turn around or in summer, wade across and continue to Chapman Beach. South from the rock, you can typically walk at least 2.2 miles south before being stopped by the tide at Silver Point; at low tide in summer you can go all the way to Arch Cape (but be aware of the tide unless you want to return on the road). If parking is full in Cannon Beach, start your walk at Tolovana Beach State Recreation Site, which has a lot more parking.

**Hug Point at low tide.** Start at Arcadia Beach State Recreation Site and walk south or start at Hug Point State Recreation Site and walk north (1.3 miles one way). But start an hour before low tide or you may not be able to get around (and back around) Hug Point. There's a lot to see here, including a waterfall tumbling onto the beach, but the big attraction is the road blasted into the rock more than a century ago, which gave horse-pulled wagons, and eventually Model Ts, a way to get around the point even if the tide was creeping up past low. On average that road is only accessible within an hour of low tide; at very low tide you can walk around the point on the beach.

**Arch Cape.** Between Hug Point and Arch Cape—the headland and the residential community—there's plenty of beach walking as far south as Beach Access 19 at Arch Cape Creek, though south of Hug Point there are a couple of headlands you won't be able to round at high tide. There's no public parking (except very limited neighborhood parking) in Arch Cape, so you're better off starting up north.

## 17 Cannon Beach Trail Loop

RATING/DIFFICULTY: **/2
LOOP: 2.3 miles
ELEV GAIN: 100 feet

**Contact:** City of Cannon Beach; **Notes:** Dogs on-leash; **GPS:** 45.88975°, –123.96167°

**The City of Cannon Beach has developed a paved trail system along Ecola Creek and around its sewer lagoons—wait! You know how critical sewage treatment is to the functioning of this busy tourist town, right? Besides, the ponds and vegetation around them are a haven for birds; a city brochure lists fifty bird species commonly observed along the trail, from bald eagles and a dozen species of ducks to little golden-crowned kinglets and Anna's hummingbirds. It's not unusual to see elk browsing along the creek. (Don't approach, especially if you are walking a dog; they can be aggressive.) Richly illustrated interpretive signs are packed with information about the area's flora, fauna, and human history. Half of this hike is a beach walk; reverse direction if the wind is blowing hard from the north on the beach and from NeCus' Park at the mouth of Ecola Creek, formerly the site of the town's elementary school. If it's drizzly or windy on the beach, this trail is a good place to get out, stretch your legs, and walk the dog, but bicycles aren't permitted.**

### GETTING THERE

From US Highway 101 southbound, take the second Cannon Beach exit between

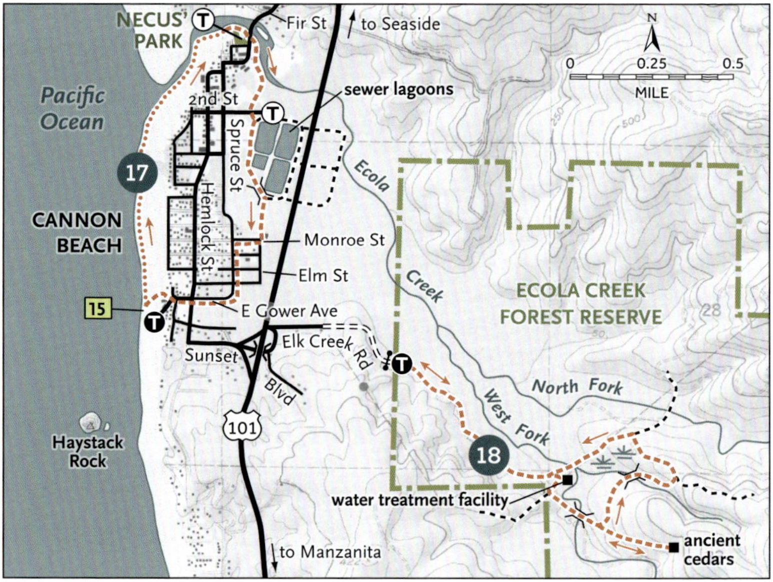

*Artist Guy Capoeman's sculpture creates a sense of welcome where the beach along Ecola Creek meets NeCus' Park at the north end of Cannon Beach.*

mileposts 29 and 30. Follow Sunset Boulevard to Hemlock Street, turn right, then turn right into public parking at E. Gower Avenue. Study the map for other options to park and start the loop.

## ON THE TRAIL

Walk west across Hemlock Street and between the hotel buildings to reach a paved path to the beach (Beach Access 15). Detour south a bit to visit Haystack Rock; otherwise walk the beach north to the mouth of Ecola Creek and follow the creek as it curves west. Where the creek beach is about to run out, head toward the 10-foot-tall welcoming pole in the dunes, carved by Native artist Guy Capoeman. The image of a young Clatsop man commemorates the time prior to the arrival of Europeans, when tribes from the Columbia River and south to the Nehalem River would visit and hold potlatches. Follow a bark chip path above the creek at NeCus' Park to Fir Street at 1.2 miles.

Cross Fir Street and pick up the paved path and boardwalk at the edge of the creek, where the path crosses 2nd Street. From here the path leads along the west side of the sewer lagoons. Cross a footbridge, climb a bit, and enter a dark forest of spruce before popping out at the corner of Elm and Monroe Streets. Walk Monroe Street west one block, then left on Spruce Street for four blocks to E. Gower Avenue; take it west to return to your starting point.

## 18 Ecola Creek Forest Reserve

RATING/DIFFICULTY: **/2
ROUNDTRIP: 3.2 miles
ELEV GAIN: 100 feet

**Contact:** City of Cannon Beach; **Notes:** Bikes allowed on hard-surface roads. Dogs on-leash or under owner's control; **GPS:** 45.88755°, –123.94974°

When the City of Cannon Beach began acquiring forest land east of town a couple of decades ago, it did more than protect its source of drinking water. It preserved groves of ancient cedars and second-growth forest, which now have the opportunity to grow into old growth. It protected salmon-bearing streams and provided residents and visitors with a close-to-town forest hiking opportunity in sight and sound of a pristine coastal creek. The trail system consists mostly of old logging roads, some of which city workers still use to access water intake and treatment facilities. In some places the trail system ducks out of the reserve and into private timberland; hikers are allowed on those roads too. Most of the elevation gain on this hike is from a brief but steep climb at the far end of the loop, where the biggest trees are; skip the big trees and this loop is much easier (and 0.6 mile shorter). This loop also requires you to wade the shallow creek; alternately, just hike out and return as you came.

## GETTING THERE

From downtown Cannon Beach, take Hemlock Street south to "midtown" and turn east on Sunset Boulevard, crossing under US Highway 101. (US Highway 101 travelers exit at Sunset Boulevard south of milepost 29 and follow signs toward the RV park.) Drive Elk Creek Road east for 0.3 mile (turns to gravel) to a parking area and gate across the road.

*Cattail sentinels line the marsh at the forest reserve.*

## A WALK IN THE RAINFOREST

*The temperate rainforest of the Pacific Northwest grows some of the largest trees on Earth.*

The temperate rainforest of the Pacific Northwest is one of the most biologically diverse ecosystems in the world, home to some of the tallest trees on Earth, from the coast redwoods of northern California to Sitka spruce, which dominate the forests closest to Oregon's seashore. The temperate rainforest isn't quite as rainy as the tropical rainforest—a mere 50 to 200 inches a year—and most rain falls from autumn through spring. But the temperate rainforest can be bathed in fog and mist any time of year; that fog condenses on tree needles year-round and contributes about as much water to stream flows as winter's rainfall does. Over eons, many fish, bird, and animal species have come to depend on the particular structure of old-growth rainforest habitat, which once covered half or more of western Oregon but now is nearly gone. The big payoff from recent conservation efforts won't be apparent for many years, when today's protected forests mature. But many of the forested coastal headlands, now protected as state parks (beginning in the 1930s), had previously been logged; you can still see evidence of that logging in the huge stumps, many of them "nurse stumps" with shrubs and trees growing out of them, as you hike through what are now maturing forests. If you conserve it, forested land will regrow. Scattered examples of very large trees hundreds of years old, including western redcedars with complex canopies, can be seen along the trail to Short Sand Beach (Hike 20) and in Ecola Creek Forest Reserve (Hike 18).

## ON THE TRAIL

Walk around the gate and down the road 0.6 mile through recovering forest (blown down in the December 2007 gale) and bear right at the first junction. Continue past the water treatment facility, across a bridge over the West Fork Ecola Creek, and past a trail on the left at 0.9 mile. Continue straight for a time. From here the road steepens considerably and passes some gorgeous ancient cedars, well worth the extra effort; turn around at the road's end at 1.2 miles and return to the prior junction, this time turning right (north). Follow this often-muddy footpath as it contours along the hillside, passing bogs filled with skunk cabbage that bloom in early spring. When the link trail ends at another old road, follow it left 0.5 mile, passing under a powerline and alongside a cattail-filled marsh to the banks of West Fork Ecola Creek. Take off your shoes, roll up your pant legs, cross the creek, and follow the old road just 0.1 mile back to that first junction; bear right to return to the parking area.

## CAPE FALCON TO TILLAMOOK BAY

Oswald West State Park, the centerpiece of this stretch of coast, is a gem. It includes two major north coast landmarks: Cape Falcon, accessible by trail from the north or south, and Neahkahnie Mountain, whose summit, also accessible from the north or south, provides spectacular views of the coastline on clear days. Both the summit of Cape Falcon and highway pullouts along Neahkahnie Mountain are good whale-watching sites during the right seasons. Between US Highway 101 and the shoreline lies a dense temperate rainforest with a handful of remnant ancient western redcedar trees, giving hikers a taste of what once was and will again someday be (nearly everything else is second-growth after logging). The park includes 4 miles of coastline, including steep seaside cliffs and the secluded Short Sand Beach, popular with surfers; tidepools appear at either end of the beach at low tide. Offshore lie the reefs and eelgrass beds of Cape Falcon Marine Reserve.

To the south just a few miles lies another large park of an entirely different character. Nehalem Bay State Park offers camping, bike and horse trails, and even a 2,400-foot airstrip just 0.25 mile from the campground entrance. It occupies 4-mile-long Nehalem Spit, dividing Nehalem Bay from the Pacific. The long, remote beach is the main feature here. It ends at the bay's narrow outlet, just a shout away from a local business that offers boat shuttles across the water for a small fee, mainly to thru hikers on the Oregon Coast Trail, but day hikers can cross the bay, have a drink and eat some fresh cooked Dungeness crab, and take the boat back north.

From Nehalem Bay, the beach continues south past the tourist town of Rockaway Beach. While here, treat yourself to a stroll on the city's Old Growth Cedar Trail at the south end of town. The trail starts at a small parking area on the east side of US 101, north of Washington Street. Follow a boardwalk winding 0.3 mile through a lush, forested wetland; just before reaching the end of the boardwalk, an often-muddy footpath takes off on the left, leading another 0.3 mile to a grove of massive, old western redcedars, the largest of which has a 49-foot circumference.

The beach ends at vast Tillamook Bay, fed by five rivers. Barview Jetty County Campground offers camping and views of the often-dramatic bay mouth, along with the seabirds and fishing boats that pass over and through it.

## 19 Cape Falcon

RATING/DIFFICULTY: ***/3

ROUNDTRIP: 4 miles

ELEV GAIN: 1,420 feet

**Contact:** Oswald West State Park; **Notes:** OPRD day-use fee. Dogs on-leash; **GPS:** 45.76308°, –123.95598°

**This out-and-back trip to Cape Falcon rolls through magnificent forest, and the ocean and shoreline views from the remote, bald cape are superb.**

### GETTING THERE

Drive south from Cannon Beach on US Highway 101 about 10 miles to Oswald West State

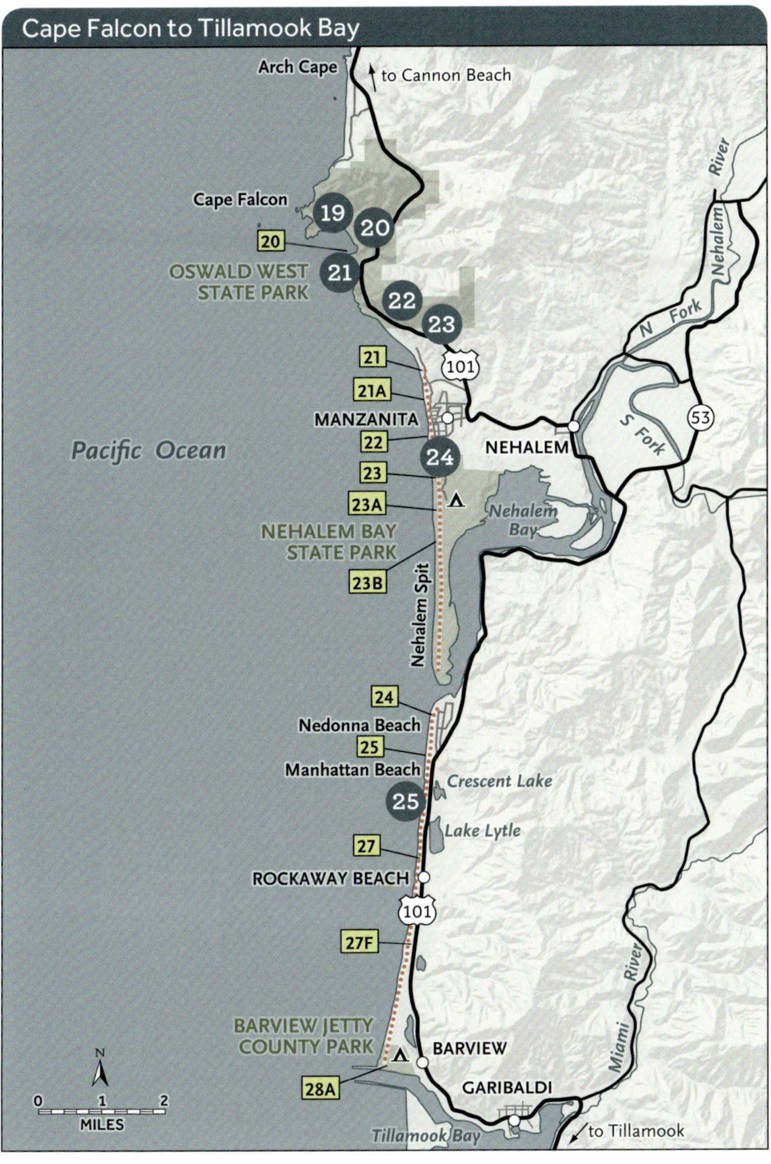
Cape Falcon to Tillamook Bay
Arch Cape
to Cannon Beach
Cape Falcon
19
20
20
21
OSWALD WEST STATE PARK
22
23
River
Nehalem
N Fork
21
101
21A
MANZANITA
22
24
NEHALEM
53
S Fork
Pacific Ocean
23
23A
Nehalem Bay
NEHALEM BAY STATE PARK
23B
Nehalem Spit
24
Nedonna Beach
25
Manhattan Beach
Crescent Lake
25
Lake Lytle
27
ROCKAWAY BEACH
101
27F
River
Miami
BARVIEW JETTY COUNTY PARK
BARVIEW
28A
GARIBALDI
N
0 1 2
MILES
Tillamook Bay
to Tillamook

Park and park on the west side of the highway at the northernmost of the park's three parking areas at milepost 39. Find restrooms and water at the next parking area south, on the east side of the highway.

## ON THE TRAIL

Pick up the trail at the north end of the parking lot and follow it 0.5 mile to a junction. Bear right and continue along the contours of the forested seaward slope, crossing Kerwin Creek at 0.6 mile. At 1.8 miles the trail enters a clearing, offering good views south to Neahkahnie Mountain and Short Sand Beach, before crossing Blumenthal Creek. At 2.5 miles a short spur trail leads left onto Cape Falcon's treeless tip; here a maze of trails cuts through the brush, leading to various viewpoints north and south. Turn around here to return as you came.

## EXTEND YOUR HIKE

For a longer hike, here are a couple of options.

**Start at Short Sand parking area.** Follow directions for the hike to Short Sand Beach (Hike 20). From here pick up the Oregon Coast Trail (OCT) northbound; in 0.2 mile you'll intersect the Cape Falcon Trail, extending your roundtrip 1.4 miles more.

**Continue to Arch Cape.** From Cape Falcon, continue north on the OCT. The trail rises gradually, with occasional ocean views, to the high point 2.3 miles from Cape Falcon; look north to catch a glimpse of Haystack Rock at Cannon Beach. Slowly descend through deep forest to where the trail crosses Falcon Cove Road (3.6 miles from Cape Falcon), meets and crosses US 101 (4.1 miles), and ends at a suspension bridge over Arch Cape Creek (5.4 miles). If you want to make it a one-way

*Neahkahnie Mountain looms to the south from the trail to Cape Falcon.*

## UNDERWATER WILDERNESS: OREGON'S MARINE RESERVES

*Undisturbed marine reserves, such as here at Cape Falcon, serve as nurseries for the rest of the nearshore ocean.* (Photo by Oregon Department of Fish and Wildlife)

If you stop to gaze at the sea from Cape Falcon or Short Sand Beach, you're looking at Cape Falcon Marine Reserve, the northernmost of Oregon's five nearshore ocean conservation zones established beginning in 2009. All ocean development and removal of marine life is prohibited in these reserves (though limited fishing is allowed in some adjacent marine protected areas). By closing these relatively small areas of the ocean to trolling and trawling, the reserves become nurseries that replenish ocean flora and fauna all along the coast. They also serve as living laboratories where scientists can explore "how ocean conditions are changing, how biological communities are changing, how fisheries are changing, and what's driving those changes, and then identifying what we can do about it," as the program's leader puts it.

The other four reserves (and hikes and beach walks overlooking them) are Cascade Head Marine Reserve (Hikes 42, 44, 45, and 46), Otter Rock Marine Reserve (Hike 49), Cape Perpetua Marine Reserve (Hikes 56 through 66), and Redfish Rocks Marine Reserve (Hike 95).

hike with a shuttle car, note that there is limited neighborhood parking in Arch Cape. The trail conditions can be iffy, depending on how recently trail crews have been able to brush the trail and cut windfall trees from winter storms.

## 20 Short Sand Beach

RATING/DIFFICULTY: **/1
ROUNDTRIP: 1 mile
ELEV GAIN: 130 feet

**Contact:** Oswald West State Park; **Notes:** OPRD day-use fee. Dogs on-leash. Toilets; **GPS:** 45.76140°, –123.95792°

**Looking for a short leg-stretcher with the kids? Join the surfers and head out to Oswald West State Park and this 0.5-mile strip of beach backed by deep woods. The waters off the park are protected as Cape Falcon Marine Reserve and the shoreline as Cape Falcon Shoreside Marine Protected Area. Harvesting is restricted: No fishing, crabbing, or clamming here.**

### GETTING THERE

From Cannon Beach, drive south on US Highway 101 about 10 miles to Oswald West State Park. Park at the large parking area on

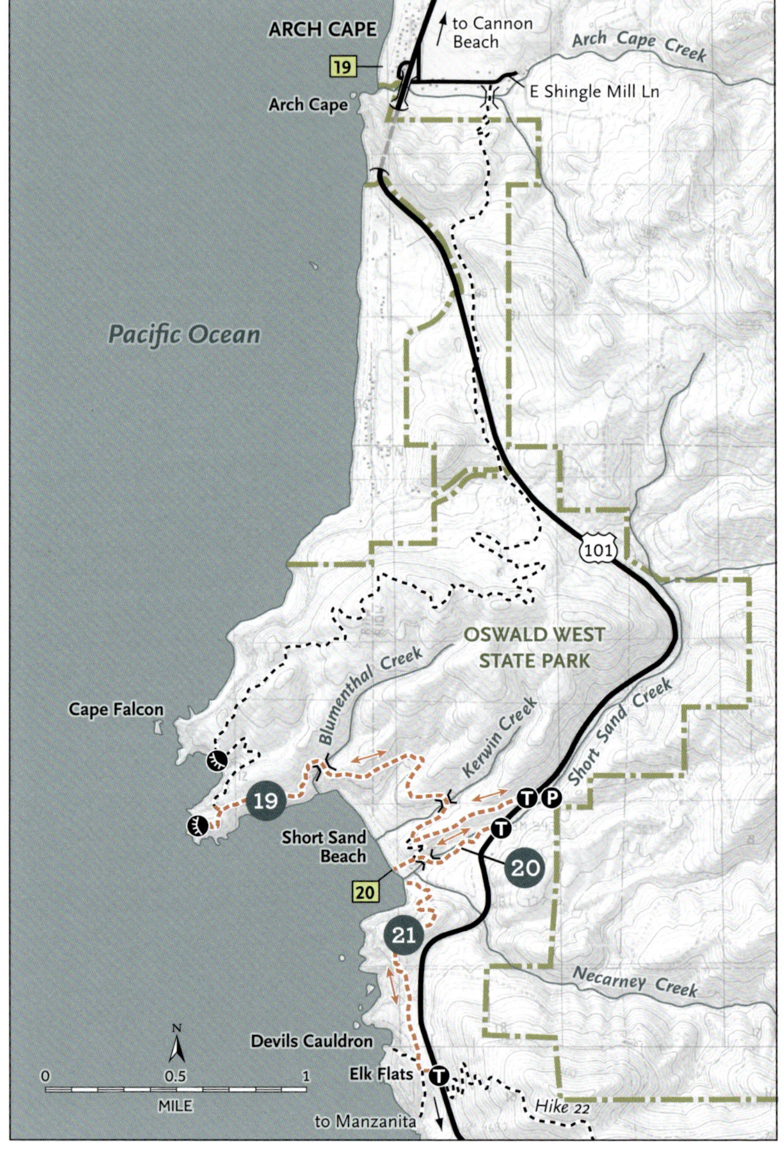
ARCH CAPE
to Cannon Beach
Arch Cape Creek
19
E Shingle Mill Ln
Arch Cape
Pacific Ocean
101
OSWALD WEST STATE PARK
Blumenthal Creek
Cape Falcon
Kerwin Creek
Short Sand Creek
19
Short Sand Beach
20
20
21
Necarney Creek
Devils Cauldron
Elk Flats
0
0.5
1
MILE
Hike 22
to Manzanita

*Driftwood piles up where Necarney Creek meets the Pacific Ocean at Short Sand Beach.*

the east side of the highway, south of milepost 39.

## ON THE TRAIL

You can get to Short Sand Beach from any of the park's three parking areas, but the route from the large, middle parking lot is the most direct. Pick up the trail behind the restrooms and follow it under US 101. It winds down toward the beach alongside Short Sand Creek, passing scattered examples of truly magnificent old-growth cedars—cedar trees many hundreds of years old with complex canopies, trees of the kind that used to dominate this shoreline. At the junction with the Old Growth Trail, either bear right to stay on the main trail or go left to see more big trees like this (in fact, you'll see more amazing old trees regardless of which route you take). The trail forks again; a right takes you over Short Sand Creek and to the beach, one of the north coast's surfing hot spots. Return as you came. There are flush toilets at the trailhead and at the beach.

# 21 Elk Flats to Short Sand Beach

RATING/DIFFICULTY: **/2
ROUNDTRIP: 2.5 miles
ELEV GAIN: 540 feet

**Contact:** Oswald West State Park; **Notes:** Dogs on-leash. Toilets at trail's end above Short Sand Beach; **GPS:** 45.74838°, –123.96250°

**In just 1 mile of hiking (and 540 feet elevation gain) west from this trailhead you can reach a couple of magnificent clifftop ocean viewpoints. Or walk all the way to Short Sand Beach. Call it the long way to Short Sand; more of a hike and not as crowded as Hike 20 can be.**

*Look for seabirds, seals, and crashing waves from the viewpoints off the trail through Elk Flats.*

## GETTING THERE

Watch for the wide turnout on the west side of US Highway 101 south of milepost 40, about 2.5 miles north of Manzanita or 12 miles south of Cannon Beach. This is also the parking area for the Neahkahnie Mountain Trail North trailhead.

## ON THE TRAIL

Follow the trail dropping down the hillside, lush with wildflowers in spring, to a junction; a left turn here takes you south to a dramatic clifftop ocean view, especially compelling in winter, at 0.3 mile with a 360-foot descent. Otherwise bear right and quickly reach another junction; turn left here to visit the Devils Cauldron viewpoint in 0.2 mile (and about 160 feet of descent). Look north to see the sea arch at the end of Cape Falcon and stay back from the fencing (it's a steep drop into the sea from here).

To go all the way to Short Sand, bear left at the last junction. The trail continues across grassy Elk Flats and heads into the woods, where the trail twists and turns, rising and falling (often over a tangle of roots), to a junction at a sharp right turn at 1.2 miles. Don't take it; it leads quickly to the site of the former Necarney Creek bridge, destroyed in a freak 2023 spring snowstorm. Instead, bear left to quickly reach the south end of Short Sand Beach. Wade across the creek to reach the picnic area above the beach. Return as you came.

## 22 Neahkahnie Mountain North Trail

RATING/DIFFICULTY: ***/3
ROUNDTRIP: 4.4 miles
ELEV GAIN: 1,600 feet

**Contact:** Oswald West State Park; **Notes:** Dogs on-leash; **GPS:** 45.74838°, –123.96250°

**Most hikers headed to the summit of Neahkahnie Mountain choose the south trail (Hike 23); the north trail starts lower, so it is more of a workout, and winds through a lovely forest. The climb is more gradual as the trail ascends with long switchbacks through the forest.**

### GETTING THERE

Watch for the wide turnout on the west side of US Highway 101 south of milepost 40, about 2.5 miles north of Manzanita or 12 miles south of Cannon Beach. Park here and cross the highway to reach the trailhead.

### ON THE TRAIL

The trail begins by traversing an open hillside meadow before entering a deep, airy forest. At about 1 mile you'll enter an area full of toppled trees, many blown over in a big storm in 2020 that closed the trail for two years. You'll see plenty of windfall for the next 0.5 mile, after which the trail nearly levels off for another 0.5 mile before making a final, steeper ascent that emerges suddenly out of the trees at the base of the summit

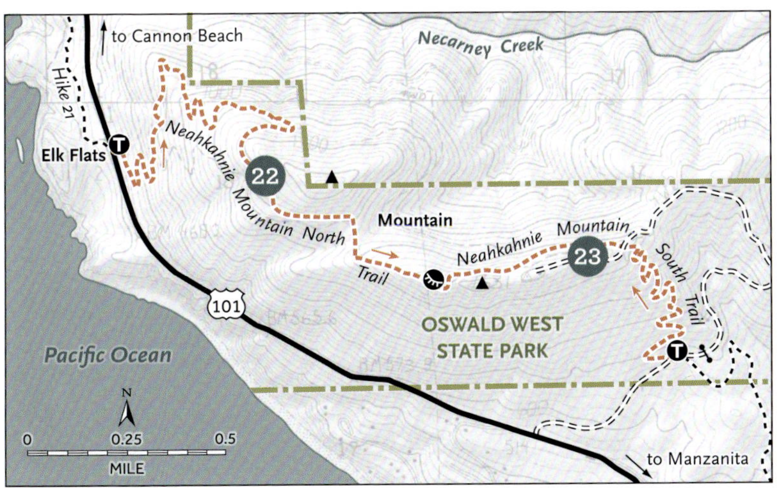

*The view from the Neahkahnie Trail summit takes in the lower Nehalem Valley and the shoreline miles to the south.*

knob. Scramble higher, above the trail, for an even better view. Return as you came, unless you've managed to arrange a shuttle, allowing you to descend on Neahkahnie Mountain South Trail.

## 23 Neahkahnie Mountain South Trail

RATING/DIFFICULTY: ***/2

ROUNDTRIP: 2.8 miles

ELEV GAIN: 960 feet

**Contact:** Oswald West State Park; **Notes:** Dogs on-leash; **GPS:** 45.74076°, –123.93457°

**Neahkahnie Mountain was reportedly a vision-quest site for Clatsop-Nehalem people; it may still be for some, but most people ascend it for the magnificent view of the Nehalem River valley and the coastline stretching to the south. Spring and early summer have the added attraction of a wildflower show in the open meadows and shaded forest glades. Most summit hikers approach Neahkahnie Mountain via the south trail; for a longer hike, check out the north trail (Hike 22).**

### GETTING THERE

Turn left at the hiker sign east of US Highway 101 about 1.5 miles north of Manzanita or 13 miles south of Cannon Beach (if the sign is missing, look for the gravel road between mileposts 41 and 42, across from the entrance to Neah-Kah-Nie Meadows). Drive 0.5 mile up the bumpy gravel road to the trailhead parking area.

### ON THE TRAIL

From the parking area, the trail climbs steadily, varying between dark stands of Sitka spruce and open, brushy slopes with outstanding views. At 0.9 mile you reach the forested summit ridge, where a road crosses the trail up to a collection of communication towers above; bypass it and continue north as the trail curves along the hillside to a sharp switchback. Follow the trail south a short distance (take great care here; unless the trail has been repaired, it would be easy to tumble at a crumbling trail section) and head up and over the summit ridge just below Neahkahnie's rocky crest. The view from here is magnificent, but some hikers aren't satisfied until they've scrambled to the top, a short, steep climb above. Return as you came.

### EXTEND YOUR HIKE

Just up a gravel road from the trailhead is the start of the Headwaters Trail, which leads 1.8 miles down (670 feet elevation loss) to US 101 across from Nehalem Road at the north end of Manzanita. The trail was built as a continuation of the Oregon Coast Trail and can be used to hike to Neahkahnie Mountain from Manzanita.

## 24 Beach Walk: Manzanita

ONE-WAY DISTANCE: 5.2 miles

The beach here stretches from near the foot of Neahkahnie Mountain south to the end of Nehalem Spit. In the middle is Manzanita, a small, upscale beach town. Locals tend to gravitate toward the quiet north end of the beach, and there's plenty of solitude at the south end of the spit too, for those willing

*Neahkahnie Mountain crouches above the beach north of Manzanita.* (Photo by Mountaineers Books)

to walk. The largest public parking lot is at Nehalem Bay State Park, just south of town.

### BEACH ACCESS

BA 21A, Laneda Avenue. Street parking. Public toilets one block up Laneda at the visitor center.

BA 23, Nehalem Bay State Park entrance. OPRD day-use fee. Parking, restrooms.

BA 23B, Nehalem Bay State Park day-use area. OPRD day-use fee. No dogs or kites on beach Mar 15–Sept 15 from here south to the end of the spit. Vault toilet.

### WHERE TO WALK

**Neahkahnie Beach.** For the quietest walk, park along Ocean Road (north of downtown Manzanita) and head north until the beach runs out.

**From downtown Manzanita.** Park on the street and follow the main street, Laneda Avenue, down to Beach Access 21A. From here you can walk for miles to the north or the south, along Nehalem Spit.

**From Nehalem Bay State Park.** Park in the large parking area near the park entrance and take a trail over the dune to the beach at Beach Access 23. Or continue south and park at the day-use area at Beach Access 23B. Either spot gives you miles of walking on Nehalem Spit. For a fun 5.4-mile roundtrip excursion, start at Beach Access 23B, walk the beach south nearly to the Nehalem's north jetty, pick up a sand trail leading south and east past the end of the jetty, scramble down to the beach, and continue another 0.4 mile or so to where you can hail (or call) a boat from Jetty Fishery (small fee) to their marina, buy a cold drink or some freshly cooked Dungeness crab, then ride the boat back to the spit and return as you came.

## 25 Beach Walk: Rockaway Beach

ONE-WAY DISTANCE: 6 miles

Rockaway Beach is one of Oregon's original beach resorts and the birthplace of the Pronto Pup, the original corndog (the first Pronto Pup outlet is still there, plus plenty of other beach food). The beach stretches from the south jetty of the Nehalem River to the north jetty of Tillamook Bay.

### BEACH ACCESS

BA 24, Nedonna Beach, north end of Beach Drive, Rockaway Beach. Large gravel parking area.

BA 25, Manhattan Beach State Recreation Site, north end of Rockaway Beach. Large parking area, restrooms.

BA 27, Rockaway Beach Wayside, at S. 1st Street, Rockaway Beach. Parking, restrooms.

BA 27F, Twin Rocks Beach Access. Small parking area.

BA 28A, Barview Jetty County Park, Tillamook Bay north jetty. Large gravel parking area, vault toilet (more restrooms in the adjacent campground).

### WHERE TO WALK

**From Nedonna Beach.** No problem finding a parking spot here, and there is a lot of quiet walking to the south.

**From Barview Jetty County Park.** Start at Barview Jetty Road and you get to watch boats (and seals and seabirds) coming and going through huge Tillamook Bay's narrow mouth. Then walk north as far as you like.

*The Twin Rocks lie just offshore from the south end of Rockaway Beach.*

## CAPE MEARES TO CAPE LOOKOUT

The Three Capes region of the Oregon coast is named for three closely clustered headlands: Cape Meares, Cape Lookout, and Cape Kiwanda. Capes Meares and Lookout are tall basalt headlands; Cape Kiwanda is a sandstone promontory described in the next section.

Cape Meares is protected as both a state park and a national wildlife refuge; the bird-watching can be excellent from the top of the cape near the historic lighthouse. Other than a few short trails and one down to the beach, it's not much of a hiking destination. Cape Lookout, on the other hand, offers one of the Oregon coast's most memorable (and muddy) hikes, leading to the very end of this cape that juts like an accusing finger into the Pacific. It offers spectacular views to the north and south even before you reach the end.

Between the two is a beach, usually accessible at low tide, stretching from Oceanside to Netarts and more sandy walking on long, remote Netarts Spit.

But first there's Bayocean Spit, enclosing Tillamook Bay. Nothing but an interpretive sign remains to tip off hikers to its brief history as the site of a bustling beach town early in the twentieth century, complete with hotels, houses, and even a narrow-gauge railroad and heated saltwater pool. Spits like this aren't meant for development, however. Natural forces of erosion, exacerbated by construction of jetties at the mouth of Tillamook Bay, caused it to fall, bit by bit, entirely into the ocean. Now hikers and mountain bikers alike enjoy traveling the dirt and gravel road out to the end of the spit through a dense coastal forest, with openings granting views of both ocean and bay.

The beaches and trails in this section are all accessed from secondary roads that compose the Three Capes Loop. If you're bypassing this scenic route and sticking to US Highway 101, consider a short detour to Munson Creek State Natural Area, 1.5 miles off the highway west of mileposts 72–73. A nearly flat 0.5-mile trail through a lush relic of ancient rainforest leads to a 319-foot waterfall.

## 26 Bayocean Spit

RATING/DIFFICULTY: **/3
ROUNDTRIP: 5.2 miles
ELEV GAIN: 60 feet

**Contact:** Tillamook County Parks Department; **Notes:** Tillamook County day-use fee. Trail open to bikes. Dogs allowed on trail but not on the beach north of the last spur trail (Mar 15–Sept 15); **GPS:** 45.51965°, –123.94756°

**In 1906, a real estate broker from Kansas City envisioned a second Atlantic City on the sand spit separating Tillamook Bay from the Pacific Ocean. By 1914 as many as six hundred building lots had been sold in what was called Bay Ocean Park, which had become a bustling community. But the unstable spit couldn't support the development. Lots began eroding steadily, and in 1950 the last house on the spit washed into the sea. Today Bayocean Spit belongs to hikers, mountain bikers, and bird-watchers who wander the beach or the forested bayside trail. (Technically it belongs to Tillamook County and several private landowners.) The hike out Bayocean Spit is an easy, flat, scenic walk;**

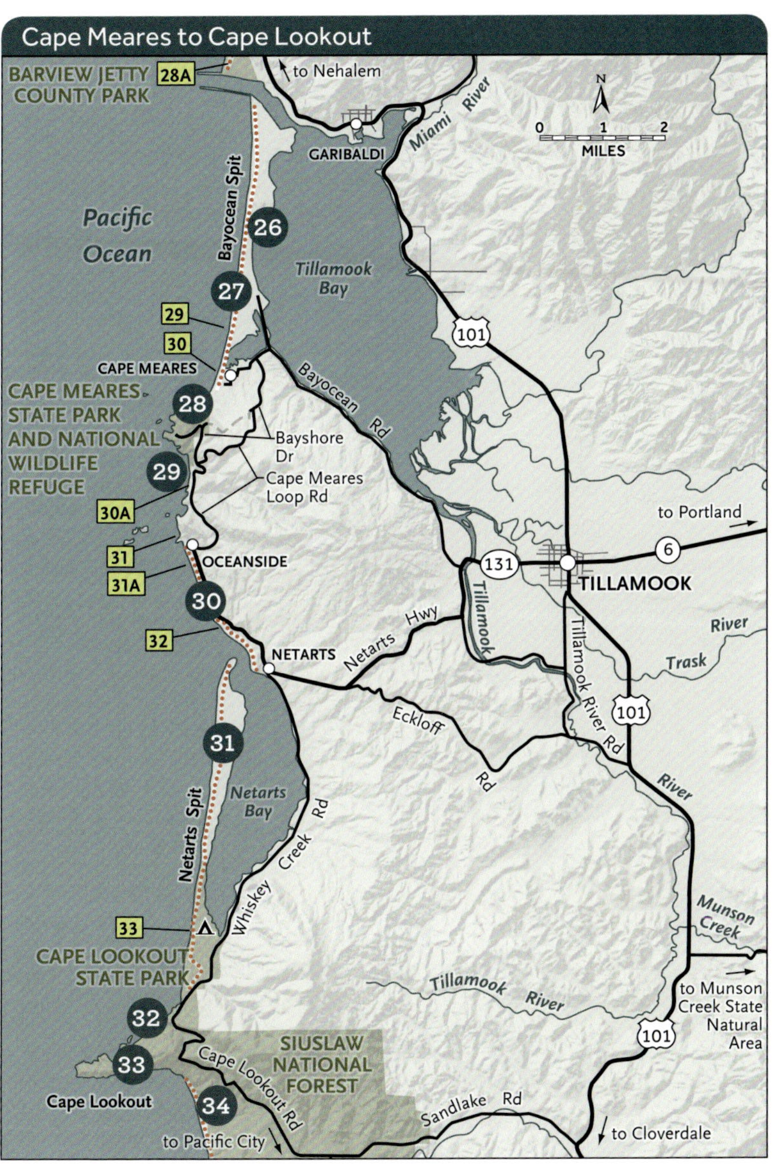
Cape Meares to Cape Lookout
BARVIEW JETTY COUNTY PARK
28A
to Nehalem
GARIBALDI
Miami River
MILES
0 1 2
Pacific Ocean
Bayocean Spit
26
27
Tillamook Bay
101
29
30
CAPE MEARES
CAPE MEARES STATE PARK AND NATIONAL WILDLIFE REFUGE
28
Bayocean Rd
Bayshore Dr
Cape Meares Loop Rd
29
30A
to Portland
6
31
OCEANSIDE
131
TILLAMOOK
31A
30
Tillamook
Tillamook River Rd
River
Trask
32
NETARTS
Netarts Hwy
101
Eckloff Rd
31
River
Netarts Bay
Netarts Spit
Whiskey Creek Rd
Munson Creek
33
CAPE LOOKOUT STATE PARK
Tillamook River
to Munson Creek State Natural Area
32
101
SIUSLAW NATIONAL FOREST
33
Cape Lookout Rd
Cape Lookout
34
Sandlake Rd
to Pacific City
to Cloverdale

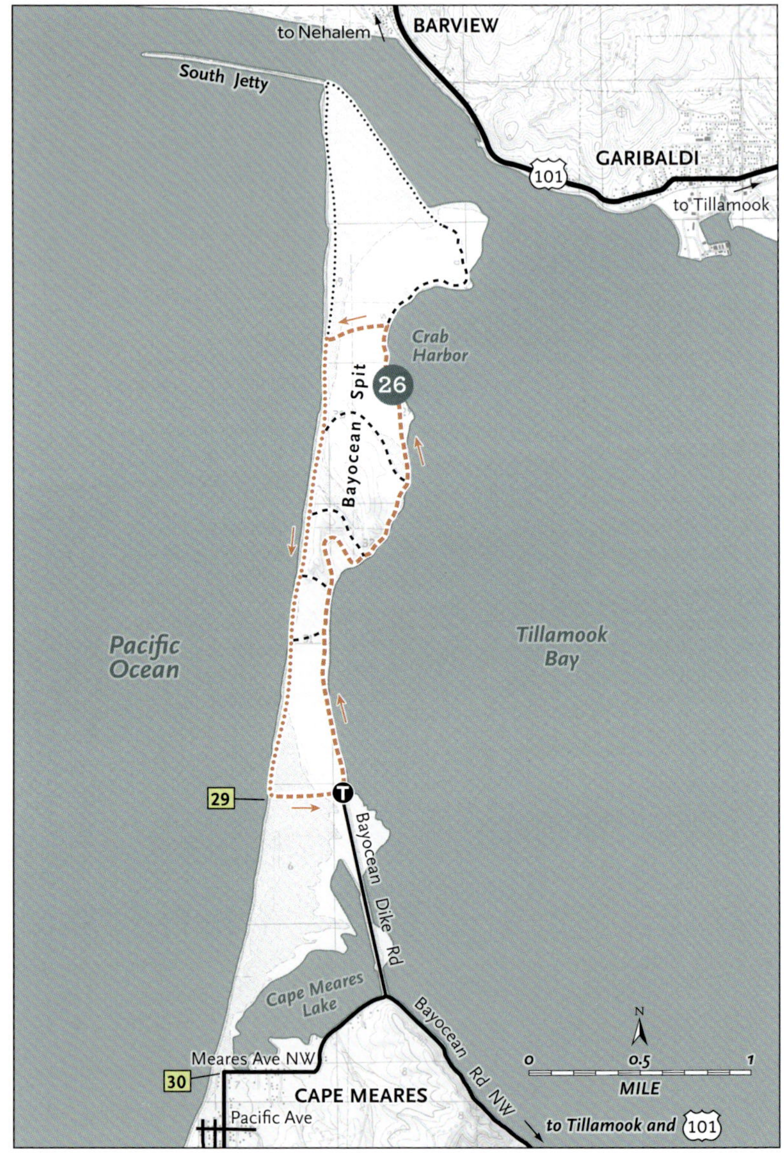

to Nehalem
BARVIEW
South Jetty
GARIBALDI
101
to Tillamook
Crab Harbor
26
Bayocean Spit
Pacific Ocean
Tillamook Bay
29
Bayocean Dike Rd
Cape Meares Lake
Bayocean Rd NW
Meares Ave NW
30
CAPE MEARES
Pacific Ave
0
0.5
1
MILE
N
to Tillamook and 101

**cut over to the ocean beach at the last of several spur trails and head back to the parking area via the shore for a satisfying 5.2-mile loop hike that can include your dog any time of year. Alternatively, take any of the other spur trails to the beach for a shorter loop. It's 8.2 miles to loop all the way to the end of the spit and back, but reconstruction of Tillamook Bay South Jetty beginning in 2024 may have altered or limited recreational access to the end of Bayocean Spit.**

## GETTING THERE

From US Highway 101 in Tillamook, follow signs to Three Capes Scenic Route, west and north, about 8 miles. Watch for the big sign describing Bayocean Spit's history on the bay side of the road. Turn off the main highway and drive north 1 mile on graveled Bayocean Dike Road, which separates the bay from Cape Meares Lake, to the trailhead parking.

## ON THE TRAIL

The trail (continuation of the gravel access road) toward the tip of the spit leads north out of the parking area; there's also a 0.3-mile trail leading straight west through the dunes to the beach from the northwest corner of the parking area (Beach Access 29). The main trail, however, takes you straight north, following the bay shore most of the way and offering expansive bay views. Additional spur trails lead west from the main trail and through the forest to the ocean beach at 0.6 mile, 0.9 mile, 1.4 miles, 1.8 miles, and 2.5 miles from the trailhead. From the beach, look for signposts marked "Trail." For a 5.2-mile loop, take the last spur trail heading west (if you reach a sharp left turn in the main trail, you've gone 0.5 mile too far). Walk the beach south about 2 miles and notice where the pine-topped dune on your left drops to merge with the grass-covered

*The flat, car-free road along the bay side of Bayocean Spit offers easy walking.*

foredune. About 25 yards from the end of the forested dune hill, look for the Beach Access 29 sign leading to a trail (barely discernible) that heads up and over the foredune and back to the parking area.

## 27 Beach Walk: Cape Meares

ONE-WAY DISTANCE: 5.4 miles

The beach bordering Bayocean Spit (Hike 26) continues south all the way to the cliffs at the base of Cape Meares.

### BEACH ACCESS

BA 29, Bayocean Peninsula County Park. Large gravel parking area. See Hike 26.

BA 30, Cape Meares community, end of Meares Avenue NW. Small parking area.

### WHERE TO WALK

**North or south from the community of Cape Meares.** Descriptions of Hikes 26 and 28 cover most of what you need to know for a walk between the north end of Bayocean Spit and Cape Meares. But there's another 2.25 miles of beach between those two beach access points available for walking as well. Cape Meares is a residential community with no commercial services.

## 28 Cape Meares Summit

RATING/DIFFICULTY: **/2

ROUNDTRIP: 4 miles

ELEV GAIN: 1,090 feet

**Contact:** Cape Lookout State Park; **Notes:** Dogs on-leash. Toilets at state park parking lot; **GPS:** 45.50179°, –123.95944°

*Walk south at Cape Meares until you hit this rock ledge, or beyond if the tide is low or can manage some scrambling.*

**A steep trail (that actually lies mostly within Cape Meares National Wildlife Refuge, adjacent to Cape Meares State Scenic Viewpoint, your destination) leads from the beach to the top of Cape Meares. It's easy to reach at low tide, but you'll have to scramble over a rock bluff to reach it at mid- or high tide (not recommended with young children or dogs). The condition of this trail varies from adequate to overgrown and slick. Adventurous day hikers can use it to get some exercise and visit the big trees and lighthouse at the top of the cape.**

## GETTING THERE

From US Highway 101 in Tillamook, follow Three Capes Scenic Route about 8 miles (becomes Meares Avenue NW) to the community of Cape Meares. Where the road turns at 4th Street NW, continue straight to a small parking area at Beach Access 30. Alternately, from Oceanside, follow Cape Meares Loop Road north 1.9 miles and turn

## LIGHTHOUSES: LIVING MARITIME HISTORY

*Walk or drive to the Coquille River Lighthouse, across the river from Bandon and the newest of Oregon's original 19th century lighthouses.*

The first lighthouse on the US West Coast was completed in 1856 at the mouth of the Columbia River, atop Cape Disappointment (Hike 1) in what later became Washington state (but was at the time still part of Oregon Territory). Oregon's first lighthouse was completed a year later and lasted only six years. Construction of the 1857 Umpqua River Lighthouse, built on the river's north bank, was prompted by an influx of settlers and miners following discovery of gold in Oregon's southwest corner. Its site on a sand spit made it vulnerable to storms and flooding, however, and in 1863 it washed away. By then the Civil War was dominating Congress' attention and pocketbook. Not until 1866 was Oregon's second lighthouse built, this one on a tiny islet south of the mouth of Coos Bay. Cape Arago Lighthouse was later rebuilt twice; the current structure, which you can't approach but can see from the Shoreline Trail (Hike 83), was completed in 1934.

A veritable flurry of lighthouse construction then commenced, prompted by an uptick in shipping between Alaska and San Francisco. The lighthouse at Cape Blanco—site of a sharp bend in the coastline and a challenge to mariners—was finished in 1870, followed by Yaquina Bay Lighthouse in 1871 and—after that charming cottage-style beacon was found to be less than helpful to mariners—a 93-foot-tall lighthouse on nearby Yaquina Head was constructed in 1873. Tillamook Rock Lighthouse, 1 mile offshore, was completed in 1881; look for it from the shoreline trails in Ecola State Park (Hikes 12 and 13). A lighthouse had been proposed for the end of long, pointy Cape Lookout (Hike 33), but it would have been difficult if not impossible to land or transport materials to the site, so a short, stocky alternative was built in 1890 on a sea cliff at Cape Meares (Hike 28), the next headland to the north. Two more lighthouses went into operation in 1894: Heceta Head (Hike 66) and one replacing the first Umpqua River Lighthouse, this one on a tall ridge south of the river. The newest of Oregon's original lighthouses, across the Coquille River from the town of Bandon, was completed in 1896.

All eight are still standing, some having barely escaped demolition. All are visible; some are also visitable. Automatic beacons, GPS, and other newer navigation technology have largely replaced the lighthouse's role in guiding mariners along the coast and in and out of harbors, but some still have lights that shine, for safety as well as nostalgia—notably Heceta Head Lighthouse, whose brilliant flashing light can be seen as far as 21 miles out to sea.

*Because it is perched high on the cliff, Cape Meares Lighthouse doesn't have to be tall.*

right to stay on this road (a left leads 0.6 mile to the park entrance). Drive another 2.7 miles to Meares Avenue NW; turn left and continue to the beach.

## ON THE TRAIL

Walk the beach south 0.6 miles; it turns to cobbles shortly before reaching a low, rocky point. Walk around it if the tide permits, scramble over it if your own condition permits, or turn around if necessary. Beyond the ledge go another 0.1 mile and look for a steep, muddy draw leading off the beach; the summit trail starts here. A couple of minutes up the trail, bear right at a trail junction. From here, the trail climbs another 0.8 mile, first through a forest dominated by alders and then into a more mature Sitka spruce forest. You'll top out near the park entrance on Cape Meares Loop Road; a short detour leads to a huge Sitka spruce. Otherwise continue another 0.5 mile down the park road (watching for cars) to the day-use area with parking, restrooms, fabulous views and bird-watching, and a short path to Cape Meares Lighthouse and the landmark Octopus Tree Trail. Return as you came.

# 29 Beach Walk: Short Beach

ONE-WAY DISTANCE: 0.7 mile

It's a short but steep walk on path, stairs, and boardwalk down to this pocket beach enclosed by tall headlands.

## BEACH ACCESS

BA 30A, Short Beach trail, off Cape Meares Loop Road. Limited roadside parking.

*Rockhounds delight at Short Sand Beach.*

## WHERE TO WALK

**Anywhere!** Winter is a good time to look for agates and jasper on the shingle beach. You may have heard of Lost Boy Cave, around the headland at the south end of the beach, but it is accessible only briefly on a very low minus tide, a few days of the year. If you choose to explore, be careful and keep an eye on the tide.

# 30 Beach Walk: Oceanside

ONE-WAY DISTANCE: 2.7 miles

Offshore rocks, a pedestrian tunnel through a headland, plenty of beach for kite-flying: The beach between Oceanside and Netarts has plenty of attractions but is still off the beaten path. A walk all the way south to Netarts is possible only at low tide.

## BEACH ACCESS

BA 31, Oceanside State Recreation Site. Parking area, restrooms.

BA 31A, Symons State Scenic Viewpoint. Limited parking along highway.

BA 32, Happy Camp, end of Happy Camp Road, off State Highway 131. Small parking area, restrooms.

Netarts Boat Ramp, Netarts. Parking, restrooms.

## WHERE TO WALK

**Oceanside south.** The state recreation site has the most parking and it's near the north end of the beach, so it's a great place to start a southbound beach walk; depending on the tide you may be able to walk as far as Netarts. The beach narrows past Happy Camp, 1.7 miles south of Oceanside and just past Fall Creek (wadeable in summer). Approaching the breakwater at Netarts, take the little trail leading off the beach to reach the boat ramp. Or go in reverse, at mid-tide or below; should you run out of beach, walk the highway north to Happy Camp to return to the wider beach.

**Oceanside north.** From the parking area it's just 0.2 mile to Maxwell Point. Here's where it gets interesting: On the other side of the point is Tunnel Beach, accessible via a pedestrian tunnel built for beachgoers in 1926. The tunnel is usually walkable at all but very high tides, but as always, keep your eye on the tide to keep from getting stuck on the wrong side of the point. The tunnel leads to an additional 0.3 mile of beach (and an adventure). You're wise to wear nonslip footwear (the rocks in the tunnel can be slippery) and bring a flashlight (or use your smartphone flashlight app).

**Lost Boy Cave.** You may have heard about a way to go farther, around or through the headland to reach what's called Lost Boy Cave. But the walkway built here years ago has long since washed away. See Short Beach description (Hike 29) for more details.

*A century-old pedestrian tunnel leads north through Maxwell Point at Oceanside to a pocket beach.*

*Netarts Spit stretches more than 5 miles north from the base of Cape Lookout.*

## 31 Beach Walk: Netarts Spit

ONE-WAY DISTANCE: 5.8 miles

This is a gem of a beach walk on the Oregon coast's longest sand spit. Few hikers go all the way to the end of the spit (more than 10 miles roundtrip), but even going a couple of miles up the beach puts you on a remote, lonely, lovely beach.

### BEACH ACCESS

BA 33, Cape Lookout State Park day-use area. OPRD day-use fee. Large parking lot, restrooms.

### WHERE TO WALK

**Northbound.** Just start at the day-use area and walk north up the beach. You'll pass a few beach access signs in the first 0.6 mile; oddly they're all labeled 33. Walk only as far as you're confident you can walk back, as there is no ready road access for at least the last two-thirds of the way to the end of the spit. Alternately take a short stroll (0.4 mile one-way) south from the day-use area to the base of Cape Lookout.

## 32 Cape Lookout North Trail

RATING/DIFFICULTY: **/3
ROUNDTRIP: 4.6 miles
ELEV GAIN: 1,820 feet

**Contact:** Cape Lookout State Park; **Notes:** OPRD day-use fee. Dogs on-leash. Toilet available; **GPS:** 45.36050°, –123.96953°

**This stretch of the Oregon Coast Trail serves day hikers and thru hikers as a link from the state park's sea-level campground to the top of Cape Lookout and the trail west to the cape's tip (Hike 33).**

### GETTING THERE

From US Highway 101 in Tillamook, follow signs west toward Three Capes Scenic Route. After crossing the Tillamook River, bear left onto Netarts Highway and follow signs to Cape Lookout State Park and its day-use area, about 10 miles from US 101. For directions to the south trailhead atop Cape Lookout (no fee), see Hike 33.

### ON THE TRAIL

Various spur trails through the day-use area confuse the trail's beginning. Look for a gravel service road crossing Jackson Creek that eventually leads onto a narrow footpath. The trail winds up and up through the woods; at 1.1 miles you'll pass a spur trail leading out to Cape Lookout Road. Stick to the main trail, crossing Cape Creek on a long footbridge at 1.3 miles. The trail steepens as it winds through a stretch damaged by heavy snowfall in 2023. It improves (but still climbs) until it emerges at the cape-top trailhead and parking area. Return as you came.

## 33 Cape Lookout Trail

RATING/DIFFICULTY: ***/3
ROUNDTRIP: 4.7 miles
ELEV GAIN: 900 feet

**Contact:** Cape Lookout State Park; **Notes:** Dogs on-leash. Toilets; **GPS:** 45.34130°, –123.97438°

*A graceful suspension bridge crosses Cape Creek on the Cape Lookout North Trail.*

Like most of the capes on the Oregon coast, Cape Lookout is built of basalt. Lava from volcanoes hundreds of miles to the east emerged some 15.5 million years ago, spread out, and followed stream valleys over what was then a very low Coast Range, one blanketed not by the Douglas-fir forests of today but by grassy savannah with ginkgos, maples, oaks, and a few pines and spruces. Where the basalt hardened, it formed casts that remained in place as the softer stone around them eroded away. Today Cape Lookout is a narrow, steep-sided promontory extending nearly 2 miles due west into the Pacific; the trail that leads to its tip is a great hiking destination and is popular year-round, but the second half of the trail is chronically muddy and tangled with tree roots. The 400-foot-high viewpoint at the end of the trail is considered one of the best sites for whale-watching on the Oregon coast (though volunteers are no longer posted there during Whale Watch Weeks). Gray whales may pass as close as 100 yards, but binoculars always improve viewing.

## GETTING THERE

From US Highway 101 in Tillamook, follow signs to Three Capes Scenic Route. After crossing the Tillamook River, bear left onto Netarts Highway to cut directly west and follow signs

*Take care once you reach the far end of Cape Lookout Trail; there's no fencing to speak of, and the cliff drops straight into the ocean. Cape Lookout had once been considered for a lighthouse location, but there was no way to get materials to it.*

to Cape Lookout State Park, about 10 miles from US 101. Pass the park's campground entrance and day-use area and continue another 2.8 miles on Cape Lookout Road to the trailhead parking area on your right.

### ON THE TRAIL

Two trails lead out of the parking area side by side; take the left-hand trail (to the right is Cape Lookout North Trail, Hike 32) and continue straight at the next junction (with Cape Lookout South Trail, Hike 34). The well-maintained trail continues west, gradually descending, passing a southward viewpoint at 0.6 mile and a northward viewpoint into Wells Cove at 1.2 miles. From here on, the trail's condition is rougher, with large pockets of mud and tree roots to negotiate. The route returns to the scenic south side of the cliffs before reaching the trail's end at the cape's tip. There is a lame cable "fence" to keep visitors away from the precipitous cliff; keep a close eye on kids and dogs. Return as you came.

## 34 Cape Lookout South Trail

RATING/DIFFICULTY: **/2
ROUNDTRIP: 3.6 miles
ELEV GAIN: 610 feet

**Contact:** Cape Lookout State Park; **Notes:** Dogs on-leash. Toilet; **GPS:** 45.34130°, –123.97438°

**From the top of Cape Lookout you can hike 1.8 deeply forested miles down to a secluded beach with a small tidepool area.**

### GETTING THERE

From US Highway 101 in Tillamook, follow signs to Three Capes Scenic Route. After crossing the Tillamook River, bear left onto

Netarts Highway to cut directly west toward Netarts and follow signs to Cape Lookout State Park, about 10 miles from US 101. Pass the park's campground entrance and continue another 2.8 miles on Cape Lookout Road to the trailhead parking area on your right.

## ON THE TRAIL

Take the left-hand trail leading west out of the trailhead parking area, and in about 75 yards make a sharp left turn down the hill at the junction with Cape Lookout Trail (Hike 33) the beach trail. From here the trail descends gently among tall Sitka spruce, crossing a creek at about the halfway point and switchbacking now and then. The trail ends close to the base of the cape. Return as you came.

## EXTEND YOUR HIKE

Extend your roundtrip hike by as much as 8.2 miles by walking the beach south to the mouth of Sand Lake estuary (see Hike 35). With a shuttle car, you could walk from the top of Cape Lookout to the estuary outlet and around the corner to Fishermans Day-Use Area at the end of Galloway Road, a 6-mile one-way hike.

*Clouds hang low over Cape Lookout on a classic Pacific Northwest day.*

## SAND LAKE TO PACIFIC CITY

The long beach stretching between Capes Lookout and Kiwanda is separated by the outlet for Sand Lake, which is not really a lake but a shallow estuary, where saltwater and freshwater mingle with the ebb and flow of the tides. Most bays are essentially wide river mouths, but Sand Lake is bar-built, formed by the sand bars at its mouth and fed only by a few small streams and the seawater that fills it and flushes it twice a day. Other than some small county and state parks, Sand Lake is virtually undeveloped. Parts of the shoreline have been logged and farmed in the past, but no more. Thanks to public and private efforts (including the latest, an acquisition of Sitka Sedge State Natural Area), Sand Lake is considered the best conserved estuary in the state, a place where native plants and animals can thrive and humans can enjoy the sights and sounds of wild nature, mingled with the distant buzzing of off-highway vehicles (OHVs) roaming the dunes to the north.

Cape Kiwanda is the only major headland on the Oregon coast composed not of basalt but of sandstone, a soft rock created by the ocean's weight compressing offshore sand and sediment and later uplifted by tectonic forces. Climb the tall parabolic (U-shaped) dune inland from the neck of the cape—that dune being another phenomenon rare on this part of the Oregon coast. Pause at the top of the dune for a view north to Cape Lookout and south to Lookout's basalt sister, Haystack Rock (the less-famous cousin of Cannon Beach's Haystack Rock). Like Cape Lookout, this Haystack Rock was once a peninsula protecting Cape Kiwanda's sandstone from winter storm waves battering it from the south. The peninsula's basalt neck gradually eroded and disappeared, stranding it as a sea stack, and as such, offering continued but lessened protection to a now quickly eroding Kiwanda. It is

*Morning sun breaks through the clouds during a walk to Sand Lake.* (Photo by Eric Halperin)

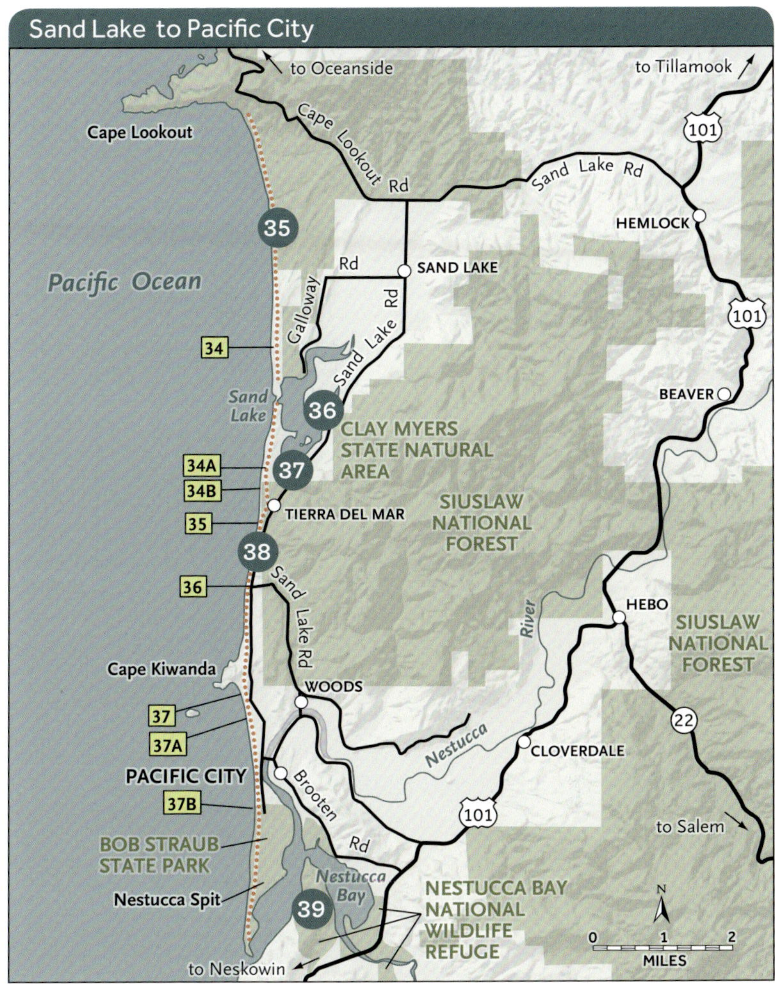


extremely dangerous to venture beyond the fencing at the top of Cape Kiwanda, with its steep cliffs and sinkholes; accidental deaths are becoming more common every year as the cape deteriorates.

There are small Tillamook County campgrounds at Whalen Island and Cape Kiwanda (Webb) and a US Forest Service campground (Sandbeach) that caters mainly to OHV enthusiasts.

## 35 Beach Walk: Cape Lookout to Sand Lake Estuary

ONE-WAY DISTANCE: 4 miles

Lovely and remote at the north end, buzzing with the sound of off-highway vehicles (OHVs) at the south end, this beach is a nice add-on to a hike down the Cape Lookout South Trail (Hike 34). The view of Cape Lookout just gets more impressive as you approach it.

### BEACH ACCESS

Bottom of Cape Lookout South Trail (see Hike 34).

Fishermans Day-Use Area, Sand Lake Recreation Area, at the end of Galloway Road. Parking, vault toilet.

### WHERE TO WALK

**From Fishermans Day-Use Area.** Walk west along Sand Lake outlet, then north up the beach. You'll pass a sign for Beach Access 34; OHVs are allowed on the beach for the next 1.6 miles to the north. Beyond that it's very quiet. You'll pass the Boy Scouts' Camp Meriwether (note the flagpole) and eventually reach the bottom of the Cape Lookout South Trail, less than 0.2 mile from the base of the cliffs.

## 36 Whalen Island

RATING/DIFFICULTY: */1
LOOP: 1.4 miles
ELEV GAIN: 140 feet

**Contact:** Clay Myers State Natural Area at Whalen Island; **Notes:** Dogs on-leash. Toilets; **GPS:** 45.27357°, –123.95039°

**Whalen Island is a tiny, densely forested island smack in the middle of Sand Lake estuary. At high tide it's surrounded by water; at low tide, by mudflats teeming with life. Forest borders the estuary to the north and south; ocean waves pound the ocean beach to the west at the entrance to the shallow bay. A pleasant loop trail circumnavigates the island.**

*Kayakers paddle along the western shore of Whalen Island on an evening low tide.*

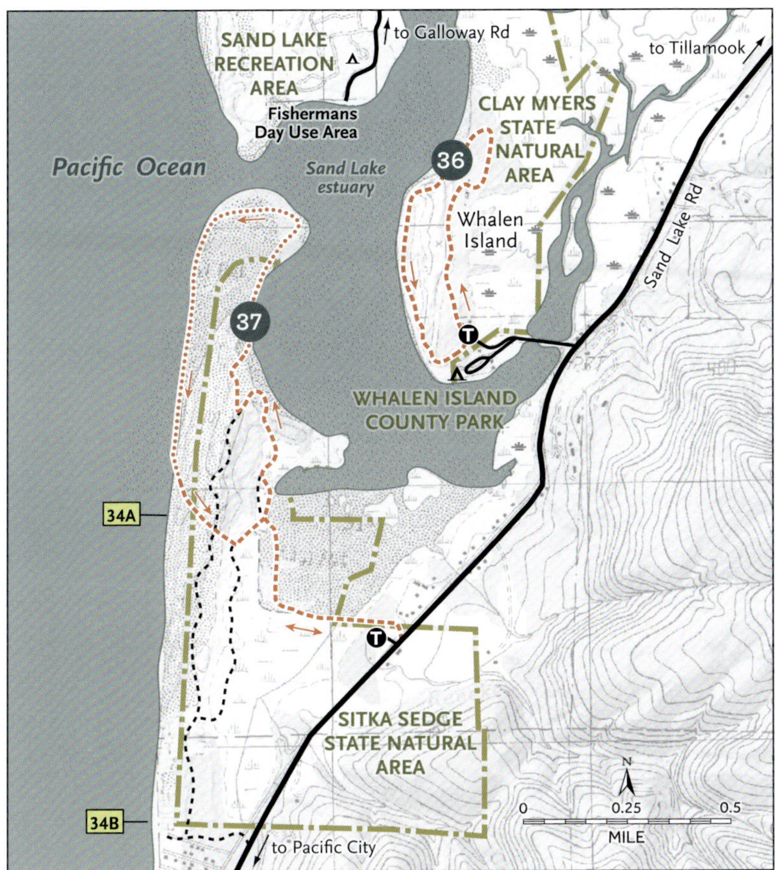


## GETTING THERE

From the stoplight in the middle of Pacific City, go west, cross the river, and turn north toward Cape Kiwanda Drive, which then becomes Sand Lake Road. The turnoff to Whalen Island is 5.5 miles north of Pacific City; take it 0.2 mile, over a channel of the estuary to Whalen Island, and bear right, passing the Whalen Island County Campground, into Clay Myers State Natural Area and the trailhead.

## ON THE TRAIL

For a counterclockwise loop, take the trail north, bearing left where a spur trail on the right leads to an overlook at the edge of the estuary. The trail continues north, along the estuary, but views are limited by the dense

## WATCHING GRAY WHALES

*You might see a gray whale breaching or spy-hopping, but you're much more likely to see the telltale vapor cloud from a whale exhaling through its blowhole.* (Photo by Tim Gage)

Of two dozen or so cetaceans—whales, dolphins, porpoises, and the like—found in the waters off Oregon, the gray whale is the species you're most likely to see from shore. Roughly 18,000 gray whales now live in the eastern north Pacific Ocean and pass by Oregon twice each year from December through May. They travel from arctic and subtropical waters—6000 miles, the longest migration of any mammal. In addition, a few hundred gray whales spend their entire summer and fall off the Oregon coast. These resident whales tend to stay closer to shore and are thus easier to spot.

As for the migrants, the number of northbound whales tends to peak around mid-March; cows with their calves start arriving from May through early June. In winter, pregnant females lead the way, reaching the Oregon coast from northern waters in mid-December; the number of passing whales builds to a peak of about thirty per hour in late December and early January.

The most common way to spot a whale is by observing it blow, exhaling water and vapor out its blowhole. Watch also for sounding (exposing tail flukes as it dives deep); spy-hopping (raising its head partially out of the water), and breaching (surging out of the ocean, then falling back with a huge splash). Occasionally dead or dying whales and other marine mammals wind up on the beach; if you come upon one, notify the Oregon Marine Mammal Stranding Network, mmi.oregonstate.edu/ommsn.

Every week between Christmas and New Year's, and again during schools' spring vacation week, trained volunteers station themselves (in all weather) at more than a dozen vantage points—from Fort Stevens State Park on the Columbia River to Harris Beach at Brookings—for a few hours at midday to help visitors spot migrating whales.

tangle of shore pine, salal, and huckleberry. The trail rises toward the island's north end, with open views of the water and hills to the north, then curves south, following the island's ocean side and offering opportunities to traipse down to the narrow sandy beach, especially as you near the island's south end. At low tide the tide flats here are exposed, allowing you to walk to the mainland at Sand Lake Recreation Area with hardly any wading, but make sure you allow time to get back to the trail before the tide rises. Finally the loop trail meets the gravel path from the parking lot at a viewpoint overlooking Sand Lake. Follow it back to the parking lot, bearing left at the spur trail leading to rustic Whalen Island County Campground, adjacent to the state natural area.

## 37 Sitka Sedge Loop

RATING/DIFFICULTY: **/1
LOOP: 3.5 miles
ELEV GAIN: 140 feet

**Contact:** Sitka Sedge State Natural Area; **Notes:** Dogs on-leash. Toilet; **GPS:** 45.26297°, –123.95455°

**In 2015 Oregon State Parks acquired 357-acre Belz Farm, in the southwest corner of Sand Lake estuary. Dikes originally built to keep out seawater and enable farming now function as hiking trails that connect with new footpaths to create a 4-mile trail system through the dense coastal forest of Sitka spruce and shore pine. At certain times of year you may see a variety of waterfowl in the estuary—even otters and elk if you're very quiet (and lucky). This 3.5-mile loop walk takes you along the estuary's edge and through the forest to the mouth of Sand Lake and the ocean beach before looping back.**

### GETTING THERE

From the stoplight in the middle of Pacific City, turn west, following signs to Three Capes Loop. Cross the river and turn north (becomes Sandlake Road). Drive 4.8 miles from Pacific City to the gravel parking area for Sitka Sedge State Natural Area, on the west side of the road. Here you'll find concrete picnic tables and benches made from redwood salvaged from an old water tank on Cape Lookout. There's even a bike station with a tire pump and bike locks, should cyclists riding down the Oregon coast wish to take a break.

### ON THE TRAIL

From the parking area, pick up the trail leading briefly north before turning west and following the dike along the water's edge. The first half-mile is accessible compacted gravel. At the first trail junction, bear right for 0.1

*Egrets fish in an arm of Sand Lake, off the dike trail at Sitka Sedge.*

mile and then straight over the boardwalk at the next junction. You'll leave the estuary and wind into the forest, hiking up a couple of switchbacks, until you reach another junction at 1 mile; turn right onto this sand trail. It ends just 0.2 mile farther at a beach near the mouth of the estuary. Follow the shore to your left in a big curve along the estuary and then south along the ocean beach until you see a yellow Beach Access 34A sign, roughly 2.6 miles from your start. Turn inland here, continuing through the dunes and going straight at a four-way trail junction. Bear left and then right at the next two trail junctions to meet the main route back along the dike to the trailhead.

## 38 Beach Walk: Sand Lake Estuary to Nestucca Spit

ONE-WAY DISTANCE: 8.5 miles

This long stretch starts at the south edge of Sand Lake estuary and stretches to the end of Nestucca Spit and includes an ascent of Cape Kiwanda. The spit lies within Bob Straub State Park, a nearly undeveloped park (no campground) best for beach walking.

### BEACH ACCESS

BA 34A, Sitka Sedge State Natural Area, off Sandlake Road. No dogs or kites on beach between Sand Lake outlet and Beach Access 34 Mar 15–Sept 15. Parking area, vault toilet.

BA 36, McPhillips Beach, off Cape Kiwanda Drive. Small gravel parking area, portable toilet.

BA 37, Cape Kiwanda State Natural Area, off Cape Kiwanda Drive. Large parking area, restrooms.

BA 37B, Bob Straub State Park day-use area. Parking area, vault toilets.

### WHERE TO WALK

**Sitka Sedge Beach Loop.** See Hike 37.

**Over Kiwanda.** Southbound, start at McPhillips Beach (or pullouts along Sandlake Road/Cape Kiwanda Drive) and walk the beach south to the base of Cape Kiwanda—then up and over. It's not tall,

*Climbable Cape Kiwanda is accessible on a beach walk between Sand Lake and Pacific City.*

but it's all sand; at the top, stay on the sand but veer just to the right of the grassy dunes (and stay behind the fencing to the west; it's not as safe as you might think). You'll soon see a clear path down to the beach just north of Cape Kiwanda State Natural Area. Grab a bite to eat; parking can be crowded so you'll be glad you walked. Northbound, start at the state natural area and do it in reverse.

**Nestucca Spit.** Park in town and walk out Pacific Avenue to the beach at Beach Access 37A, or park at the day-use area at Bob Straub State Park. It's 3 miles one-way from Pacific Avenue (2.3 miles from the park day-use area) to the end of the spit—a dramatic spot with the steep cliffs of Porter Point across the Nestucca River's mouth.

## 39 Two Rivers Peninsula Loop

RATING/DIFFICULTY: **/2
LOOP: 2.5 miles
ELEV GAIN: 180 feet

**Contact:** Nestucca Bay National Wildlife Refuge; **Notes:** Open daily dawn to dusk. Dogs not allowed. Vault toilets; **GPS:** 45.16649°, –123.95281°

**For decades, the high Cannery Hill peninsula at the confluence of the Little Nestucca and Nestucca Rivers south of Pacific City served as a Catholic retreat center welcoming people of all faiths. Today it is part of Nestucca Bay National Wildlife Refuge. The area now known as Two Rivers peninsula offers gently graded trails winding through meadows, coastal prairie, and alder forest, with views of the Pacific Ocean. The pastures around the wildlife refuge provide important wintering habitat for Canada geese, while the peninsula's uplands serve as homes or stopping places for migratory songbirds, bald eagles, peregrine falcons, bobcat, black-tailed deer, and other wildlife.**

*A viewing platform at the end of the trail system at Two Rivers Peninsula gives you a look at the confluence of the Nestucca River and the Little Nestucca.*

### GETTING THERE

From the intersection of US Highway 101 and Brooten Road (the road leading west to Pacific City), follow the highway south 2.2 miles and turn right (north) on Christiansen Road. Follow it 0.4 mile to the first parking area, which offers views, a vault toilet, and a covered viewing platform with interpretive displays. Hikers should continue another 0.6 mile up the road (turns to gravel) and park at the upper trailhead.

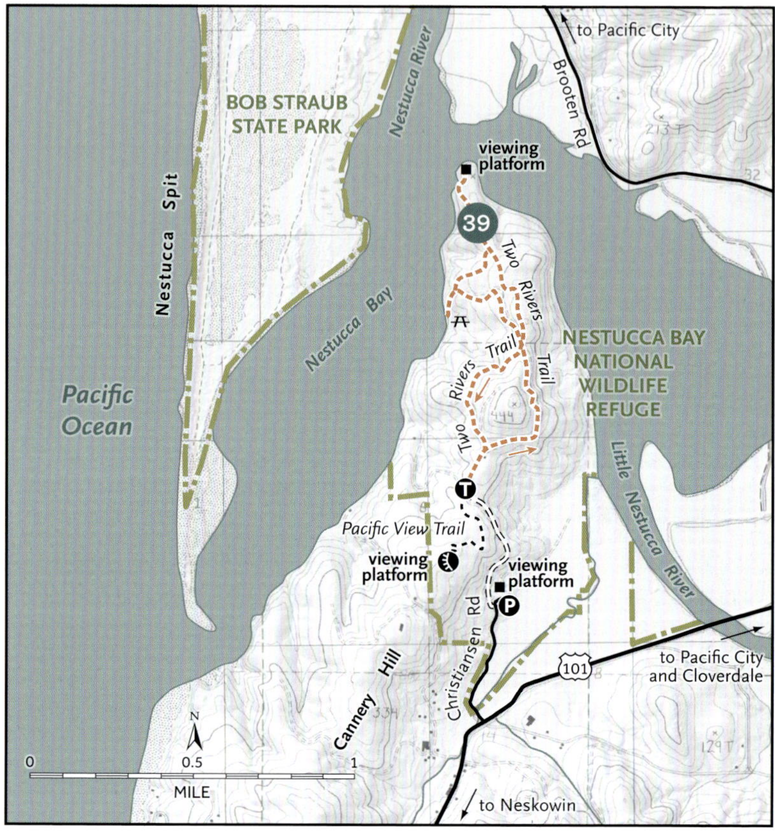


## ON THE TRAIL

From the trailhead you have a couple of options. The paved Pacific View Trail leads south 0.3 mile up through a meadow to a boardwalk and large viewing platform where you can spot the ocean or, with binoculars, scan the surrounding grasslands and skies for a variety of birds.

For a longer walk, follow the old gravel roads and Two Rivers Trail north to the tip of the peninsula—about 1.25 miles one-way via the shortest route—where a viewing platform overlooks the meeting of the rivers. Return as you came for a 2.5-mile roundtrip or consider returning on a different route. See the map here or one posted at the trailhead for options. The spur winding out to the northwest corner of the peninsula leads past a picnic area and a short path anglers can take to reach the water's edge.

## NESKOWIN TO ROADS END, LINCOLN CITY

The centerpiece of this stretch of the Oregon coast is Cascade Head. Notwithstanding the many headlands on the Oregon coast with spectacular trailside views, Cascade Head is still a standout, with its views of the Salmon River estuary from its steep, wildflower-strewn meadows facing the sea and vast forests of hemlock and spruce stretching inland. In 1974 Congress designated 9,670 acres on Cascade Head as a scenic research area. Another 12,000 acres, including the Salmon River estuary, had already been set aside as an experimental forest in 1934; all of it is now recognized as a United Nations Biosphere Reserve. This protection means whole watersheds in this stunning chunk of temperate rainforest have been conserved and are being studied to better understand forest and estuarine ecology as well as the impacts of global climate change. The Nature Conservancy manages and allows the public to access trails on another 270 acres of the headland. A variety of trails lead up and over Cascade Head, each with its own rewards, from deep forest to remote shoreline coves to broad ocean vistas.

Unfortunately, access to some trails and trailheads on Cascade Head has been limited since 2021, when landslides led to closure of Forest Road 1861, which provides access to Harts Cove Trail, the upper Nature Conservancy trailhead, and the upper trailheads for both the north and south Rainforest Trails. Currently the USFS is collecting data and starting preliminary engineering designs as three options are considered: rebuild the road in its current location; rebuild the first mile or so of road from US 101 from a point farther north, in a more geologically stable location; or convert the existing (closed) road to a trail. That phase may extend into or beyond 2027, and it could take several more years before a new road or trail is completed. For updates on the road repair project, search online for "Cascade Head Road 1861 road repair." For now these trails are still open, and the road and trail are occasionally cleared by volunteer trail crews, but they may not have been recently maintained when you arrive.

South of Cascade Head, across the Salmon River, is another unnamed headland just north of Lincoln City. A trail network here through a patchwork of city-owned and Forest Service lands offers more forest hiking and more ocean views. There is no camping on Cascade Head; the closest public campground is at Devils Lake State Park in Lincoln City.

## 40 Beach Walk: Nestucca Bay to Neskowin

ONE-WAY DISTANCE: 4.8 miles

The middle of this beach is typically the quietest. Residents and vacationers staying in Neskowin, day visitors to landmark Proposal Rock, and a good-sized public parking area draw a lot of beachgoers to the south end. At the north it's mostly folks from a small church camp and a few others. Oceanfront houses are mostly arrayed high above the beach. Proposal Rock—so named at the successful conclusion to a turn-of-the-century coastal settler's courtship—is especially fun to visit during minus tides in summer, when you might even be able to walk all around this tree-topped haystack rock and see the creatures not usually visible to us.

## BEACH ACCESS

BA 38, End of Wi Ne Ma Road, 0.6 mile from US 101 south of Pacific City. Limited parking.

BA 39B, Neskowin Beach State Recreation Site, Neskowin. Parking, restrooms.

## WHERE TO WALK

**Porter Point and beyond.** From Beach Access 38, at low tide, venture north 0.75 mile to the large rocks at Porter Point; continue around the point to the mouth of the Nestucca River as far as the tide (and

*Proposal Rock lies at the edge of the shore near the community of Nestucca; only at the lowest tides can you walk all the way around the rock.*

cliffs) allow. South from Beach Access 38, it's about 3.5 miles to Proposal Rock. If high tide blocks the beach as you approach Neskowin, turn around or leave the beach at Beach Access 39A (end of Mount Angel Avenue, Neskowin) and follow neighborhood streets into town.

**Proposal Rock and beyond.** From parking at Neskowin Beach State Recreation Site, walk the sidewalk and then creekside trail a short distance to the beach. Proposal Rock is before you. To the south lies Neskowin Creek, easy to wade in summer; a "ghost forest" of three-century-old tsunami-killed stumps (sometimes visible); and the base of towering Cascade Head. To the north the wide (at high tide) beach beckons.

## 41 Cascade Head North Rainforest Trail

RATING/DIFFICULTY: */2
ROUNDTRIP: 5 miles
ELEV GAIN: 1,120 feet

**Contact:** Hebo Ranger District, Siuslaw National Forest; **Notes:** Closed to hikers Jan 1–July 15 to protect sensitive species. Dogs on-leash; **GPS:** 45.08372°, –123.96087°

**The Cascade Head Rainforest Trail is part of the Oregon Coast Trail. It serves mainly to get hikers off the highway and up and over Cascade Head but not out to the shoreline, so there are no ocean views (but plenty of forest views).**

### GETTING THERE

From Neskowin Beach State Recreation Site, drive US Highway 101 south 1.9 miles and turn right into a very small trailhead parking area, possibly unsigned, with room for just a few vehicles. At this time the upper trailhead is not accessible by car due to closure of Forest Road 1861.

### ON THE TRAIL

The hike begins as a nearly flat path above Fall Creek. At 0.6 mile it makes a sharp left turn and steepens into a steady ascent of the

*Switchbacks get you quickly up to the summit of the North Rainforest Trail.*

north side of the headland with a few switchbacks but mostly following the hillside's contours. At 2.5 miles you reach the top of the trail at FR 1861. The South Rainforest Trail (Hike 43) begins across the road. Return as you came or cross the road and pick up the South Rainforest Trail for a 6-mile one-way hike (with a shuttle car) or 12-mile roundtrip.

### EXTEND YOUR HIKE

More options all may involve negotiating around fallen trees and other obstacles due to lack of maintenance on (closed) FR 1861. Hike the road west 2 miles to the upper trailhead for the Nature Conservancy Trail (see Hike 44). From here it's a 0.9-mile walk through the forest to the viewpoint at the top of the headland's grassy overlook.

Continue west on the road 0.9 mile more to the Hart's Cove trailhead (Hike 42).

Hike the road east 1.2 miles to reach US 101 for a one-way hike with a shuttle vehicle. (User trails skirt the upper edges of landslides across the road.)

## 42 Harts Cove

RATING/DIFFICULTY: ***/3
ROUNDTRIP: 13.4 miles
ELEV GAIN: 3,580 feet

**Contact:** Hebo Ranger District, Siuslaw National Forest; **Notes:** Closed to hikers Jan 1–July 15 to protect sensitive species. Dogs on-leash; **GPS:** 45.06591°, –123.94857°

**Harts Cove Trail is one of the most spectacular trails on the coast but one that is currently out of reach for most hikers. Normally a 5.2-mile (and 1400 feet elevation gain) roundtrip, closure of FR 1861 means you must walk the road 4.1 miles each way just to reach the trailhead. (A mountain bike is another option, but you may have to walk it much of the way.) Crews of volunteers from Trailkeepers of Oregon sometimes open up the road (and trail) with saws and loppers, but you can't count on the road and trail being cleared when you arrive. If you decide to take it on, you'll roll through gorgeous Sitka spruce and western hemlock forest, sometimes to a chorus of California sea lions on the offshore rocks, to end at a large open meadow with views of a dramatic ocean cove and stunningly remote rocky shoreline. Given the lack of cell phone coverage and accessibility by emergency services, the trail in its current condition should be undertaken only by experienced**

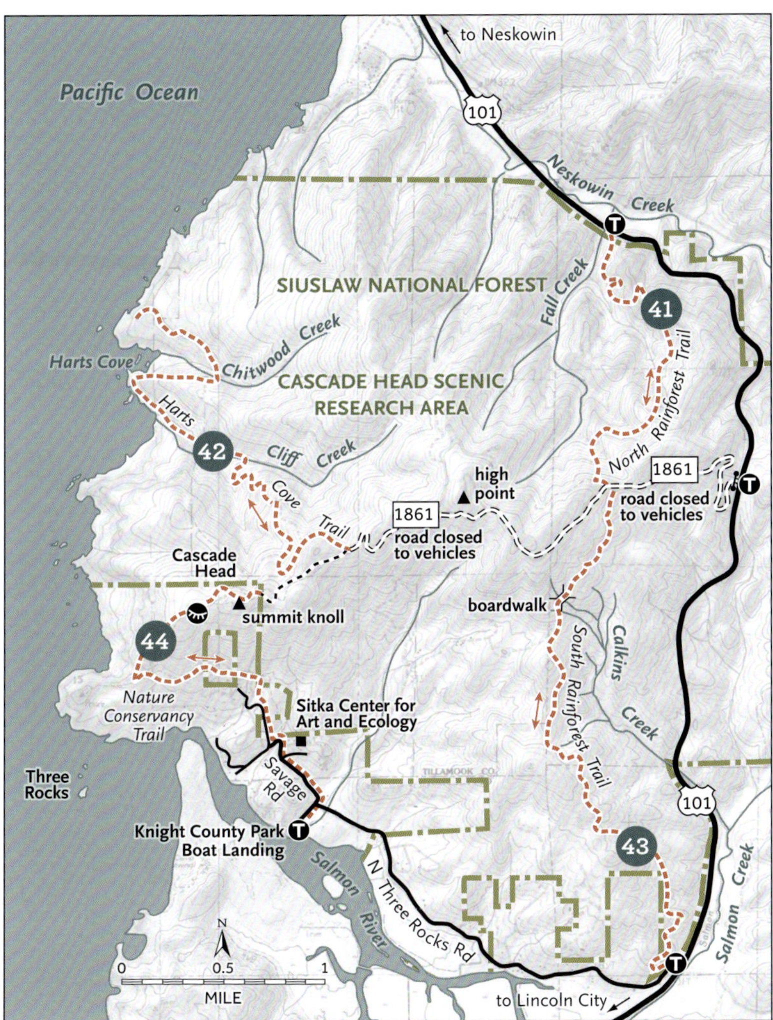


**and well-equipped hikers. The trail is listed here mainly as a placeholder in hopes that easier access will be reestablished in the foreseeable future.**

## GETTING THERE

About 4 miles north of the junction of US Highway 101 and State Hwy 18, at the crest of the highway, pull over at the east end of gravel

*The trail to Harts Cove winds through gorgeous old-growth forest with glimpses of the nearby ocean.*

Forest Road 1861 and park. The trailhead is at the end of this road, which is currently closed to vehicles since it was hit with landslides in 2021.

### ON THE TRAIL

For the first 0.7 mile from the trailhead, the trail switchbacks down steeply, dropping more than 500 feet in elevation, before crossing Cliff Creek, continuing more gently down, then ascending slowly as it follows the slope's contours north. A sign announces the trail's entry into Neskowin Crest Research Natural Area; just beyond the sign there's a bench and a view of Harts Cove from the south. The trail then travels deep into a ravine to cross Chitwood Creek at not quite 2 miles and emerge from the forest at 2.4 miles. Follow the trail down the open prairie another 0.2 mile to a view of the steep-walled cove and Chitwood Creek cascading into the sea. Return as you came.

## 43 Cascade Head South Rainforest Trail

RATING/DIFFICULTY: **/3

ROUNDTRIP: 7 miles

ELEV GAIN: 1,150 feet

**Contact:** Hebo Ranger District, Siuslaw National Forest; **Notes:** Closed to hikers Jan 1–July 15 to protect sensitive species. Dogs on-leash; **GPS:** 45.03068°, –123.95552°

**The Cascade Head Rainforest Trail is part of the Oregon Coast Trail. It leads up and over Cascade Head but not out to the shoreline; the views are all forest views. The south trail described here is the best part, especially its upper half, with its mature spruce and hemlock forest and bonus wetland traversed via boardwalk.**

### GETTING THERE

From the junction of US Highway 101 and State Hwy 18, drive north 1.3 miles; turn west on Three Rocks Road, then immediately turn right into the small trailhead parking area with room for about four vehicles. At this time the upper trailhead is not accessible by car due to closure of Forest Road 1861.

### ON THE TRAIL

From the lower trailhead, the trail switchbacks a couple of times to gain elevation through a mostly alder forest before beginning a gradual ascent alongside hills nearly

## A COASTWIDE REFUGE FOR BIRDS AND MORE

Every offshore rock along the Oregon coast is protected as part of Oregon Islands National Wildlife Refuge—every one. So are a handful of headlands such as Crook Point and Coquille Point and nearshore sea stacks such as Haystack Rock at Cannon Beach and Proposal Rock at Neskowin. These hundreds of rocks, reefs, and islands provide breeding and resting habitat for birds, marine mammals, and more living things. Hundreds of thousands of seabirds nest on them in early summer, from tufted puffins that burrow into the soil on Haystack Rock to vast colonies of common murres that nest on bare rock on relatively flat-topped rocks along the coast (the pear shape of their eggs helps keep them from rolling away). Bring binoculars when you visit; to protect the wildlife and help keep their populations strong, these rocks are all off-limits to humans.

*Many flat-topped rocks off the Oregon Coast serve as nesting sites for common murres. Young murres are flightless when they leave the nest to swim off with their father.* (Photo by Peter Pearsall/USFWS)

the entire way up. The size of Sitka spruce, and overall beauty of the forest, increases as you ascend. At about 2.4 miles the trail drops briefly, then resumes its uphill march, at about 2.8 miles, to a lovely bog at the headwaters of Calkins Creek, brilliant with yellow skunk cabbage in early spring, and crosses a long (and slippery when wet) wooden boardwalk. You'll cross another finger of Calkins Creek before resuming the trail's ascent, at 3.5 miles, to FR 1861, your turnaround point. Return as you came.

For a 4.7-mile one-way hike with a shuttle car, start your hike at the east end of FR 1861, about 4 miles north of the junction of US 101 and Hwy 18 at the crest of the highway. The road, currently closed to vehicles, can be walked with care, skirting the tops

*No ocean views on the South (or North) Rainforest Trail; here, it's all forest, ranging from young alders to tall, old, lichen-covered spruce.*

of landslides and ducking around and over fallen trees. Walk 1.2 miles to reach the upper trailhead and follow the trail south to the parking area off Three Rocks Road.

## 44 Cascade Head Preserve

RATING/DIFFICULTY: ***/2–3
ROUNDTRIP: 4.8 miles
ELEV GAIN: 1,050 feet

**Contact:** The Nature Conservancy, Oregon; **Notes:** No dogs allowed. Toilets; **GPS:** 45.04156°, –123.99262°

**The Nature Conservancy's Cascade Head Preserve is pure magic. Trails on the headland traverse a deep hemlock and spruce forest and open coastal prairie. Bobcats roam the forest, Pacific giant salamanders—the largest salamanders in the world—creep along the alder-shaded stream banks, salmon run up the Salmon River in the fall, and Oregon silverspot butterflies flit over the grassy headland in the summer. This hike, approaching the headland's tip from the south, is the most popular route on Cascade Head—so please stick to the trail, especially for the first 0.5 mile while it parallels the road, where it runs near private homes, and on the open meadow to avoid trampling valuable habitat for native butterflies and other creatures. Hikers may see hawks circling in the updrafts or deer grazing on the open headland late and early in the day. The view of the estuary and coastline to the south is breathtaking.**

### GETTING THERE

From the junction of US Highway 101 and State Hwy 18 near Lincoln City, drive north 1.3 miles and turn west onto Three Rocks Road, following it 2.5 miles to parking (just past Savage Road) at Knight County Park. Note that parking can be tight here, especially on summer weekends or during fishing seasons. The Upper Meadow trailhead, 3.2 miles west of US 101 off Forest Road 1861, is currently closed to vehicles and can only be reached on foot.

### ON THE TRAIL

From Knight County Park, walk back up Three Rocks Road to Savage Road, watching for a boardwalk on the right signaling the start of a little access trail. Follow the signed route 0.5 mile, past the turnoff to the Sitka Center for Art and Ecology, to where it

The hilly headland and the sandbar at the mouth of the Salmon River dominate the view from Cascade Head Preserve.

becomes a forest path up a steep hillside. It levels off shortly, crossing several small creeks on wooden footbridges and boardwalks. Gently ascending, the trail follows the hillside's contours through the forest, crossing the first of several footbridges at 0.75 mile and getting your first ocean views at 1.5 miles. Continue another 0.3 mile for a broader view at the trail's westernmost end, at 1.8 miles.

Many hikers stop here for a satisfying 3.6-mile roundtrip hike. If you wish to challenge yourself further, continue another 0.6 mile (and 600 more feet in elevation) as the trail switchbacks up the steep open hillside to the Upper Meadow with an even more magnificent view. Return as you came.

## 45 The Knoll

RATING/DIFFICULTY: **/2

LOOP: 3.1 miles

ELEV GAIN: 610 feet

**Contact:** City of Lincoln City; **Notes:** Dogs on-leash; **GPS:** 45.01089°, –123.99775°

**If it wasn't so close to spectacular Cascade Head, the Knoll at the north end of Lincoln City would be a destination vista; instead it's just another awesome ocean viewpoint on the Oregon coast. Still it's a more accessible and shorter hike than Cascade Head Preserve, well worth an out-and-back trek on a combination of**

**trails and quiet roads. Better yet, make it a loop, as described here. Better still, extend your hike to get a view of what's known as Gods Thumb, or to some, just the Thumb. I urge you to view but not touch the Thumb, tempting as it is. Why? See Extend Your Hike.**

## GETTING THERE

At the north end of Lincoln City, turn north off US Highway 101 onto Northeast Devils Lake Boulevard (at the traffic light southwest of milepost 112) and continue for 1.2 miles to the cul-de-sac at the road's end, built for a housing development that instead became part of a large city-owned open space. An alternative trailhead mentioned in this trail description is at Roads End State Recreation Site; near US 101 milepost 113, turn west at the light onto Logan Road and follow it 1 mile to the beach access parking area. Parking here adds 0.8 mile to this roundtrip hike by adding a walk up Northeast Sal La Sea Drive to connect with the loop (see map). Avoid parking on neighborhood streets.

## ON THE TRAIL

Look for a faint trail on the west side of the cul-de-sac, leading into the woods. The trail quickly turns into a wide gravel road. Follow it 0.25 mile, crossing Logan Creek on a wide footbridge and walking around a gate to a junction with gravel Northeast Sal La Sea Drive. Go right and walk up the road 0.25 mile, past the junction with Northeast Port Drive, to a gate. Go around the gate, but rather than continuing straight (the road ends shortly at a quarry), bear right up a path angling up the middle of an old road. It ascends steadily 0.5 mile to a landing where you will bear left through an open meadow to the top of the Knoll and the best viewpoints.

You could turn around here for a 2-mile out-and-back hike, but you can make it a loop hike with just a bit more walking. From the landing, continue north on the trail for 0.3 mile to a trail junction; go right and follow this trail east and south through airy forest. At the next junction, turn right and follow the trail 0.6 mile to where it ends at Northeast Devils Lake Boulevard. Go right a short distance on the road to return to where you started.

## EXTEND YOUR HIKE

Heard about Gods Thumb and want to see it? From the landing at the Knoll, continue north 0.3 mile, but at the junction bear left through forest and meadow. At the junction in 0.6

*From the Knoll's summit, you can see Lincoln City (and a glimpse of Devils Lake) stretching to the south.*

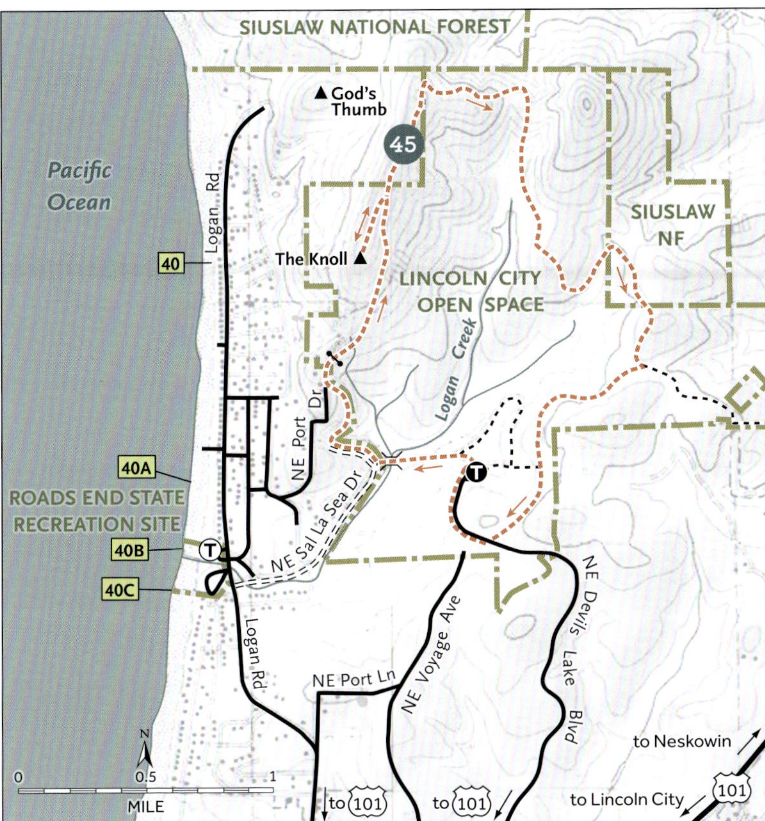


mile, wander west through the meadow a short distance until you see the Thumb looming above the ocean. Ideally return as you came or on the loop described (see On the Trail).

Most people can't resist walking the narrow ridge from here to the base of the Thumb and up to the top. Actually most Thumb-bound hikers approach via Logan Road and a rough trail from the south after parking at Roads End. Please consider skipping a hike up the Thumb. (Not only is the route not signed, but US Forest Service [USFS] officials explain that it is technically not on public land; the USFS has an administrative easement, not a public easement.) The trail from the south to the summit is maintained, but it is very steep and unsafe for children, dogs, and most of the rest of us. If that just makes you more eager to conquer it, consider that use—*overuse*—is severely degrading the Thumb and the trails leading to it.

## LINCOLN CITY AND DEPOE BAY

Lincoln City began as six distinct beachfront communities and incorporated as one big town in 1965. They're strung along one long beach that ends at the mouth of Siletz Bay. The town is anchored by two tourist attractions: Chinook Winds Casino at the north and an outlet mall at the south. The next town south is Depoe Bay, smaller and just as tourist-driven; it hangs its hat on whale-watching (for gray whales), which you can do from the seawall or from tour boats departing from the town's tiny harbor. There's a state park campground at Devils Lake State Park, in the middle of Lincoln City.

Hiking in this section of the coast consists mainly of beach walking on the busy beach fronting Lincoln City or on the less populated beaches south of Siletz Bay, including Salishan Spit and the beach leading past the communities of Gleneden Beach and Lincoln Beach. For forest hiking, consider driving a half-hour or so off US Highway 101 to the trailhead for Drift Creek Falls (Hike 47), a moderate hike to a surprising suspension bridge with views of a plunging waterfall. For a short, close-to-town hike, consider Alder Island Nature Trail at Siletz Bay National Wildlife Refuge, just south of Lincoln City. This nearly flat, 0.5-mile path winds along the Siletz River and Millport Slough. The trailhead is just off US 101 on Millport Slough Lane; dogs are not allowed.

Consider a stop at Rocky Creek State Scenic Viewpoint, south of Depoe Bay. A short trail leads to a view of otherwise hidden Whale Cove, where you may not see whales but will surely see seals and seabirds in this conserved marine gem (no pedestrian access to the cove itself; it really is just for wildlife). Some believe Whale Cove is the true site of Sir Francis Drake's New Albion, the short-lived colonial outpost (Britain's first)

### STONE SNAILS: FOSSILS ON THE BEACH

*Winter is a good season for collecting fossils on the beach, after storms erode shorefront cliffs.*

Tens of millions of years ago, what we think of as western Oregon was under the sea. When sea creatures died, their bodies settled on the seafloor and were covered with sediments that, over time, were compressed into sandstone or mudstone by the weight of the water. The animals' soft tissue decomposed, but dissolved minerals seeped into their shells. Look for rock-hard remnants of ancient snails, clams, and other invertebrates in sea cliffs (uplifted by the movement of tectonic plates) around Coos Bay, between Waldport and Lincoln City, in the Three Capes area, and north and south of Cannon Beach, especially after winter storms.

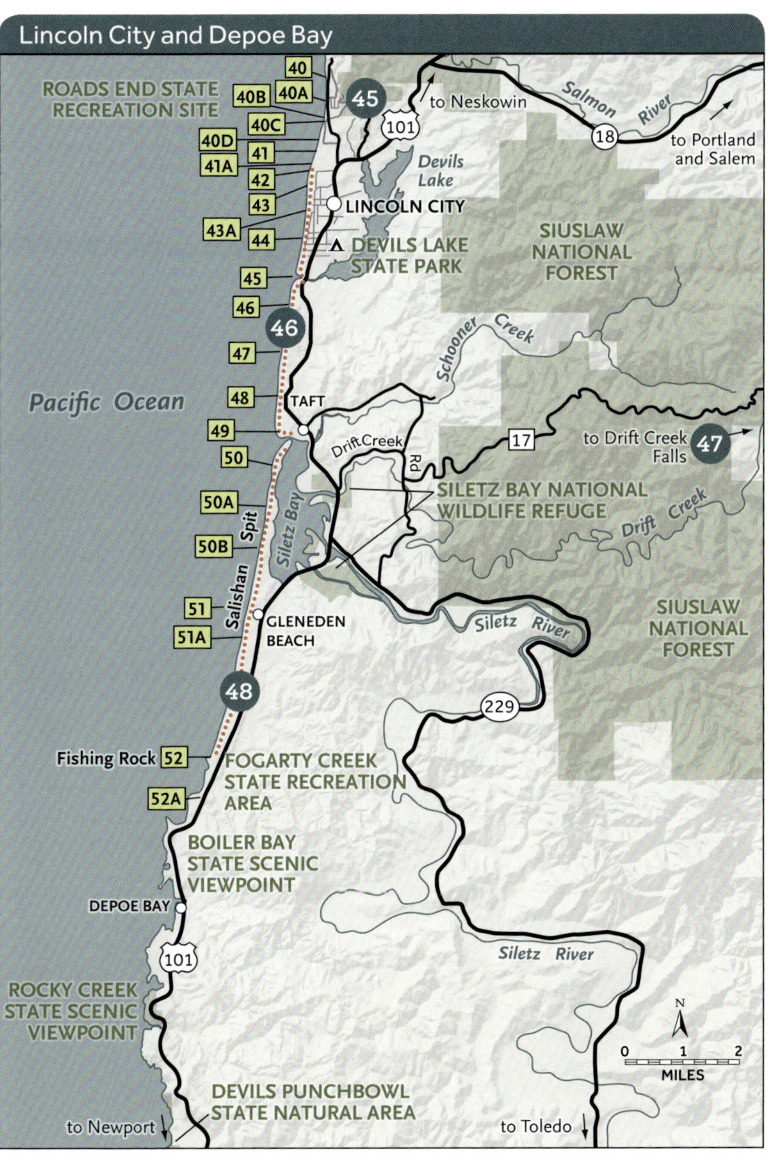
Lincoln City and Depoe Bay
ROADS END STATE RECREATION SITE
40
40A
40B
40C
40D
41
41A
42
43
43A
44
45
46
47
48
49
50
50A
50B
51
51A
52
52A
45
46
47
48
to Neskowin
101
Salmon River
18
to Portland and Salem
Devils Lake
LINCOLN CITY
DEVILS LAKE STATE PARK
SIUSLAW NATIONAL FOREST
Schooner Creek
Pacific Ocean
TAFT
Drift Creek Rd
17
to Drift Creek Falls
SILETZ BAY NATIONAL WILDLIFE REFUGE
Drift Creek
Siletz Bay
Salishan Spit
GLENEDEN BEACH
Siletz River
SIUSLAW NATIONAL FOREST
229
Fishing Rock
FOGARTY CREEK STATE RECREATION AREA
BOILER BAY STATE SCENIC VIEWPOINT
DEPOE BAY
101
Siletz River
ROCKY CREEK STATE SCENIC VIEWPOINT
N
0 1 2
MILES
DEVILS PUNCHBOWL STATE NATURAL AREA
to Newport
to Toledo

*The mouth of the D River is kite central in Lincoln City: there's a kite festival here in late June, and there's a kite shop right across the highway.*

where Drake spent the summer of 1579 on his landmark circumnavigation of the earth. (Others believe Drake landed in Nehalem Bay, though most historians pinpoint Point Reyes north of San Francisco.)

## 46 Beach Walk: Lincoln City

ONE-WAY DISTANCE: 7.5 miles

US Highway 101 through Lincoln City is lined with motels, shops, and restaurants, but step onto the beach and you're in another world, one defined not by commerce but by the sound of the surf. No headlands stop you from walking this entire beach (except perhaps at a high winter tide). The beach stretches from the cliffs north of Roads End State Recreation Site to the mouth of Siletz Bay. You will see additional beach access signs as you walk the beach, but these are neighborhood access points with little or no parking.

### BEACH ACCESS

BA 40C, Roads End State Recreation Site, off NE Logan Road, Lincoln City. Parking, restrooms.

BA 45, D River State Recreation Site, off US 101 at SE 1st Street, Lincoln City. Parking, restrooms.

BA 46, Canyon Drive Park, end of SW 11th Drive, Lincoln City. Parking, restrooms, and outdoor surfer shower.

BA 49, Taft Beach Access Wayside, end of SW 51st Street, Lincoln City. Parking, restrooms.

### WHERE TO WALK

**From Roads End State Recreation Site.** Walk north (it's 1.25 miles before the beach runs out) for the closest thing to a quiet beach stretch here. Or head south as far as Siletz Bay.

**From D River State Recreation Site.** Parking can be at a premium here in summer; it's popular for kite-flying (there's a kite shop across US 101). Walk north or south; it's in about the middle of the beach.

**From Taft.** If the tide's in, watch the recreational crabbers in Siletz Bay before heading north up the beach.

## 47 Drift Creek Falls

RATING/DIFFICULTY: **/2

ROUNDTRIP: 3.5 miles

ELEV GAIN: 930 feet

**Contact:** Hebo Ranger District, Siuslaw National Forest; **Notes:** USFS day-use fee. Dogs on-leash. Vault toilets available; **GPS:** 44.93550°, –123.85561°

**This hike is named for the waterfall, and it's dramatic enough: A tributary of Drift Creek pours over a mossy cliff to free-fall 75 feet into a pool in Drift Creek. But it's the massive suspension bridge near the trail's end that's the real draw. It hangs between support towers, each nearly 30 feet tall, and is anchored to the bedrock on either side of Drift Creek. From the middle of the bridge, you get a good look at the falls (some will find the high bridge's gentle swaying motion a bit unnerving). The trailhead is a good 20 minutes off US 101 east of Lincoln City, but worth the drive. The mostly paved route is well signed.**

## GETTING THERE

From US Highway 101 at the south end of Lincoln City, turn east just south of milepost 119 onto Drift Creek Road; follow it for 1.5 miles and bear right onto South Drift Creek Road. In 0.4 mile, veer left at the sign to Drift Creek Trail (Forest Road 17) and, in another 0.9 mile, left again.

*A solidly built suspension footbridge lies deep in the forest east of Lincoln City, next to a 75-foot waterfall.*

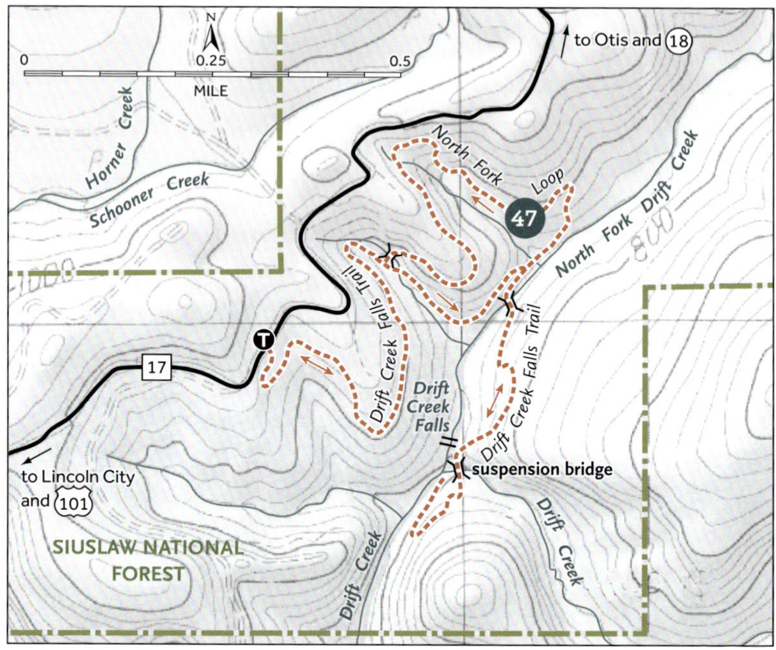


Continue following the main paved road another 9.5 miles to the trailhead parking area on the right. Alternatively, from State Hwy 18 at Rose Lodge (just west of milepost 5), turn south onto Bear Creek Road (which becomes FR 17) and follow the main road, bearing right at the fork at 4.6 miles and reaching the trailhead at 9 miles.

## ON THE TRAIL

The hike to the falls descends gently through a recovering forest; stumps testify to the logging that occurred here a few decades ago, but the replanted Douglas-firs are tall and the forest feels lush. About 0.75 mile into the hike you'll start to hear the rush of water down below; shortly the North Fork Loop takes off to the left (your return route). Continuing straight you'll pass the other end of the North Fork Loop and, after a sharp right, a small footbridge crossing North Fork Drift Creek. At 1.25 miles the trail reaches the suspension bridge, the star attraction of this hike. The trail continues another 0.25 mile, switchbacking down the hill nearly 100 feet in elevation to reach the edge of Drift Creek.

Return as you came, but this time, take the 0.8-mile North Fork Loop right to wind up through a magnificent stand of old forest that has grown since a fire here more than a hundred years ago. The loop ascends, steeply in places, before leveling off and dropping to meet the main trail; bear right to return to the trailhead.

# 48 Beach Walk: Gleneden Beach

ONE-WAY DISTANCE: 5.7 miles

Gleneden Beach stretches from the northern tip of Salishan Spit—part of the Salishan resort community but public like every other Oregon beach—south to Fishing Rock, just north of Fogarty Creek State Recreation Area. There's a little pocket beach at the end of Fogarty Creek too. You're mostly walking past residential communities with no headlands to get in your way.

## BEACH ACCESS

BA 51A, Gleneden Beach State Recreation Site, off Wesler Street, Gleneden Beach. Parking, restrooms.

BA 52, Fishing Rock State Recreation Site, off Fishing Rock Street, Lincoln Beach. Limited parking.

BA 52A, Fogarty Creek State Recreation Area, off US 101, Lincoln Beach. Parking, restrooms.

## WHERE TO WALK

**Salishan Spit.** If you're in the mood for walking the spit, start at Gleneden Beach and walk 3.5 miles north to where the ocean pours in and out of shallow Siletz Bay. Expect to share the end of the spit with harbor seals.

**Fishing Rock.** It's a 2.2-mile walk between Gleneden Beach and Fishing Rock, a minor headland. A trail leads up from the beach and through a tangle of coastal forest to the parking area at the top of the bluff.

**Fogarty Creek Beach.** This pocket beach is a surprise. Park at Fogarty Creek and look for paved paths on either side of Fogarty Creek leading from a footbridge out to the beach. It doesn't take long to explore this tiny beach, but it's a nice find, and you may find shelter from the wind at the base of the cliffs.

*Homes line the shoreline much of the way from Siletz Bay to Fishing Rock. Beach walkers might have to navigate some small creeks, especially in winter.*

## NEWPORT TO BEAVER CREEK

There's a lot going on in Newport: fishing, marine research, interpretive centers, a busy bayfront, and not one but two lighthouses. It's also the home port for the National Oceanic and Atmospheric Administration (NOAA) Pacific Fleet. In addition to beaches stretching north and south of Yaquina Bay, the Newport area offers several other options for short hikes, some of which could be combined with visits to one of the town's three interpretive centers, beginning with one at Yaquina Head Outstanding Natural Area, which also has a lighthouse, tidepools, and great summer seabird-watching. Bigger and better known is the Oregon Coast Aquarium on the south shore of Yaquina Bay, with its displays of sea otters and seabirds and jellies (better known as jellyfish) and its walk-through tank featuring other ocean species such as sharks and rays. The 0.5-mile paved interpretive Estuary Trail allows you to walk between the aquarium and the (much less expensive) Hatfield Visitor Center, the public wing of Oregon State University's Hatfield Marine Science Center, where family-friendly exhibits and docents help you explore current research about the ocean, the beaches, and the flora and fauna that live here.

To the south a few miles, the broad wetland where Beaver Creek approaches the Pacific Ocean is slowly returning to its presettlement native condition, thanks to the efforts of Oregon Parks and Recreation Department and the Wetlands Conservancy. Just east of US Highway 101 is a canoe and kayak put-in, granting access to the quiet, slow-moving creek; a short distance upstream is Beaver Creek State Natural Area, where hikers can enjoy a network of trails lacing a forested hillock rising from the marsh. West of US 101, Ona Beach offers access to miles of beach via a short trail through the trees and over Beaver Creek. The trail network at Beaver Creek and Ona Beach are both part of Brian Booth State Park. No camping here, but camping is available just north of Newport (Beverly Beach State Park) and south (South Beach State Park).

## 49 Beach Walk: North of Newport

ONE-WAY DISTANCE: 6 miles

The beach between the community of Otter Rock and Yaquina Head offers surfer sightings and quiet walking, despite its proximity to US Highway 101 most of the way. Devils Punchbowl at Otter Rock is a must-see at high tide in winter; formed by the collapse of the roof over two intersecting sea caves, it churns wildly when the surf charges in (there's not much to see in summer). About 1 mile past Moolack Beach, Schooner Point (and its rock tunnel) typically cannot be rounded or walked through at high tide.

### BEACH ACCESS

BA 53A, Devils Punchbowl State Natural Area, Otter Rock. Parking, restrooms, outdoor surfer shower, and stairs that drop 340 feet to reach the beach.

BA 54, Beverly Beach State Park day-use area, off US 101 north of Newport. OPRD day-use fee. Parking, restrooms.

BA 55, Moolack Beach, pullout on west side of US 101 between mileposts 135 and 136. Limited parking.

Newport to Beaver Creek
DEVILS PUNCHBOWL STATE NATURAL AREA
101
53A
BEVERLY BEACH STATE PARK
54
49
55
YAQUINA HEAD OUTSTANDING NATURAL AREA
229
Yaquina Head Lighthouse
Yaquina Head
AGATE BEACH STATE RECREATION SITE
58
Pacific Ocean
50
to Corvallis
59
NEWPORT
20
60
Hatfield Visitor Center
Yaquina Bay Lighthouse
TOLEDO
Yaquina Bay
60A
Oregon Coast Aquarium
61
61A
SOUTH BEACH STATE PARK
61B
Yaquina River
51
101
LOST CREEK STATE RECREATION SITE
62
62A
SIUSLAW NATIONAL FOREST
BRIAN BOOTH STATE PARK
Ona Beach
62B
63
Beaver Creek
52
Seal Rocks
SEAL ROCK
N
SEAL ROCK STATE RECREATION SITE
64
0 1 2
MILES
to Waldport

*You may be able to walk through or around Schooner Point, depending on the tide.*

## WHERE TO WALK

**From Devils Punchbowl.** Climb down the stairs and walk south; surfers often congregate in the water at the base of the cliffs here. There's also a small tidepool area just north of Devils Punchbowl (Beach Access 53). Or skip the stairs and park at Beverly Beach.

**From the south end.** Park at Moolack Beach and scramble down a short, slick trail to the beach. You can walk south 1 mile to Schooner Point—and another mile or so to Yaquina Head, if the tide permits. Or head north toward Beverly Beach.

# 50 Beach Walk: Between the Newport Lighthouses

ONE-WAY DISTANCE: 3.9 miles

In 1871 a lighthouse was built at the entrance to Yaquina Bay, the first lighthouse north of the Umpqua River on the Oregon coast and the oldest wood-frame lighthouse in Oregon. It functioned as both lighthouse and keeper's quarters, with a 40-foot tower rising above the roof of the Cape Cod–style house. Three years after it went into service, it was mothballed when the taller, more effective Yaquina Head Lighthouse went into service about 4 miles north. The beach between the two lighthouses is accessible in several places, including at Nye Beach, with its shops, cafés, and art center.

## BEACH ACCESS

Ernest Bloch Memorial Wayside, off US 101 just south of Lighthouse Drive, Newport. Parking, restrooms, and outdoor surfer shower.

BA 58, Agate Beach State Recreation Site, off US 101, Newport. Parking, restrooms.

BA 59, Nye Beach Public Access, NW Coast Street and Beach Drive, Newport. Parking, restrooms.

BA 60 and 60A, Yaquina Bay State Recreation Site, immediately north of Yaquina Bay Bridge, Newport. Parking, restrooms.

## WHERE TO WALK

**Agate Beach.** If parking is a concern, which it can be in summer, start at Agate Beach State Recreation Site with its huge parking area.

**Surfers' choice.** Join the surfers who park at Bloch Wayside, walk down the stairs behind the restrooms, walk a block north, and then descend the stairs to the beach at the very foot of Yaquina Head, passing an installation commemorating the start of surfing at Agate Beach in the mid-1960s. Alternately take Lucky Gap Trail, which starts at the south end of the same parking area. It's about 1 mile from here to Agate Beach State Recreation Site.

**Nye Beach.** Parking can be a challenge at this beach access site in midsummer, but it's a fun place to start a beach walk, with shops and cafes and the Newport Visual Arts Center nearby. It's also a fun place to stop on a walk from either end of this beach.

**Yaquina Bay State Recreation Site.** From the parking area below the old lighthouse, follow either of the two paths and stairs 180 feet down to the beach. Walk south a short distance to the north jetty or north as far as Yaquina Head.

*The path leading to the beach from Ernest Bloch Memorial Wayside passes an installation that commemorates the start of surfing south of Yaquina Head in the 1960s.*

## HIKING TO THE COAST: CORVALLIS TO THE SEA TRAIL

*The Corvallis to the Sea Trail uses existing and newly built roads and trails through state park, national forest, and private timberlands.*

How would you like to walk, not just *on* the coast, but *to* the coast from the Willamette Valley? It took decades of work by generations of volunteers, but by the early 2020s a viable route for hikers and mountain bikers was completed from the Corvallis riverfront to the ocean shore at Ona Beach, south of Newport. The C2C Trail crosses a patchwork of private timberland, national forest, and state parks using gravel roads, old and new trails, and even a municipal bike path. You'll walk through deep forests of old trees, recent clear-cuts, and meadows strewn with blooming wildflowers in spring. One short stretch requires a (free) permit from the landowner to transit. In places, the route splits, with hikers and bikers following different trails. Water is scarce in places, as are legal campsites, but with some planning it's doable in less than a week by a reasonably fit backpacker. Visit c2ctrail.org for details.

What about other valley-to-coast routes? Portland author James Thayer pioneered somewhat aspirational walking routes (remote and undeveloped much of the way) from Portland to Seaside and Tillamook and has written them up in his *Hiking from Portland to the Coast* (Oregon State University Press, 2016). A third option, still mostly aspirational: a recreational rail-to-trail through the Salmonberry River corridor, from the Banks-Vernonia State Trail near the town of Banks west across the Coast Range to Nehalem Bay and south to Tillamook; find project updates at salmonberrytrail.org.

## 51 Beach Walk: South Beach to Seal Rock

ONE-WAY DISTANCE: 8 miles

This long beach starts at the mouth of Yaquina Bay and stretches south nearly to Seal Rock State Recreation Site. Beaver Creek, typically wadeable in summer, meets the ocean in the middle of this long beach.

### BEACH ACCESS

BA 61, Yaquina South Jetty, west end of SW Jetty Way, Newport. Gravel parking area.

BA 61B, South Beach State Park day-use area, Newport. OPRD day-use fee. Parking, restrooms.

BA 62, Lost Creek State Recreation Site, off US 101, 7 miles south of Newport. Parking, restrooms.

*A tall footbridge crosses Beaver Creek, linking Ona Beach parking area with the beach.*

BA 62B, Ona Beach day-use area, at Brian Booth State Park, off US 101 south of Newport. Parking, restrooms.

## WHERE TO WALK

**South Beach to Beaver Creek.** Park at the South Beach State Park day-use area and follow the trail out to the beach; from here it's a 4.6-mile roundtrip walk to Lost Creek State Recreation Site. Or go all the way to the north side of Beaver Creek; park a second vehicle at Beach Access 62A (a gravel pullout just north of the Ona Beach parking lot) for a 5.5-mile one-way walk.

**Beaver Creek to Seal Rock.** From the parking area at Ona Beach, follow the path to a long footbridge across the creek to the beach, then follow the sand south until you run out of beach as you approach Seal Rock, a 4.2-mile roundtrip walk.

## 52 Beaver Creek Loop

RATING/DIFFICULTY: **/2
LOOP: 3.6 miles
ELEV GAIN: 480 feet

**Contact:** Brian Booth State Park; **Notes:** Dogs on-leash. Toilet available on trail (and at nearby welcome center and marsh trailhead parking area off N. Beaver Creek Road); **GPS:** 44.50212°, –124.04198°

**Don't let the inauspicious start to this hike scare you off. This trail system is a gem. There's no formal trailhead parking area; Oregon State Parks owns the forested upland but not the access road, so hikers have to walk up a private road (with easement) to get to the trail system. Those trails are a combination of old roads, dirt trails, and mown paths that wind around and over a forested hill like an island in the middle of Beaver Creek marsh. When it's blowing cold on the beach, it could be 10°F warmer here. This suggested route follows the scenic perimeter trail, with a detour to the summit at Snaggy Point. But you needn't hike the whole thing or limit yourself to this route. Junctions are well-marked with flexible brown trail posts.**

## GETTING THERE

Look for signs to Beaver Creek State Natural Area between Waldport and Newport at milepost 149 on US Highway 101, just across the highway from Ona Beach day-use area. Follow North Beaver Creek Road east 1 mile,

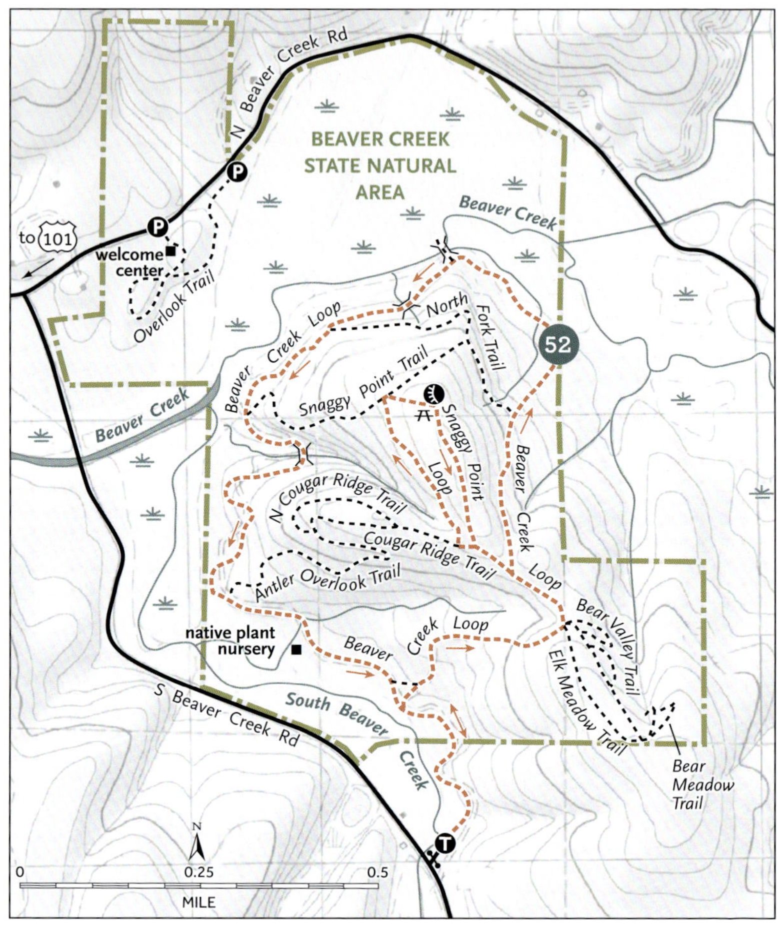


turn right onto South Beaver Creek Road (0.2 mile before reaching the welcome center), and follow it 1 mile to a small dirt turnout on the right with room for four or five cars across the road from a gated service road. Note: The welcome center on North Beaver Creek Road has a few interpretive displays (and not much else); 0.2 mile farther (by road or on a footpath from the center) is a wayside with vault toilets and what appears to be the trailhead for an alternate route to the Beaver Creek trail network. A path leads into the marsh, crossing a channel of the creek on a footbridge, and plans call for a

*A large snag on a knoll marks the aptly named Snaggy Point in Beaver Creek Marsh.*

second footbridge to be installed closer to the uplands. But we have found the trail too wet to be walked even at low tide at the driest time of year, with or without a second footbridge.

## ON THE TRAIL

Walk around the gate and follow the road 0.3 mile, to where it splits and rises to meet Beaver Creek Loop. For a counterclockwise walk, bear right and follow the trail up and up—eventually rather steeply—to a four-way junction at 0.7 mile; bear left to stay on Beaver Creek Loop. A left at the next junction will lead to the start of Snaggy Point Loop on your right; the map (and trail posts) will help you navigate the various trail junctions on the way to the summit and back. On top are two picnic tables and a distant view of the ocean. Follow the loop back to Beaver Creek Loop and continue counterclockwise to, at 2 miles, a plank footbridge on the right leads over an arm of Beaver Creek to the Marsh Trail. Plans call for a footbridge on the Marsh Trail that will facilitate hikes to a secondary trailhead on North Beaver Creek Road, but don't count on keeping your feet dry in any case. Continuing on the main trail, bear right at all junctions. At 3 miles you'll pass a native plant nursery (and a portable toilet). Less than 0.2 mile farther you'll complete the loop; bear right to return to your vehicle.

**OPPOSITE:** *South of Heceta Head, the Coos Bay Dune Sheet offers hikers days of often remote beach walking opportunities interrupted by rivers and creeks but no headlands.*

# THE CENTRAL COAST

## Seal Rock to Cape Perpetua

NORTH OF THE SIUSLAW RIVER NEAR Florence, most of the trails on Oregon's central coast are clustered around Cape Perpetua and Heceta Head. Cape Perpetua Scenic Area offers trails of varying length that access the shoreline and lead up to creeks and ridges rising into the forest. More trails lead over Heceta Head, with its iconic lighthouse, and into the adjacent forest. South of the Siuslaw lie 40 miles of remote beaches and mounds of sand protected as Oregon Dunes National Recreation Area. Here "trail" often means a route marked by posts planted in open dunes. The dunes separate US Highway 101 from the beach, with trails providing the only beach access along much of this stretch. Off-highway vehicles are also allowed to roar over parts of the dunes, but not any parts near established footpaths, leaving the trails quiet and most beaches wild and uncrowded.

## SEAL ROCK TO CAPE PERPETUA

Between Newport and Yachats lie 13 miles of beach walking that is interrupted only by the mouth of Alsea Bay at Waldport. Where the beach ends at Yachats, the shoreline Yachats 804 Trail begins, leading all the way into town. Yachats (*YA-hots*) is a charming village with active trail volunteers who supported not only development of the Yachats 804 Trail but also improvements to Amanda Trail south of town and, at the north end of town, the Ya'Xaik–Gerdemann Botanic Preserve Loop that starts at the top of Diversity Drive, leads up the hillside, then winds down through a lush and lovely private botanical garden. Return a short distance along the highway and up Diversity Drive for a 1.6-mile loop with 370 feet of elevation gain.

The name Cape Perpetua Scenic Area says it all: With its craggy punchbowl-strewn shoreline, tide pools, dramatic vistas, and deep Sitka spruce forest, Cape Perpetua and neighboring Cummins Creek Wilderness area are—for hikers—the centerpiece of the central coast. A varied network of trails offers hikes for every interest and ability, from paved paths along the shore to narrow forest trails leading to remote ridges. It was known to the Native Alsea people as Halaqaik, reportedly meaning an open or exposed place, possibly referring to the open coastal prairies that the Alsea maintained with regular burning. The name Cape Perpetua was bestowed by Captain James Cook as he sailed past it on the feast day for Saint Perpetua in March 1778. Cummins Creek Wilderness, adjacent to Cape Perpetua, and Rock Creek Wilderness, a few miles to the south, were created to conserve some of the last major virgin stands of temperate rainforest on the Oregon coast—mature western hemlock, western redcedar, and Douglas-fir, as well as Sitka spruce along the shore. Cummins Ridge Trail requires a long drive (or hike) to reach, but for lovers of trees, it's worth the effort. Public camping is available at a small state park (Beachside) and small US Forest Service campground (Tillicum) between Waldport and Yachats and a USFS campground at Cape Perpetua.

### 53 Beach Walk: Seal Rock

ONE-WAY DISTANCE: 0.6 mile

This short beach is named for the partially submerged rocks that lie about 0.5 mile offshore and extend north and south more than 2.5 miles.

*This pocket beach at Seal Rock is named for the string of rocks offshore.*

### BEACH ACCESS

BA 64, Seal Rock State Recreation Site, in the community of Seal Rock. Dogs on-leash. Parking, restrooms.

### WHERE TO WALK

**To the beach.** Paths lead 0.2 mile down to the beach, which stretches from Elephant Rock at the north end to a small beach-ending headland at the south. A rocky ledge splits the beach, but it's easy to clamber over at most tides to get to more walking. A scramble trail here leads up the hillside to a small highway turnout.

## 54 Beach Walk: North of Alsea Bay

ONE-WAY DISTANCE: 3.2 miles

The beach north of Alsea Bay is rarely crowded, especially the farther north you go and even at the south end adjacent to a neighborhood of mostly vacation homes. Best access for this beach (the only one with plenty of parking) is at Driftwood Beach State Recreation Site. There are several additional signed beach access points along NW Oceania Drive in the Bayshore neighborhood north of Alsea, but there is limited roadside parking at each.

### BEACH ACCESS

West end of Quail Road, just north of US 101 milepost 152. Very limited street parking.

BA 66, Driftwood Beach State Recreation Site, just south of US 101 milepost 153, north of Waldport. Parking, restrooms.

### WHERE TO WALK

**North from Driftwood.** Enjoy this quiet 1.7-mile walk to the rocks that separate this beach from the Seal Rock beach.

**South from Driftwood.** Follow this wide beach as much as 2.5 miles, past the Bayshore development to the end of the spit (past BA 67D) marking the entrance to Alsea Bay. Curve around the end of the spit, if tide permits, for a sea-level view of Alsea Bay Bridge.

## 55 Beach Walk: Alsea Bay to Yachats

ONE-WAY DISTANCE: 6.4 miles

The highway is never far away here, but the surf drowns out traffic sounds. You'll pass neighborhoods on the bluff, especially at the south end, but this beach is never crowded. It's a good place for a long walk.

### BEACH ACCESS

Waldport Heritage Museum, south end of Alsea Bay Bridge. Parking here and along bluff to south.

Keady Wayside, south end of Waldport. Limited parking, restrooms.

BA 68, Patterson State Recreation Site, south of Waldport. Parking, restrooms.

BA 70, Beachside State Recreation Site day-use area (BA 70A sign located adjacent to campground). Parking, restrooms in campground.

BA 71, Tillicum Beach Campground day-use area (sign located adjacent to campground). USFS day-use pass. Parking, restrooms in campground.

End of Yachats 804 Trail (see Hike 56).

### WHERE TO WALK

**Low-tide access at Waldport Heritage Museum or Keady Wayside.** You can start walking the beach south from either access site right in Waldport, but only if the tide is low enough at the seawall at Keady Wayside. If so, you can get around Yaquina John Point to the south and be able to keep going. If you're out too long and the tide rises, you may need to return along the highway from Patterson State Recreation Site.

*Where there is driftwood you are likely to find a driftwood fort, such as here north of Alsea Bay. If not, build your own!*

*The beach north of Yachats starts at the end of the Yachats 804 Trail and leads to Waldport.*

**North or south from Patterson State Recreation Site.** Plenty of walkable beach northward or southward at nearly any tide.

**Extend a hike on the Yachats 804 Trail.** If you have someone willing to pick you up, start at Smelt Sands State Recreation Site in Yachats and take Hike 56 north to the beach, then continue to Tillicum Beach Campground (3.7 miles one-way), Beachside State Recreation Site (4.4 miles), or Patterson State Recreation Site (6.5 miles). Or turn around where you choose for a roundtrip trail and beach hike as long as you like.

## 56 Yachats 804 Trail

RATING/DIFFICULTY: **/1
ROUNDTRIP: 1.4 miles
ELEV GAIN: 100 feet

**Contact:** Smelt Sands State Recreation Site; **Notes:** Dogs on-leash. Toilets; **GPS:** 44.32201°, –124.10575°

This trail is named for the county road right-of-way upon which it is built, dedicated back in 1890 but abandoned in the 1930s. Local residents fought all the way to the Oregon Supreme Court to return it to public use in the late 1980s. Its main attraction is a long, wave-sculpted shelf of sandstone north of Smelt Sands, with chasms and blowholes that, at high tide, shoot seawater into the air with the pulse of the waves. The trail's compacted gravel surface makes it passable for wheelchairs. The rocks and cliffs are tempting to explore, but they're slippery when wet, and a fall into the water here can quickly turn tragic (as a memorial at the trailhead clearly reminds visitors).

### GETTING THERE

From US Highway 101, at the north end of the town of Yachats between mileposts 163 and 164, turn west at the sign to Smelt Sands State Recreation Site (Beach Access 75).

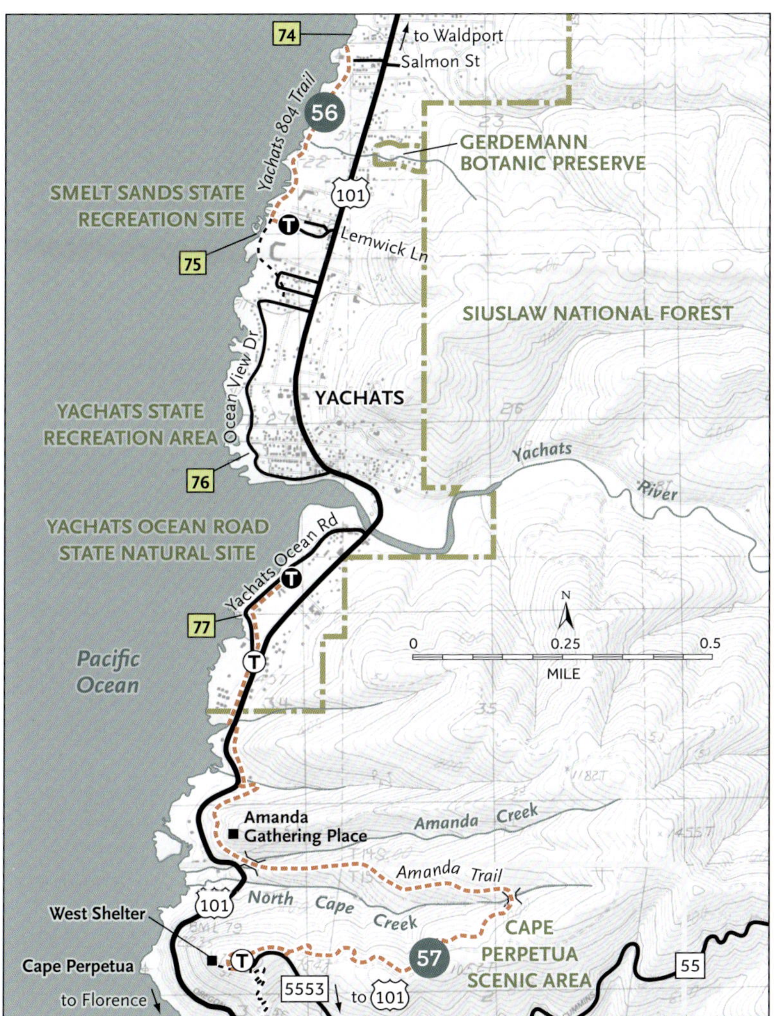


## ON THE TRAIL

From Smelt Sands, the trail portion most often used by day visitors leads north along a low bluff, passing a pocket beach (where smelt have been dip-netted for eons—hence the name) and a rocky shelf, with motels and private homes on your right. The trail leads into a stand of shore pines and skirts a

*Take a short walk on this wide shoreline path or follow it north to the beach or south to trails leading up Cape Perpetua.*

narrow chasm at about 0.4 mile. After crossing Perch Street, the trail crosses Salmon Street (Beach Access 74, no parking) and leads down a ravine on a set of wooden stairs to the beach at 0.7 mile. From here the beach stretches north more than 7 miles to the outskirts of Waldport; for details, see Beach Walk: Alsea Bay to Yachats. Otherwise, return as you came.

### EXTEND YOUR HIKE

Alternately or in addition, you can walk the 804 Trail 1 mile south from Smelt Sands, though this stretch is mainly used by locals and long-distance Oregon Coast Trail hikers. Follow signs across a little footbridge, along the grassy bluff in front of the Adobe Resort, and inland between a pair of fences. The route turns right at the street and continues zigzagging on a gravel path along neighborhood streets until reaching Ocean View Drive; from here, follow the road shoulder south 0.6 mile more to parking at Yachats State Recreation Area.

## 57 Amanda Trail

RATING/DIFFICULTY: **/3
ROUNDTRIP: 5.4 miles
ELEV GAIN: 1,240 feet

**Contact:** Cape Perpetua Scenic Area, Siuslaw National Forest; **Notes:** Dogs on-leash. Vault toilets at upper trailhead; **GPS:** 44.30581°, –124.10534°

**Amanda Trail is a leafy link in the Oregon Coast Trail that connects the small town of Yachats with the top of Cape Perpetua. Its name commemorates a dark chapter in the history of this coast. In 1864 members of the Coos and Lower**

**Umpqua tribes were rounded up by the US Cavalry in order to open the land up for white settlement. They were forced to walk more than 70 miles from Coos Bay to the Alsea Subagency reservation at Yachats, which was really nothing more than a prison camp. Amanda De-Cuys, a blind Coos elder, was among those seized, bound, forced to abandon her daughter, and driven barefoot to Yachats on terrain ranging from sand to sharp basalt rocks that tore her feet to shreds. Nothing more is known of her fate, but most of those who made the trek died before the reservation was dismantled twelve years later. A wooden statue memorializing Amanda and her people stands alongside the trail where it crosses Amanda Creek.**

## GETTING THERE

There is no formal parking area at the bottom of this hike, where the trail actually begins. From southbound US Highway 101 in Yachats, cross the Yachats River and make an immediate right turn on Yachats Ocean Road. Drive 0.3 mile to a small pullout on the right side. Walk along this quiet road south, then just before it reaches US Highway 101, bear right at the sign for the Oregon Coast Trail (OCT); it leads 0.4 mile south (above the west side of the highway, then across it, and then above the east side) to the start of the trail, 0.8 mile from where you started. (You might also find parking on the side of an unsigned road leading east just south of US 101 milepost 166; pick up the trail where it crosses just below a gate a few steps before it drops into Amanda Gathering Place.) To start at the upper trailhead, turn east off US 101 about 0.25 mile north from the Cape Perpetua Visitor Center road (about 3 miles south of Yachats) onto Forest Road 55; in 0.8 mile, turn left onto FR 5553. Park at the first and lowest parking area in 0.8 mile or continue 0.1 mile to more parking at the top of Cape Perpetua (USFS day-use fee required).

*A suspension footbridge leads past the Amanda Gathering Place, memorializing a 19th century Coos Indian woman and honoring her people past and present.*

## ON THE TRAIL

From the lower trailhead along US 101 (0.8 mile from parking on Yachats Ocean Road), head into the woods and walk just above the highway for 0.5 mile to where the trail crosses a gravel road (and potential parking spot). It quickly drops down into an area known as Amanda Gathering Place, where visitors often leave offerings at a statue honoring Amanda's memory and where a substantial footbridge crosses Amanda Creek. The trail ascends fairly steeply, crossing North Cape Creek, for about 1 mile, then descending for most of the next mile to a junction with a short spur trail leading left to the lower of the two upper trailhead parking areas. If you parked at the higher one, bear right and continue to the next junction, where a left turn leads to the upper parking area. Or continue bearing right to reach the West Shelter viewpoint; it ultimately winds back to the upper parking area as well. Return as you came. Alternately, park at the top (parking is easier, but a parking pass is required) and walk down to Amanda Gathering Place before returning, for a 4.2-mile roundtrip.

# 58 Cape Perpetua: Four Short Hikes

**Contact:** Cape Perpetua Scenic Area, Siuslaw National Forest; **Notes:** USFS day-use fee. Dogs on-leash. Toilets. Parking; **GPS:** 44.28090°, –124.10826°

**The longer signature hikes in Cape Perpetua all climb up into the forest east of the shore, but there are some great short hikes along the shoreline and a short distance up Cape Creek that are worth your time; do them all or just one. Each has charms specific to the season, the weather, or the tide. During winter and spring Whale Watch Weeks, volunteers can help you spot whales from the highway turnout below the visitor center.**

## GETTING THERE

Turn east off US Highway 101 at Cape Perpetua Visitor Center, about 3 miles south of Yachats. Park in one of the lots on the hillside south of the visitor center.

### Cooks Ridge Discovery Loop

RATING/DIFFICULTY: **/2
LOOP: 1.3 miles
ELEV GAIN: 680 feet

**Cooks Ridge Trail gives you a taste of a coastal forest in transition (from being logged many years ago); the Discovery Loop makes a nice destination for this short hike.**

### On the Trail

Look for the start of the trail at the top of the parking lot above the visitor center. It begins in dense Douglas-fir and Sitka spruce and then leads into a stand of older spruce at 0.4 mile, where a junction signals the start of the 0.7-mile mid-trail Discovery Loop. Follow the loop either direction to the junction and return as you came.

### Giant Spruce

RATING/DIFFICULTY: **/1
ROUNDTRIP: 2.2 miles
ELEV GAIN: 160 feet

**You'll see plenty of large Sitka spruce along this trail—ducking under at least**

**one and walking between cuts in others that have fallen across the trail—but keep going to the end to see *the* Giant Spruce, which manages to dwarf the others. Campers in the campground can take a shortcut to the trail via a footbridge over Cape Creek.**

## On the Trail

From the visitor center, follow the asphalt path (quickly turns to dirt) down toward Cape Creek and continue as it follows the creek upstream along its south bank, crossing the occasional footbridge. At 0.9 mile bear right (a left leads over the creek to the end of the campground road). You'll cross one more footbridge before reaching the trail's end at 1.1 miles. Note how the Giant seems to be standing on legs; Sitka spruce typically take root only in spruce stumps or fallen logs, which eventually rot away and leave what look like stilts. Look up to see a cluster of licorice ferns: epiphytic plants, which rely on air for their food and nutrients and are part of the unique canopy habitat old trees like this provide to insects and other critters far off the ground. Return as you came.

### Spouting Horn

RATING/DIFFICULTY: **/1
ROUNDTRIP: 0.9 mile
ELEV GAIN: 220 feet

**Check out this paved trail at high tide, especially during or after a storm when the seas are churning. Or come at low tide to explore the tidepools in this state-protected marine garden. It's walkable with a stroller if you can handle some short steep sections.**

## On the Trail

From the visitor center, follow the path that leads south and west and under the highway; just past the tunnel, bear left at the trail junction. In another 0.1 mile you'll connect with Captain Cook Trail loop; bearing left, it leads to a viewpoint at 0.4 mile above Spouting Horn, a hole in the top of a sea cave at the end of Cooks Chasm. At high tide, air and water burst out when incoming waves build pressure inside the cave. Continuing, you'll reach a footbridge at 0.5 mile and then a spur trail down to the tidepools. In another 0.1 mile you'll complete the loop; turn left to reach the tunnel and the path back to the visitor center.

*The tree at the end of the Giant Spruce Trail is more than 185 feet tall and nearly 600 years old. It's one of a half-dozen designated Oregon Heritage Trees on the coast (more at oregontic .com/oregon-heritage-trees).*

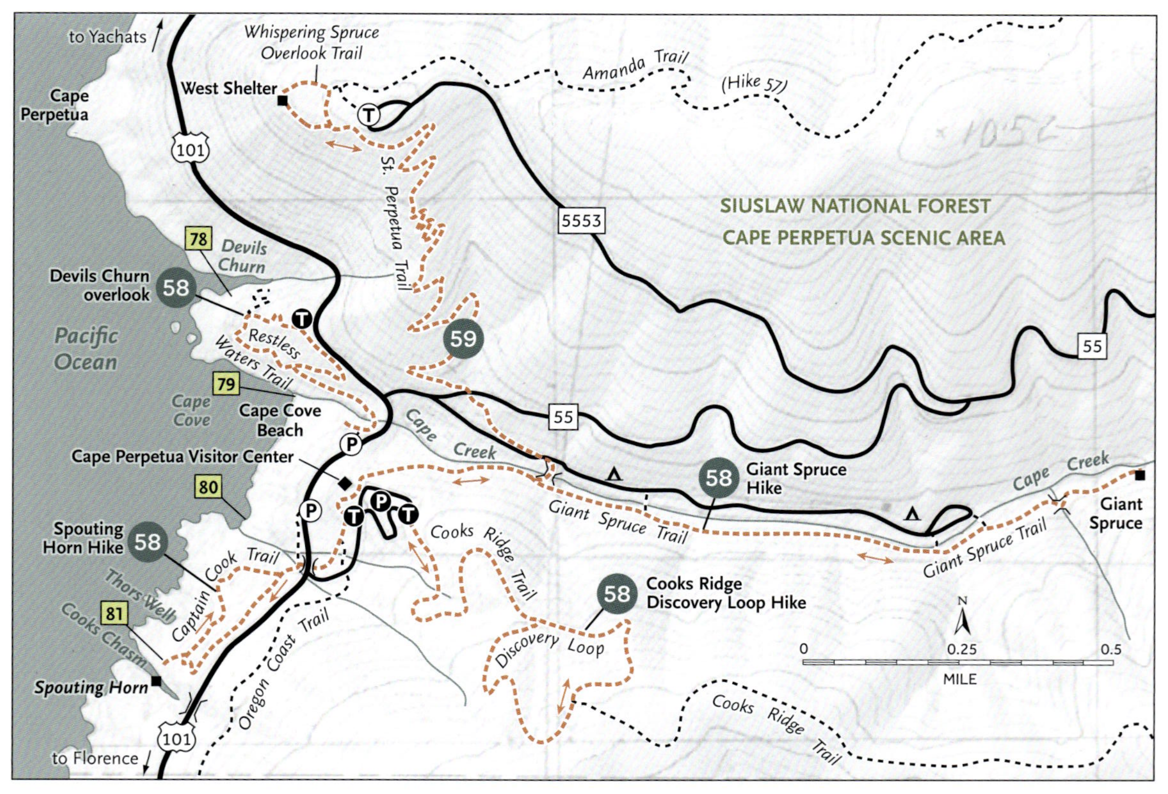
to Yachats
Whispering Spruce Overlook Trail
Amanda Trail
(Hike 57)
Cape Perpetua
West Shelter
101
St. Perpetua Trail
5553
SIUSLAW NATIONAL FOREST
CAPE PERPETUA SCENIC AREA
78
Devils Churn
Devils Churn overlook
58
Pacific Ocean
Restless Waters Trail
59
55
79
Cape Cove
Cape Cove Beach
55
Cape Creek
Cape Perpetua Visitor Center
58
Giant Spruce Hike
Cape Creek
Giant Spruce
80
Giant Spruce Trail
Giant Spruce Trail
Spouting Horn Hike
58
Cooks Ridge Trail
Captain Cook Trail
Thors Well
58
Cooks Ridge Discovery Loop Hike
81
Cooks Chasm
Discovery Loop
N
0
0.25
0.5
MILE
Oregon Coast Trail
Spouting Horn
Cooks Ridge Trail
101
to Florence

### Devils Churn

RATING/DIFFICULTY: **/1
ROUNDTRIP: 0.7 mile
ELEV GAIN: 180

**This 0.7-mile Devils Churn loop hike has charms at both low and high tide. The parking area is 0.4 mile north up US 101 from the visitor center turnoff.**

### On the Trail

Follow the paved Restless Waters Trail loop downhill a short distance to the top of the stairs to Devils Churn, a narrow rock chute where waves rush in, smash the wall, and shoot seawater into the air. There's nothing to see at low tide, but it's high drama at high tide, and you can see most of the action from the top of the stairs. Or continue another 0.2 mile on the main trail and bear right at a trail junction that leads a short distance to a spur down to Cape Cove Beach, a pocket beach that is most expansive at low tide. Expect to negotiate a field of cobbles and driftwood to reach the sand. To loop back to the parking area, turn right at the main loop trail and follow it back to the trailhead.

## 59 St. Perpetua Trail

RATING/DIFFICULTY: **/3
ROUNDTRIP: 3.2 miles
ELEV GAIN: 1,030 feet

**Contact:** Cape Perpetua Scenic Area, Siuslaw National Forest; **Notes:** USFS day-use fee. Dogs on-leash. Toilets; **GPS:** 44.28090°, –124.10826°

**Steep, forested Cape Perpetua dominates the coastline south of Yachats. It was formed by layers of lava cooled into basalt and uplifted millions of years ago.**

*The rock shelter at the top of Cape Perpetua, which was a Coast Guard lookout during World War II, is today an all-weather overlook.*

## BORN OF LAVA: AGATES

Among the treasures you might find on a beach walk in Oregon are agates in a wide range of hues, from milky-clear to fiery orange. They typically form in cavities in ancient lava rock, where silica-rich groundwater accumulates over millions of years. These little gems erode out of cliffs along the shore or flow down rivers to the sea and get tumbled in the waves, causing the softer rock surrounding them to get rubbed away. The agates you find in souvenir shops have been further smoothed in electric tumblers that imitate, in a fraction of the time, the effect of ocean waves.

*Oregon coast beaches produce agates in a range of colors.*

Agates are relatively plentiful near Cape Meares and Cape Lookout, Haystack Rock at Pacific City, and Yaquina Head, particularly in late fall through early spring after storms have begun moving sand to offshore sandbars, leaving a pebbly beach behind.

**This trail up to the cape's summit is one of several options available to hikers in Cape Perpetua Scenic Area. You could drive to the top of the cape, but then you'd miss the slow unfurling of the view to the south.**

### GETTING THERE

To reach the lower (southern) trailhead, turn off US Highway 101 at the Cape Perpetua Visitor Center, about 3 miles south of Yachats. To reach the upper (northern) trailhead, turn east off US 101 onto Forest Road 55 about 0.25 mile north of the visitor center then bear left onto FR 5553, which ends at the cape's summit viewpoint.

### ON THE TRAIL

From the lower trailhead at the visitor center, follow an asphalt path north and down to Cape Creek. Turn left and cross the creek, continuing across the campground road (at an alternative trailhead parking area) and FR 55. Steep at first, the trail switchbacks through forest up the cape's south side. About 0.2 mile from the top, a spectacular view opens to the south. Continue up the grassy hillside to the West Shelter, a lookout built of stone. Extend your outing with a stroll around paved, 0.25-mile Whispering Spruce Overlook Trail. It loops around the summit and links to Amanda Trail (Hike 57). A good spot for whale-watching is the rock shelter on the west side, built in 1933 by the Civilian Conservation Corps and used as a Coast Guard lookout during World War II (Whale Watch volunteers are posted at the visitor center during Whale Watch Weeks). Unless you've left a second car at the top for a one-way hike, return as you came.

## 60 Cooks Ridge

RATING/DIFFICULTY: **/3
ROUNDTRIP: 7.2 miles
ELEV GAIN: 1,720 feet

**Contact:** Cape Perpetua Scenic Area, Siuslaw National Forest; **Notes:** USFS day-use fee. Dogs on-leash. Toilets. Parking; **GPS:** 44.28052°, –124.10741°

**Cooks Ridge Trail is one of several forest trails in Cape Perpetua Scenic Area. Hike 58 describes the short Discovery Loop at the lower end of this trail. For a longer hike, keep going to the ridge and return as you came or loop back on another trail.**

*The reward of a hike up to Cooks Ridge is a rolling stroll through an airy forest of big trees.*

### GETTING THERE

Turn off US Highway 101 at Cape Perpetua Visitor Center, about 3 miles south of Yachats. To reach the upper trailhead, turn off US 101 just north of the visitor center onto Forest Road 55 and follow it 4 miles to the signed trailhead parking area.

### ON THE TRAIL

Pick up the Cooks Ridge Trail at the top of the visitor center parking area. In 0.4 mile you'll reach the mid-trail loop; a left turn leads 0.3 mile to another junction (or take a right and go 0.4 mile). Where the loop ends meet, take the main trail heading slightly up and east. It levels off, ascends, and levels again to reach a junction with Gwynn Creek Trail at 2.3 miles; follow the directions in Hike 61 (Gwynn Creek) to return to the visitor center. Otherwise, continue ascending steadily on Cooks Ridge Trail another 1.1 miles to Cummins Creek Trail. (For an 8.7-mile loop, take Cummins Creek Trail to its lower trailhead, bearing right at two junctions to stay on the main trail to the trailhead, then continue on a gravel road 0.3 mile and turn north on the Oregon Coast Trail for 1.3 miles to return to the visitor center and the lower Cooks Ridge trailhead.) From the Cummins Creek junction, the upper Cooks Ridge trailhead is 0.2 mile ahead on FR 55. Return as you came, unless you are looping back on other trails.

## 61 Gwynn Creek–Cooks Ridge Loop

RATING/DIFFICULTY: ***/3
LOOP: 6.3 miles
ELEV GAIN: 2,100 feet

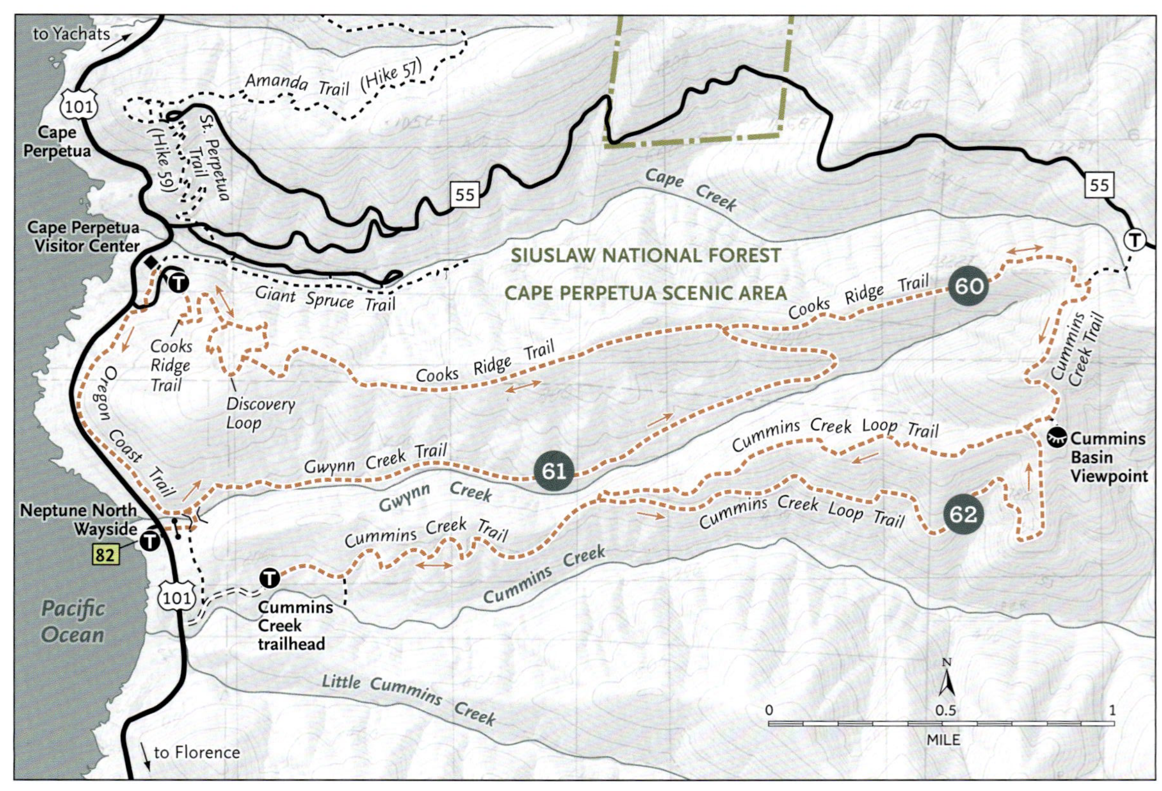
to Yachats
Amanda Trail (Hike 57)
101
Cape Perpetua
(Hike 59)
St. Perpetua Trail
55
Cape Creek
Cape Perpetua Visitor Center
SIUSLAW NATIONAL FOREST
CAPE PERPETUA SCENIC AREA
Giant Spruce Trail
Cooks Ridge Trail
60
Cooks Ridge Trail
Discovery Loop
Cummins Creek Trail
Oregon Coast Trail
Cummins Creek Loop Trail
Cummins Basin Viewpoint
Gwynn Creek Trail
61
Gwynn Creek
Neptune North Wayside
82
Cummins Creek Trail
Cummins Creek Loop Trail
62
Cummins Creek
101
Cummins Creek trailhead
Pacific Ocean
Little Cummins Creek
N
0
0.5
1
MILE
to Florence

*The walk up Gwynn Creek ascends through a forest of old Sitka spruce, to the creek's musical accompaniment.*

**Contact:** Cape Perpetua Scenic Area, Siuslaw National Forest; **Notes:** Dogs on-leash. Toilets at visitor center; **GPS:** 44.26982°, –124.10811°

**The trail up Gwynn Creek may be the prettiest on Cape Perpetua. It follows the hillside above the creek, gently climbing through deep forest, much of it mature hemlocks, spruces, and Douglas-firs. You can hike it a mile or two up and back or link with Cooks Ridge Trail for a satisfying loop.**

## GETTING THERE

From Yachats, take US Highway 101 south 4 miles, passing Cape Perpetua Visitor Center, and park at the wide Neptune North Wayside (Beach Access 82) west of the highway. Alternately start the loop at the Cape Perpetua Visitor Center (USFS day-use fee).

## ON THE TRAIL

Cross US 101, walk around a gate and up a grassy clearing, and look left for the footbridge crossing Gwynn Creek. Cross it, then bear right. The trail immediately begins a slow climb up the hillside on the north bank of the creek. The trail crosses several side creeks; one at about 1.5 miles is especially pretty, cascading in a fan down a rock face. At about 2.5 miles the trail switchbacks left, leading out of the protected valley and up to Cooks Ridge. At 3 miles Gwynn Creek Trail intersects the Cooks Ridge Trail; turn left here and follow Cooks Ridge Trail west and down to the visitor center parking lot. In front of the visitor center, pick up Cape Cove Trail, which begins as a paved path parallel to and just west of the entrance road. Follow it for 1 mile as it crosses the entrance road and becomes the unpaved Oregon Coast Trail leading south just above the highway to the footbridge crossing Gwynn Creek, completing the loop. Return as you came, via the path through the clearing out to the highway, cross it, and back to your starting point.

## 62 Cummins Creek Loop

RATING/DIFFICULTY: ***/3
ROUNDTRIP: 6.2 miles
ELEV GAIN: 2,040 feet

**Contact:** Cape Perpetua Scenic Area, Siuslaw National Forest; **Notes:** USFS day-use fee. Open to bikes. Dogs on-leash; **GPS:** 44.26809°, –124.10157°

**Most of Cummins Creek Trail follows an old road, making it inviting for off-road cycling and easy for hikers and bikers to share the trail. Despite the name, the trail stays well above the creek. It passes through a lush forest, though the forest tends to form a wall on either side of the roadbed, making it feel less intimate than forest footpaths such as Gwynn Creek. The best part of this hike is the upper 3.3-mile loop.**

### GETTING THERE

From US Highway 101 about 4 miles south of Yachats, pass the Cape Perpetua Visitor Center, then turn east at the sign to Cummins Creek trailhead and drive 0.3 mile to the road's end.

*The view from Cummins Basin Viewpoint stretches from forested Coast Range foothills to the Pacific.*

## ON THE TRAIL

The trail travels a gentle uphill grade following the old roadbed. At 0.2 mile an unsigned, unmaintained trail takes off to the right and leads 0.25 mile to a lovely spot on Cummins Creek, shallow and tranquil in late summer (but no doubt boisterous in December). Continuing, the main trail enters a beautiful grove of mature Sitka spruce at about 0.5 mile. The trail continues to ascend through the deep coastal forest. At 1.3 miles, bear right at the junction to start the loop. At 2.7 miles the trail diverges from the old road and bears left up a narrower, rockier, steeper footpath. At 3.2 miles you'll meet a junction signifying the top of the loop. Bear right and continue another 0.1 mile, then take the spur on the right 0.1 mile more to see a sea of trees at Cummins Basin Viewpoint. To return, backtrack 0.2 mile to the junction and bear right to complete the loop. The trail soon emerges onto a grassy ridge, revealing a blue-green panorama of forested ridges to the south. It returns to forest—big Douglas-firs and western redcedars—and winds downhill, steeply in places, to meet the main trail at 4.9 miles. Bear right to return as you came on the main trail.

## EXTEND YOUR HIKE

For a longer loop, see Hike 60 or 61.

## 63 Cummins Ridge

RATING/DIFFICULTY: **/3
ROUNDTRIP: 11.6 miles
ELEV GAIN: 1,770 feet

**Contact:** Central Coast Ranger District, Siuslaw National Forest; **Notes:** Dogs on-leash; **GPS:** Lower trailhead 44.25446°, –124.09385°; upper trailhead 44.23952°, –123.99739°

**The only trail through Cummins Creek Wilderness is Cummins Ridge Trail (not to be confused with Cummins Creek Trail), a 5.8-mile route of which the lower 2.9 miles originated as a logging road. Some 2.2 miles of footpath were added to the upper end of the old road to take the trail all the way to the edge of the wilderness, where an upper trailhead was established. As the regenerating forest on the lower portion of the trail has matured, it has grown prettier and prettier, though you need to get to the upper half to see the really old trees. The**

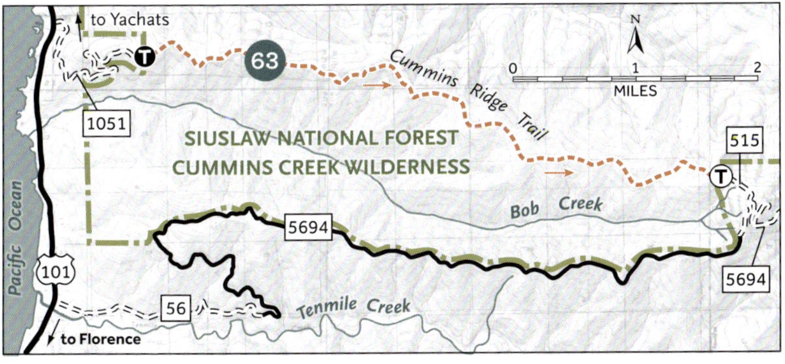

*The ascent up Cummins Ridge is a mostly gentle climb on a narrow forest path.*

**trail is described as an out-and-back 11.6-mile hike from the lower trailhead (though you could of course turn around at any point for a shorter hike); another option, if you have a shuttle vehicle, is a one-way, not-quite-all-downhill (or nearly all uphill!) hike. This little-used trail is never steep; it's similar in feel to Gwynn Creek Trail (Hike 61) but much less used.**

## GETTING THERE

To start a hike at the lower (western) trailhead, from US Highway 101 turn east on Forest Road 1051 at the sign to Cummins Ridge trailhead (2 miles south of Cape Perpetua Visitor Center and about 5 miles south of Yachats) and drive 2.2 miles to the trailhead at the end of the gravel road. To start a hike at the upper (eastern) trailhead, turn off US Highway 101 about 7 miles south of Yachats on gravel FR 56 just north of Tenmile Creek. At 2 miles, turn left onto narrow, paved FR 5694. Where a spur road comes in from the right in 7.8 miles, continue straight on FR 5694; shortly after the road turns to gravel, turn left on FR 515 and follow it about 0.2 mile to where it ends at the trailhead.

## ON THE TRAIL

From the lower trail, begin a gradual climb on the former road through the lush forest, watching the predominately Sitka spruce forest slowly give way to a mix of tree species. At 2.9 miles the trail narrows to a footpath and continues up, reaching the ridge at about 3.7 miles. From here the trail rolls along the ridge before making a final ascent to the eastern trailhead in the final 0.6 mile. Return as you came, unless you've made shuttle arrangements for a one-way hike.

## HECETA HEAD TO FLORENCE

With its lighthouse and charming nineteenth-century lightkeepers' house, Heceta Head may be the most photographed site on the Oregon coast. Hikers know it as part of an extensive trail system with options for loops of several lengths that wind into the forest north of the lighthouse and east of the highway to access the relatively remote beach to the north.

I say "relatively remote" because many people seem to think that Hobbit Beach is their own secret beach. It's not actually a secret (there's a sign on US Highway 101 pointing to it), but it does require a short hike to access, which limits the number of visitors and lends it that well-kept-secret feel. The loop route to China Creek and north through Washburne State Park and out to the beach, finishing on the Hobbit Trail, is one of my favorite hikes on the Oregon coast. Washburne State Park offers camping; for more primitive car camping, consider the US Forest Service (USFS) Rock Creek Campground north of Washburne.

The longest stretch of Oregon beach unbroken by headlands is the 56 miles of sand running from Heceta Head south to Cape Arago. North of Florence, most people access the beach from the parking area at the north jetty of the Siuslaw River. I prefer the more remote Sutton day-use area. But unless winter high water has floated a log to just the right spot for fording, you may have to wade the creek to get to the short trail through the dunes and onto the beach. A trail through the Sutton Creek corridor between the day-use area and US 101 offers fine one-way or out-and-back hiking. Camping is available at the USFS Sutton Campground and Rock Creek campgrounds, Washburne State Park, and Harbor Vista County Park.

## 64 Beach Walk: Rock Creek to Hobbit Beach

ONE-WAY DISTANCE: 3 miles

The shoreline bordering the beach here is almost entirely undeveloped state park or national forest land, so it's lovely and wild. Hobbit Beach at the south end is very popular with families seeking a short hike to a remote-ish beach. In the winter the creeks on the northern part of this beach (China Creek, Big Creek, and Rock Creek) may not be wadeable and effectively shorten the beach walk potential here.

### BEACH ACCESS

BA 90, Muriel O. Ponsler Memorial State Scenic Viewpoint, north of entrance to Carl G. Washburne Memorial State Park. Parking.

BA 92, Washburne State Park day-use area, across US 101 from Washburne Campground entrance. Parking, restrooms.

BA 93, Hobbit Beach trailhead, east side of US 101 south of Washburne Campground entrance. Limited roadside parking.

### WHERE TO WALK

**To Hobbit Beach.** It's 0.5 mile and 175 feet elevation down a tunnel-like trail to the beach on this popular trail. Hang out here or add in a stroll to the north.

**From Ponsler or Washburne day-use areas.** Skip the hike and get right on the beach from either of these sites; see China Creek Loop (Hike 65). Perhaps the best way for hikers to enjoy this beach is on a loop walk—north

Heceta Head to Florence
to Waldport
56
86
87
88
Rock Creek Campground
ROCK CREEK WILDERNESS
89
90
CARL G WASHBURNE MEMORIAL STATE PARK
91
92
Hobbit Beach
93
64
65
Heceta Head
66
HECETA HEAD LIGHTHOUSE STATE SCENIC VIEWPOINT
94
SIUSLAW NATIONAL FOREST
Berry Creek
Bailey Creek
Pacific Ocean
95
67
Baker Beach
95A
101
68
95B
Sutton Lake
69
Sutton Campground
Mercer Lake
96
96A
DARLINGTONIA STATE WAYSIDE
Heceta Beach
97
Clear Lake
to Eugene
HARBOR VISTA COUNTY PARK
98
99
100
Munsel Lake
Siuslaw River
101
102
126
103
FLORENCE
104
OREGON DUNES NATIONAL RECREATION AREA
105
Port of Siuslaw RV Park
70
106
107
S Jetty Rd
to Reedsport
0 1 2
MILES
N

*Heceta Head marks the southern end of the beach that lies south of Rock Creek.*

through the forest east of the highway and back south down on the sand.

## 65 China Creek Loop

RATING/DIFFICULTY: ***/2

LOOP: 3.9 miles

ELEV GAIN: 440 feet

**Contact:** Carl G. Washburne Memorial State Park; **Notes:** Dogs on-leash. Toilets at day-use area and campground; **GPS:** 44.14357°, –124.11758°

**Most of the people parked at the Hobbit Beach trailhead go straight to the beach. It's rare to encounter another hiker on this lovely trail that loops into the forest east of the highway and circles back on the beach.**

### GETTING THERE

Look for trailhead parking 12.5 miles north of Florence in a wide turnout (Beach Access 93) along the east side of US Highway 101 just south of milepost 177 (and 1.2 miles south of the entrance to Washburne State Park). Alternately pick up the loop at the Washburne day-use area (Beach Access 92), where you may find more parking.

### ON THE TRAIL

Pick up the trail on the east side of the highway next to the parking area. It drops down briefly, then levels off, following slow-moving Blowout Creek. At 0.5 mile, the trail passes a couple of ponds; look for evidence of beavers. It crosses the creek and then continues north through the woods. At 1 mile, there is a trail junction; go right to take the 0.8-mile Creek–Valley Loop, not to be missed. It leads into a gorgeous Sitka spruce forest with inviting creek crossings. After crossing a small creek, the trail ascends briefly, then zigzags south and east across a carpet of moss to the accompaniment of the ocean's roar. It descends and veers north, crossing a footbridge across babbling China Creek at

1.5 miles, then follows the creek's east bank to a broad, open prairie called Valley Meadow and another footbridge at 1.8 miles, where the Creek–Valley Loop rejoins the main trail.

To continue, head north, walking briefly on an old road lined with shore pines, turning right at a signed spur trail and meeting the paved road into Washburne State Park at 2.1 miles. Follow it out to US 101, cross the highway, and cut through the parking loop at the day-use area to get to the beach (at 2.4 miles). Walk the beach south about 1 mile and look for the west end of the Hobbit Trail at Beach Access 93, about 0.25 north of the cliffs at the end of the beach; follow it 0.5 mile back to your starting point.

## EXTEND YOUR HIKE

To lengthen the loop hike to 4.8 miles, rather than having to walk out the park entrance road and run across US 101, continue north on the paved campground road to campsite B-40 and pick up the paved path heading north. It leads along China Creek and under US 101 to end at Beach Access 91, just south of Muriel O. Ponsler Memorial State Scenic Viewpoint. Turn south and walk the beach 1.6 miles to the end of the Hobbit Trail, returning you to the start of the loop.

## 66 Heceta Head Lighthouse

RATING/DIFFICULTY: **/2

ROUNDTRIP: 2.4 miles

ELEV GAIN: 870 feet

**Contact:** Heceta Head Lighthouse State Scenic Viewpoint; **Notes:** Dogs on-leash; **GPS:** 44.14357°, –124.11758°

**This hike leads to possibly the most-photographed lighthouse on the Oregon**

*A substantial footbridge crosses a gully near the south end of the China Creek Loop.*

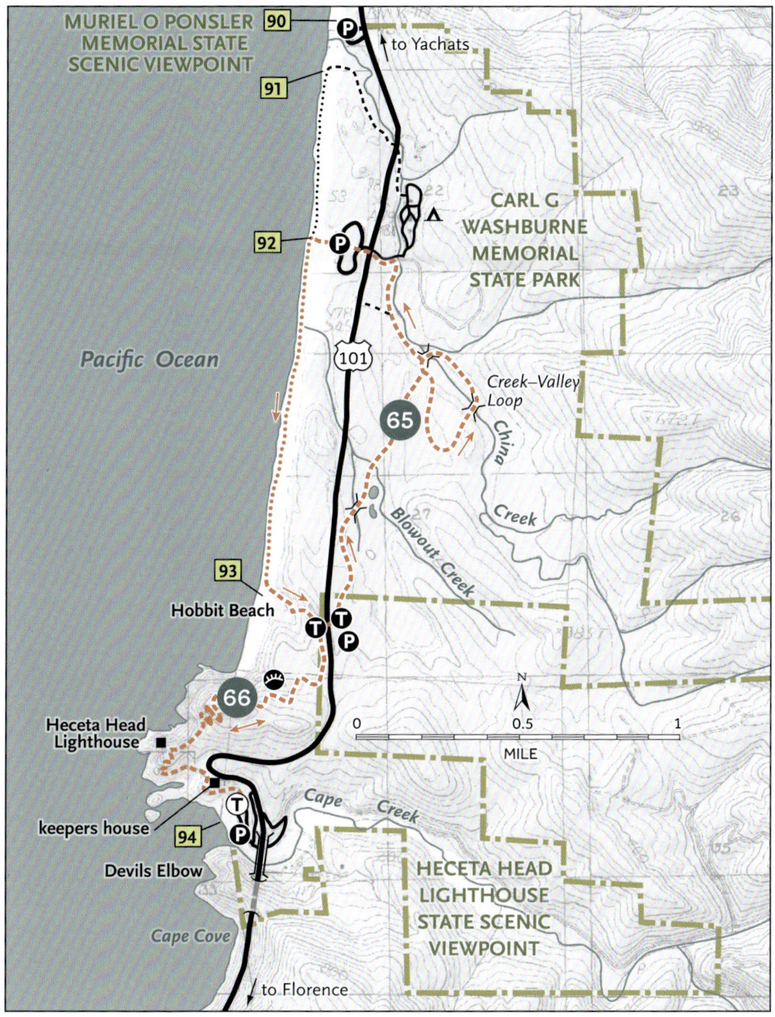


coast, open for tours daily, weather and staff permitting. Whale Watch volunteers are posted at the lighthouse during Whale Watch Weeks in winter and spring. Walk a little farther south to pass the vintage white Queen Anne–style lightkeepers house. There's a shorter way to get here (from the parking area at Heceta Head

*To reach the lighthouse, take a short walk from the parking lot at Heceta Head Lighthouse State Scenic Viewpoint, or take a longer hike from the parking lot shared with the Hobbit Trail.*

**Lighthouse State Scenic Viewpoint) if you're not seeking much of a hike.**

## GETTING THERE

North of Florence, look for trailhead parking for Hobbit Beach in a wide turnout along the east side of US Highway 101 just south of milepost 177 (and 1.2 miles south of the entrance to Washburne State Park).

## ON THE TRAIL

Cross the highway and start down the Hobbit Trail but take an immediate left. The lighthouse trail runs parallel to the highway for a short distance, then it veers away into a draw and starts up the airy forested hillside, first on steps and then on a series of switchbacks. At 0.75 mile, it levels off at a view of the coastline to the north, then drops down into a dark spruce forest, switchbacking before reaching the 1893 lighthouse. From the grassy flat at its base, hikers can look west to watch for fishing boats, whales, or seabirds nesting on the offshore rocks, or look back east to watch the huge original Fresnel lens still turning slowly in the lighthouse tower. Return as you came.

## EXTEND YOUR HIKE

Continue south on the trail to pass the assistant lighthouse keepers' house and all the way down the hill to the parking area for Heceta Head Lighthouse State Scenic Viewpoint and its pocket beach (and vault toilet), adding 1 mile to your roundtrip hike. Parking here requires an OPRD day-use permit.

# 67 Cape Mountain Loop

RATING/DIFFICULTY: **/3
LOOP: 7.5 miles
ELEV GAIN: 1,300 feet

**Contact:** Central Coast Ranger District, Siuslaw National Forest; **Notes:** Dogs on-leash. Vault toilet; **GPS:** 44.09641°, –124.07060°

**Hikers' opinions of this trail range widely: Some call it buggy and boring, lacking grand views; others love the forest and the lack of crowds. My own opinion has improved as what were once clear-cuts have matured into some impressive groves. The trails here, best known as the Coast Horse Trails, were built mainly for equestrians but are well maintained, nicely graded, and inviting for hikers, especially since they seem to be sparsely used by horses.**

**Note that there are some 17 miles of trails here; this loop is just one of many, some shorter and some longer, that you could try. Consider an out-and-back as far as you like on relatively level Princess Tasha Trail. Or take kids on a short out-and-back to the top of Cape Mountain, though that's hardly worth the drive. This loop is satisfying, scenic, and not too taxing if you're in shape for it.**

## GETTING THERE

North of Florence, turn off US Highway 101 between mileposts 182 and 183 on Herman Cape Road. After 1.1 miles of sinuous pavement, it becomes narrow, gravel Forest Road 789. Continue 1.7 miles and turn left at the sign to Dry Lake Trailhead.

## ON THE TRAIL

From the trailhead, follow the trail up between the two horse corrals and continue to a four-way junction at 0.4 mile. To make a counterclockwise loop, go right on Princess Tasha Trail. It rolls along the ridge for not quite 2 miles, passing a small picnic

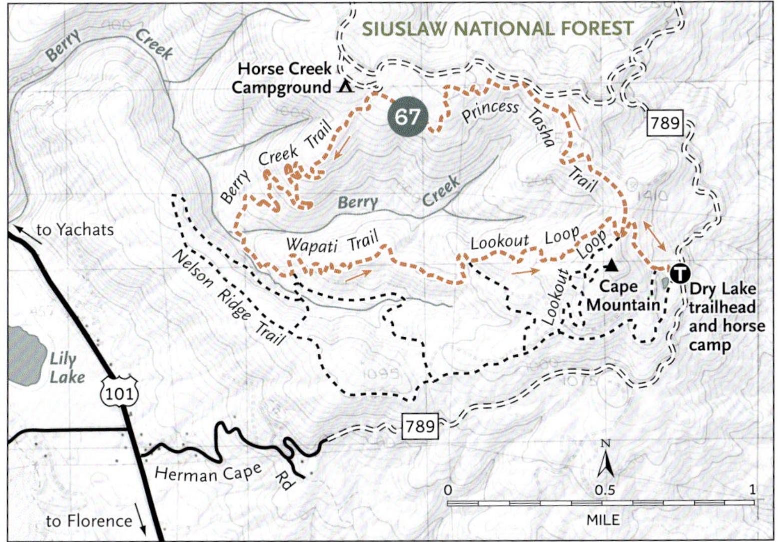

*On the Berry Creek Trail you'll need to rock-hop across shallow Berry Creek.*

area memorializing the owner of the trail's namesake, to a short spur leading to the right to Horse Creek Campground. Continuing, follow the sign to "horse water," which puts you on the Berry Creek Trail. Soon you'll enter an avenue of alder trees and start to hear the ocean (and maybe traffic on US 101) before reentering older, lusher forest. The trail descends with a series of switchbacks to reach Berry Creek at 4.2 miles. Cross it by stepping from rock to rock, then ascend, steeply at first, to a junction at 4.6 miles. Bear left onto the Wapati Trail, which switchbacks back up the hill until it reaches the ridge at 5.3 miles. Bear left at the next junction, at 6 miles, onto Lookout Loop, which leads back to that four-way junction with Princess Tasha Trail at 7 miles. Cross it to return to the trailhead.

From this junction, the top of Cape Mountain is two left turns and about 0.5 mile farther; consider making it the destination of a short hike or a highlight of this loop hike. The summit is a big tree-ringed meadow; no distant views, but a couple of benches and interpretive panels mark it as the former site of a fire lookout and homestead.

## 68 Beach Walk: Baker Beach to the Siuslaw River

ONE-WAY DISTANCE: 6.4 miles

This beach represents the north end of the Coos Bay Dune Sheet, a vast shoreline of beach and dunes interrupted only by three large rivers and bays and a number of smaller creeks. This section stretches south to the mouth of the Siuslaw River. There are a couple of creeks that are generally wadeable in summer but not in winter. Note: No dogs or kites on the beach March 15–September 15 from the north end of beach south to about 0.5 mile from the mouth of Sutton Creek (watch for fencing and signage).

## BEACH ACCESS

BA 95, US 101 pullout off US 101 just south of milepost 181. Beach is 0.2 mile down the hillside on a narrow trail. Limited parking.

BA 95A, Baker Beach, end of Baker Beach Road, north of Florence. Beach is 0.4 mile away via a sand trail. USFS day-use fee. Limited parking, vault toilet.

BA 95B, Holman Vista day-use area, end of Sutton Beach Road, north of Florence. Beach is 0.3 mile away via a sand trail; requires wading Sutton Creek or crossing on a log. USFS day-use fee. Parking.

BA 96, Heceta Beach North, end of Heceta Beach Road, Florence. Lane County day-use fee. Parking, restrooms.

BA 96A, Heceta Beach South, end of Heceta Beach Road, Florence. Parking.

BA 97, Siuslaw River North Jetty, end of North Jetty Road, Florence. Parking, vault toilet.

## WHERE TO WALK

**Adventurous.** Start at any of the northern three access points; each requires a bit of a walk to get to the beach and grants access to miles of fairly remote shoreline. Berry Creek and Sutton Creek are typically wadeable in summer, not in winter.

**Easy.** Start at Heceta Beach, or at the North Jetty, and walk north. From the north

*You can walk south on Baker Beach as far as Sutton Creek, where you can turn around or wade across in summer.*

jetty it's a 2.25-mile walk (less than 1 mile from Heceta Beach access points) before you reach Sutton Creek, which is a good turnaround point if you want to keep your feet dry.

## 69 Sutton Creek Trail

RATING/DIFFICULTY: ***/3

LOOP: 5.4 miles

ELEV GAIN: 190 feet

**Contact:** Central Coast Ranger District, Siuslaw National Forest; **Notes:** USFS day-use fee. Dogs on-leash. Toilets; **GPS:** 44.05359°, –124.09760°

**Sutton Creek flows out of Sutton Lake north of Florence, winding through mostly forested dunes before spilling into the Pacific. A relatively easy loop trail (other than some tricky wayfinding) follows it much of the way, traversing terrain ranging from dense forest to lush creekside meadows to pockets of open sand dunes. This loop hike takes in the entire trail system on either side of the creek, but with**

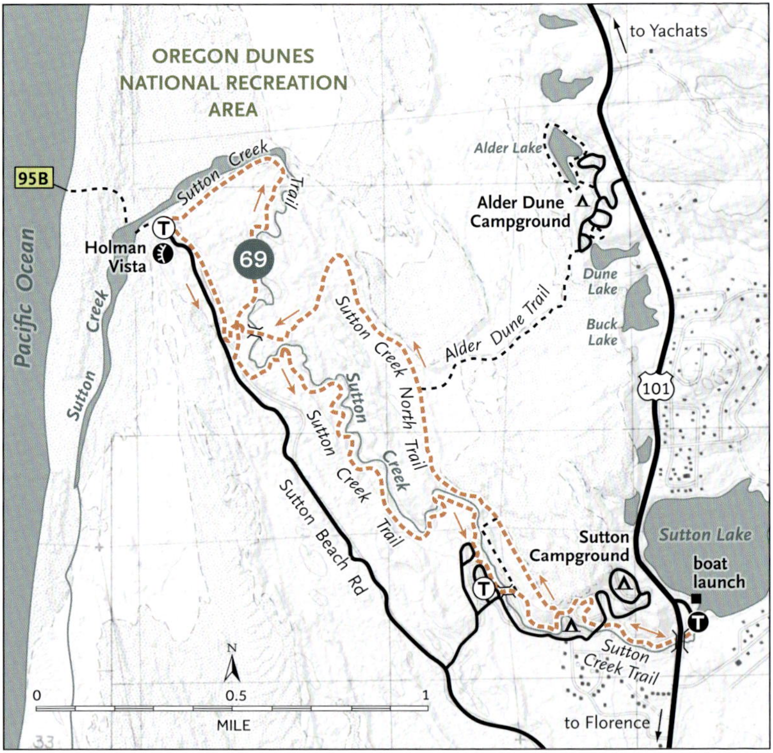

## BOG-DWELLING BUG EATERS

Two species of carnivorous plants can be found in bogs on the Oregon coast. The hooded leaves of the pitcher plant, or cobra lily (*Darlingtonia californica*), are what lure, capture, and digest the insects the plant uses to supplement its diet. The plant's purple and yellow flower rises above the bulbous leaf in late spring. Look for dense stands of *Darlingtonia* on a spur off the Sutton Creek Loop (Hike 69) and along a short boardwalk trail in nearby Darlingtonia Wayside (off US 101 south of milepost 185, just north of Sutton Beach Road) as well as on the Lost Lake trail (Hike 88).

Darlingtonia *is best recognized by its hood-like, bug-catching leaf; look closely to see its pale green and dark purple flower jutting above it.*

Less common and harder to spot is the roundleaf sundew (*Drosera rotundifolia*), which grows in freshwater bogs and fens, usually on sphagnum moss. Only 2 to 10 inches tall, the plant's upper leaf surface is covered with sticky pink hairs that capture bugs and hold them as the plant digests its prey with enzymes and bacteria. You might spot some near the dikes along Coos Bay South Slough Loop (Hike 85). If you come across them, be thoughtful of these rare and wondrous plants.

**its many trail junctions, there are plenty of options for shorter loop hikes.**

### GETTING THERE

Park at the Sutton Lake Boat Launch, 0.5 mile north of Sutton Beach Road on the east side of US Highway 101, north of milepost 185. Other trailhead options include Holman Vista, at the end of 2.5-mile Sutton Beach Road (off US 101, south of milepost 185) and trail crossings inside Sutton Campground, accessed by turning east to the campground off the Sutton Beach Road. All require a USFS day-use fee.

### ON THE TRAIL

Park at the boat launch and pick up the trail where it leads under US 101; follow it along the creek 0.3 mile to Loop D of Sutton Campground. Cross the road and bear left up the paved road marked "Wrong Way" a short distance until the signed foot trail leads left. At 0.5 mile you'll reach your first trail junction; bear right to begin a counterclockwise loop. The trail rolls through forest just above the creek, then heads up a sandy hillside to a trail junction at 0.8 mile. Continue straight, in and out of open and forested dunes, to pass a spur trail leading northeast to Alder Dune Campground at 1 mile. The trail continues in dunes, with soft sand underfoot in places, to a footbridge at 1.8 miles; cross it, bear right, and follow the trail a short distance to another trail junction; go right. The trail treats you to more

*The Sutton Creek Trail never veers far from the creek itself.*

up and down, now on the west side of the creek, until you pass a junction to emerge at Holman Vista and the trailhead at the end of Sutton Beach Road at 2.8 miles (Beach Access 95B).

To complete the loop, pick up the trail to your left, off the parking loop, and follow it to a junction 3.2 miles, completing the upper loop. Go right, pass the footbridge, and closely follow the west side of the creek, until you emerge onto Loop A of Sutton Campground at 4.4 miles. Here's where it can get a little confusing. Walk left around the campground loop and take the short wood-chip path on your left, across from campsite A12, to the Loop B road; follow it around to the left to a small trailhead parking area past campsite B18. Here an asphalt path leads left to another footbridge over Sutton Creek; cross it and go right, then right again (after climbing some concrete stairs), to complete the loop and return to the boat launch. Hikers starting at Sutton Campground (or from the end of Sutton Beach Road) can cut off the spur to the boat launch and trim their loop hike to 4.4 miles.

## OREGON DUNES NORTH

From the Siuslaw River at Florence south to the mouth of the Umpqua River, most of the land between the shore and highway is part of Oregon Dunes National Recreation Area. It's the largest expanse of coastal sand dunes in the United States, with some dunes as tall as 500 feet. But numbers can't express the essence of the dunes' appeal: the play of light and shadow across the open sand, the lazy curve of a tannin-stained creek through the forest, the stillness found in the lee of a hummock on a blustery day.

Several roads allow entry to the beach; in between, hiking trails provide access to more remote dune stretches. Many trails consist of established paths up tree islands—steep-sloped mini-forests isolated by shifting sands—and across the deflation plain—the wet, densely vegetated depression inland from the beachgrass-covered foredune. These are linked by stretches of open sand where the route is marked only with blue-tipped wooden posts. You can also forgo signed trails entirely and just strike out on your own. But that's getting harder to do, as the areas of open sand contract and vegetation covers more of the dunes—a consequence of the widespread planting of European beachgrass used to stabilize the dunes.

First-time visitors to the Oregon Dunes are sometimes taken aback by the presence of off-road vehicles. Dune buggies have been a fixture on the dunes for years and are fiercely defended by a contingent of local residents and visitors. Their use is closely managed and generally restricted to areas well away from hiking trails.

Note that dogs and kite-flying are not allowed on the beach on most of this stretch from March 15 to September 15 to protect nesting snowy plovers.

## 70 Beach Walk: Siuslaw River to Siltcoos River

ONE-WAY DISTANCE: 9.7 miles

The long finger of sand stretching south from the rock jetty at the mouth of Siuslaw River—a stretch of beach locally referred to as the "south jetty"—is a great pick for no-hassle beach walking—at least on the north half, where off-highway vehicles (OHVs) aren't allowed. Dogs are allowed on nearly all of it (just not in the vicinity of the Siltcoos River), unlike much of the beach bordering Oregon Dunes National Recreation Area, due to snowy plover nesting. OHVs are restricted to the 5-mile stretch of beach and dunes from Beach Access 105 south to Beach Access 110 at the mouth of the Siltcoos.

### BEACH ACCESS

(see map on p.156)

BA 98, Siuslaw River South Jetty, end of Sand Dunes Road. Limited parking and rough access road; park at BA 99.

BA 99, South Jetty parking area 7. Northernmost parking on Sand Dunes Road.

BA 100, 101, 102, 103, 104, 105, South Jetty parking areas 1–6, along Sand Dunes Road. USFS day-use fee. Vault toilets at parking areas 1, 2, and 6.

BA 110, mouth of Siltcoos River, end of Siltcoos Beach Access Road. USFS day-use fee. Parking, vault toilet (flush toilets available in nearby campgrounds).

## Oregon Dunes North

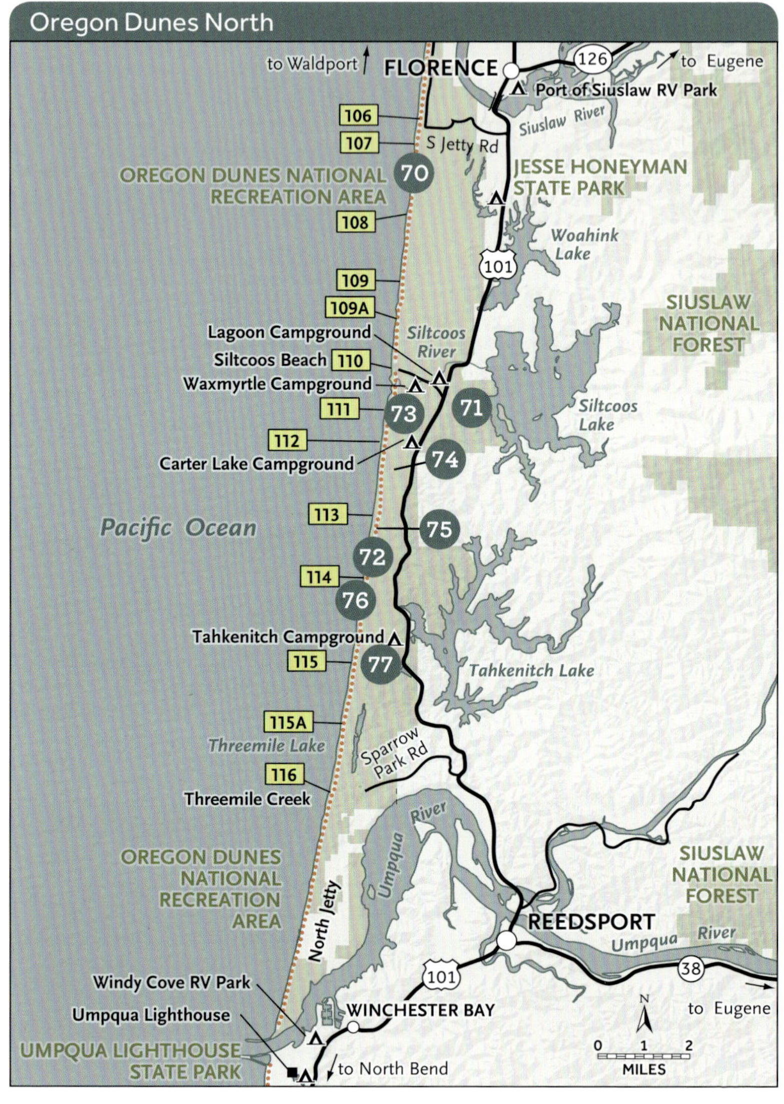

*To reach the beach south of the Siuslaw South Jetty, you'll have to climb a tall foredune.*

## WHERE TO WALK

**North of Beach Access 105.** It's about 4.2 miles from here (the southernmost of the beach parking lots used by hikers rather than off-highway vehicles) to the rock jetty at Beach Access 98. Pick any of these parking lots, walk up and over the dunes, and as long as you stay between these points, you won't be bothered by the buzz and roar of OHVs.

**South of Beach Access 110.** It's about a 0.4-mile walk to the mouth of the Siltcoos River from here. During snowy plover nesting season, the dunes themselves are off-limits (to humans and dogs), but it's a wildlife-watcher's dream if you stick to the wet sand: You may see seals, bald eagles, and maybe even a plover. The river mouth itself can usually be waded in summer, at least from low to about mid-tide, vastly extending the potential distance of your walk (see Beach Walk: Siltcoos River to Umpqua River) as long as you watch the tide for your return wade; otherwise check the map for trails leading to a bridge over the Siltcoos at Waxmyrtle Campground.

## 71 Siltcoos Lake

RATING/DIFFICULTY: **/2
ROUNDTRIP: 5 miles
ELEV GAIN: 740 feet

**Contact:** Oregon Dunes National Recreation Area, Siuslaw National Forest; **Notes:** USFS day-use fee. Vault toilet; **GPS:** 43.86900°, –124.13336°

**On a warm summer's day, there's nothing like hiking a couple of miles through deep coastal forest, with shafts of sunlight**

*With tall trees lining the way, the Siltcoos Lake Trail is appealing in all seasons.*

**filtering through the conifers, and then plunging into freshwater Siltcoos Lake, the largest lake on the Oregon coast. You might encounter boaters at campsites along the lakeshore when you arrive. The trail is equally appealing on a drizzly winter day, with the deep forest buffering the rain.**

## GETTING THERE

From Florence, take US Highway 101 south about 7 miles and turn east at the sign to the Siltcoos Lake trailhead, across the highway from Siltcoos Beach Road.

## ON THE TRAIL

Begin hiking up a steady but gentle incline through dense shrubbery and tall trees. The trail levels off and then splits into two forks at about 0.8 mile. Either direction leads to little lakeside campsites in about another mile. Taking the left-hand trail, the route descends slowly over a couple of boardwalks and through second-growth forest logged long ago; look for old-time loggers' springboard notches cut in large, decaying stumps. At about 2.7 miles a spur trail leads left to a group of five lakeside campsites; stay right to continue around the lakeshore to a single (lovely) primitive campsite. (In our experience they are not often in use; there are a couple of outhouses nearby, but they appear to be abandoned and unmaintained.) The campground loops are a bit confusing here but bear left and you'll eventually wind around to a sign, at 3.5 miles,

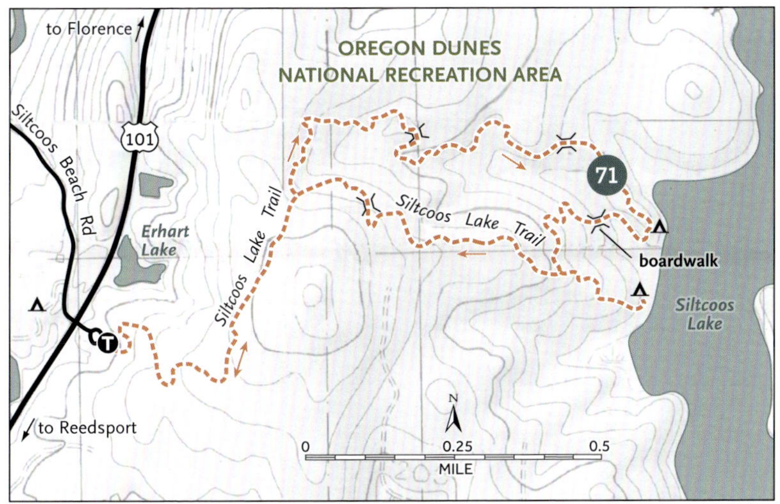


indicating a left turn leads to the "south camp" in 0.25 mile. Check it out or bear right to stay on the main trail. It leads over a long boardwalk and up a set of stairs then skirts the bottom of a regenerating clear-cut before reaching your first junction and completing the loop portion of this lollipop trail. Bear left to return to the trailhead.

## 72 Beach Walk: Siltcoos River to Umpqua River

ONE-WAY DISTANCE: 14.1 miles

This long stretch of beach can only be reached on foot—or Sparrow Park Road, too rough in at least one spot for most passenger cars. Off-highway vehicles aren't allowed on the beach or nearby dunes here, making this stretch of beach one of the Oregon coast's best for hikers—remote and uncrowded. Note that dogs and kite-flying aren't allowed March 15–September 15 for most of this beach (see Where to Walk).

### BEACH ACCESS

Hike 73, Waxmyrtle Trail
Hike 74, Taylor and Carter Dunes
Hike 75, Oregon Dunes Loop
Hike 76, Tahkenitch Creek Loop
Hike 77, Tahkenitch–Threemile Lake Loop
BA 116, end of Sparrow Park Road, 3.9 miles west of US 101 between mileposts 207 and 208, Gardiner. The road is rough in places and is recommended for high-clearance vehicles only. Roadside parking.

### WHERE TO WALK

**Hikes 73–77 to the beach.** Pick any of the hikes listed above to get to the beach; some of them are loop hikes that incorporate a mile or two of beach walking into the hike. Or, once you reach the beach, just take off to the north or south. Respect snowy plover recovery efforts and don't bring dogs in spring or summer (except near the end of Sparrow Park Road). Instead, come

*You're likely to see seals at the mouth of the Siltcoos River. It's often wadeable at low tide in summer; otherwise, reach the beach to the south from one of a few trails leading across the dunes.*

mid-September through mid-March for a lovely, lonely off-season walk with your dog. Be aware of the tides, however; winter's highest tides can obliterate the beach and have you scrambling up a steep foredune to stay dry.

**Sparrow Park Road to the Umpqua north jetty.** If your vehicle can handle the road, park at the road's end and enjoy 3-plus miles of beach with your dog year-round; dogs are allowed from about 0.6 mile north of Sparrow Park Road to about 2.6 miles south. During plover nesting season, if you leave your pooch at home, you can walk as far south as the jetty at the mouth of the Umpqua River, 5.5 remote miles one-way.

## 73 Waxmyrtle Trail

RATING/DIFFICULTY: **/2
ROUNDTRIP: 2.4 miles
ELEV GAIN: 120 feet

**Contact:** Oregon Dunes National Recreation Area, Siuslaw National Forest; **Notes:** USFS day-use fee. No dogs or kites on beach Mar 15–Sept 15. Toilets and water available in adjacent campground; **GPS:** 43.87766°, –124.14559°

**Follow a woodsy trail above the Siltcoos River to a quiet stretch of beach near the river's mouth. The trees provide a natural blind behind which to observe the birdlife in the estuary. The second half of the trail is a somewhat tedious slog on a soft sand road, but you're rewarded with a sparkling beach a short walk from the river's mouth. The name (of the trail and campground) is the common name for *Morella californica*, a native shrub that grows widely on the Oregon coast, especially in the Oregon Dunes. It is characterized by its clusters of long, pointed leaves and dark purple berries popular with birds. The name is similar, but it's only distantly related to Oregon myrtlewood (*Umbellularia californica*, or California bay laurel), which also grows widely on the southern Oregon coast; it's best known for its fragrant leaves and its lovely, hard wood popular for salad bowls and other gift items.**

### GETTING THERE

From US Highway 101 about 7 miles south of Florence, take Siltcoos Beach Road west 1 mile to the Stagecoach Trailhead parking area just west of the entrance to Waxmyrtle Campground.

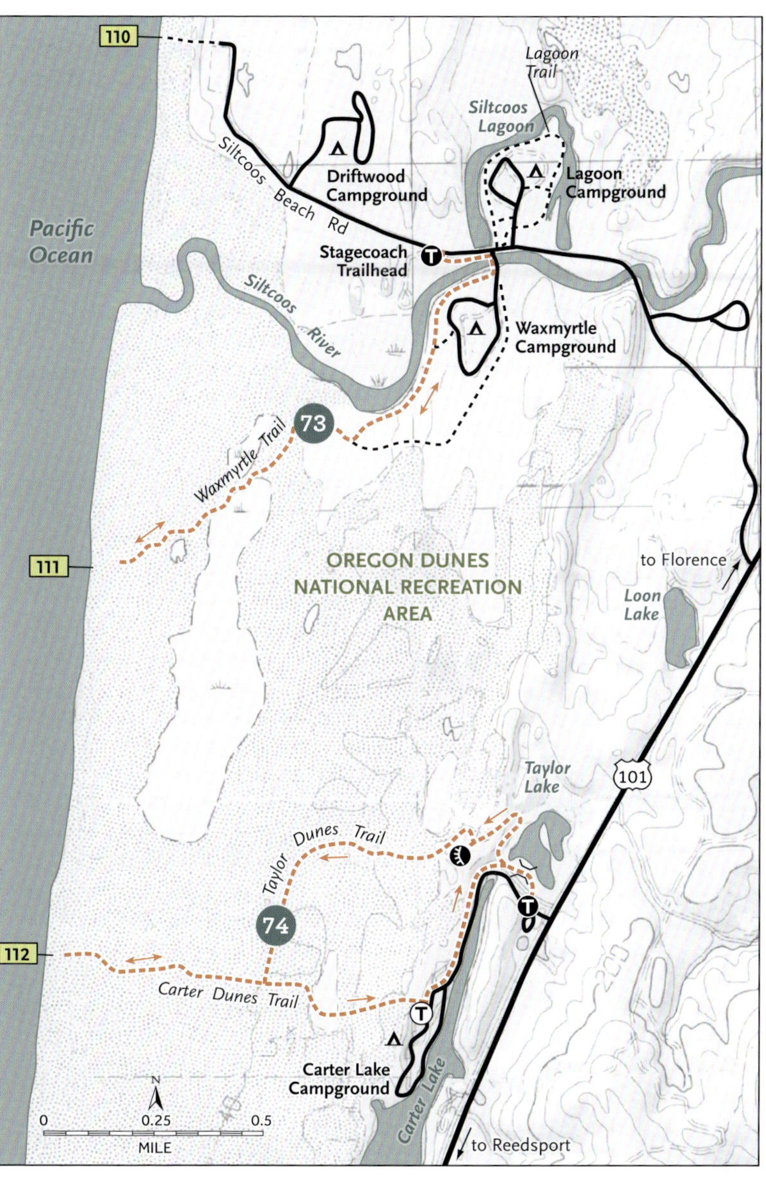

110
Lagoon Trail
Siltcoos Lagoon
Driftwood Campground
Lagoon Campground
Siltcoos Beach Rd
Pacific Ocean
Stagecoach Trailhead
Siltcoos River
Waxmyrtle Campground
73
Waxmyrtle Trail
111
OREGON DUNES NATIONAL RECREATION AREA
to Florence
Loon Lake
Taylor Lake
101
Taylor Dunes Trail
74
112
Carter Dunes Trail
Carter Lake Campground
Carter Lake
to Reedsport
N
0
0.25
0.5
MILE

## ON THE TRAIL

From the trailhead parking area, follow the trail 0.1 mile east to the Waxmyrtle Campground road, cross the Siltcoos River, and immediately turn right where the trail begins following the river's south bank. Climb stairs up a short hill forested with shore pines. At 0.5 mile the trail veers south 0.1 mile, then west again on a sand road leading 0.6 mile out to the beach, steering hikers away from snowy plover habitat adjacent to the river's mouth. To reach the mouth of the Siltcoos River, walk the beach north about 0.4 mile. Return as you came.

## EXTEND YOUR HIKE

Across the road and river from Waxmyrtle Campground is the 1-mile Lagoon Trail, which follows an old arm of the Siltcoos River that was cut off when Siltcoos Beach Road was built, hence the nickname "the river of no return." It is an appealing little trail; the bird-watching here can be spectacular, and the boardwalk at the start, plus numerous wooden observation platforms, help propel hikers along the route.

# 74 Taylor and Carter Dunes

RATING/DIFFICULTY: **/2
LOOP: 2.7 miles
ELEV GAIN: 275 feet

**Contact:** Oregon Dunes National Recreation Area, Siuslaw National Forest; **Notes:** USFS day-use fee. No dogs or kites on beach Mar 15–Sept 15. Toilets; **GPS:** 43.86069°, –124.14199°

**The Taylor and Carter Dunes Trails begin in the forest but mostly traverse sand dunes; hikers used to find their way by walking from trail post to trail post, but as vegetation has overtaken the open dunes, the route is now an easy-to-follow footpath. Not many people use these trails, making the stretch of beach they lead to one of the quietest on this part of the coast. The first 0.5 mile of Taylor Dunes Trail leads up a gently graded, accessible gravel path to a scenic overlook—a fine destination for a short out-and-back view hike. If you have a dog with you, enjoy the loop but skip the 0.4-mile spur to the beach during**

*The Waxmyrtle Trail closely follows the lower Siltcoos River, offering glimpses of the creek and salt marsh.*

*You may see birds from the viewing platform near the start of Taylor Dunes Trail.*

**the spring-to-fall snowy plover nesting season. Water is available when Carter Lake Campground is open (summers).**

## GETTING THERE

From Florence, take US Highway 101 south about 8 miles and turn west at the road to Carter Lake Campground; immediately turn left into the Taylor Dunes parking area.

## ON THE TRAIL

A counterclockwise loop allows a gradual ascent to the dune ridge. Cross the campground road and begin walking along Taylor Lake. A boardwalk viewing platform invites hikers to pause at the pond and watch for osprey and other birds. Continue as the trail slowly ascends the hillside. At 0.5 mile the trail splits; detour left a short distance to a viewpoint at the edge of the forest. Bear right to continue on the trail route down and across the dunes.

Follow the trail another 0.5 mile through dense stands of Scotch broom to where the trail meets Carter Dunes Trail. To reach the beach, go west through a tunnel of shore pines. The trail here can be very soggy in winter. Emerging from the trees, head up and over the foredune to the beach at the Beach Access 112 sign. To complete the loop, return on Carter Dunes Trail, bearing right at the intersection with the Taylor Dunes Trail and following footprints and blue-tipped trail posts up to the dune ridge and down through the forest to reach the end of Carter Dunes Trail in the Carter Lake Campground; follow the campground road north 0.4 mile to return to the trailhead.

# 75 Oregon Dunes Loop

RATING/DIFFICULTY: **/2
LOOP: 4.5 miles
ELEV GAIN: 300 feet

**Contact:** Oregon Dunes National Recreation Area, Siuslaw National Forest; **Notes:** USFS day-use fee. No dogs or kites on beach Mar 15–Sept 15. Toilets. **GPS:** 43.83337°, –124.15181°

**Oregon Dunes Day-Use Area offers a view of the ocean (otherwise rare on this stretch of US 101) and an opportunity to take a vigorous but not-too-long hike to and along the beach. The loop takes in the many and varied habitats found in the dunes: open sand dunes, boggy deflation plain, tree islands, grassy foredune, and the beach itself. With nearly half the hike on soft sand, you may find this to be more of a workout than a same-distance hike on a forest path.**

## GETTING THERE

From US Highway 101 about midway between Florence and Reedsport, turn off at the Oregon Dunes Day-Use Area between mileposts 200 and 201.

## ON THE TRAIL

Two routes lead out of the parking area and converge on the sand below. Follow the asphalt path heading north past the restrooms; it makes a sharp left and continues as a dirt path down to the sand. Alternately, climb the stairs or ramp to the upper viewing deck and follow a winding sand path a short distance through the trees, then walk or slide to the bottom of the tall sand dune. Posts mark the way from here; to make a counterclockwise loop, head west across

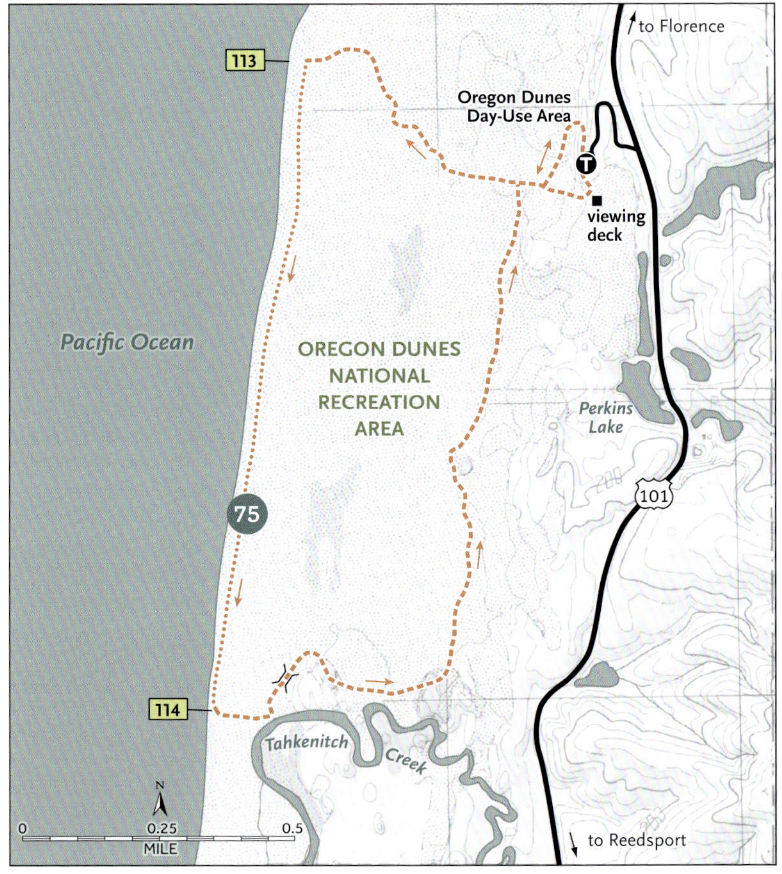

*Start your walk on this loop route by crossing mostly open sand dunes to the vegetated dunes and, eventually, the ocean beach.*

about 0.25 mile of sand to where a footpath resumes in the vegetation. Bear right into what's called the deflation plain; small bridges get you across most boggy spots. It veers west over the foredune to land you at the beach in 1 mile, at Beach Access 113.

Walk the beach south, keeping your eyes open for the remains of a fishing boat that ran aground here in 1983 and sometimes reemerges from the sand, particularly in the spring after a stormy winter (more details in my 2008 book, *Strand: An Odyssey of Pacific Ocean Debris*). At 1.5 miles, look for Beach Access 114 and a trail post in the dune to the east (if you reach the mouth of Tahkenitch Creek, you've gone too far—about 1.5 miles too far). Climb past the trail post and follow the path along a bend in Tahkenitch Creek, over a footbridge, up and over a tree island, to a view of an oxbow turn in the creek.

From here posts help mark the way north across any open dunes to another tree island about 1 mile from where you left the beach. Skirt west of a third tree island (the posts may not always be easy to see) and you will find yourself back in the sand below the overlook. The easiest way back is to bear left up the gradually ascending path to the day-use parking area.

## 76 Tahkenitch Creek Loop

RATING/DIFFICULTY: **3

LOOP: 5.1 miles

ELEV GAIN: 180 feet

**Contact:** Oregon Dunes National Recreation Area, Siuslaw National Forest; **Notes:** USFS day-use fee. No dogs or kites on beach Mar 15–Sept 15. Toilets; **GPS:** 43.81305°, –124.15435°

*On a hot day, look for spots to veer off the Tahkenitch Creek Trail and take a dip.*

**On its way from Tahkenitch Lake to the ocean, Tahkenitch Creek twists and turns through the dunes. A trail system twists and loops to follow the creek's east bank and final few miles through a landscape of forest, marsh, and open dunes, with rare glimpses of the creek itself. Check out the map for shorter and much shorter loop options. The route may not be well signed and thus can be confusing. The mouth of Tahkenitch Creek is remote and lovely; depending on the season and time of day, expect to see shorebirds on the sand, kingfishers in the estuary, and even coho salmon entering the creek to spawn during high tides in November or December. The trail can be soggy during winter high-water periods; we've hiked the trail barefoot on a mild January day through pools the color of French onion soup. In summer's snowy plover nesting season, dogs are allowed on the trail but not on the beach.**

## GETTING THERE

The signed trailhead for Tahkenitch Creek is west of US Highway 101, 1.6 miles south of the Oregon Dunes Day-Use Area and about 8 miles north of Reedsport.

## ON THE TRAIL

From the parking area, the trail descends 0.1 mile to a footbridge at a bend in the creek. Continue a short distance to a junction, the first of several; bear right and look for a spur leading right to a sweet wading spot at the creek's edge. A left at 0.9 mile cuts 0.2 mile across the loop; go left, then right, for a little 1.8-mile loop walk. Otherwise, continue straight (south) and make a sharp left with the main trail and reach a junction with Tahkenitch Dunes Trail at 1.4 miles, where

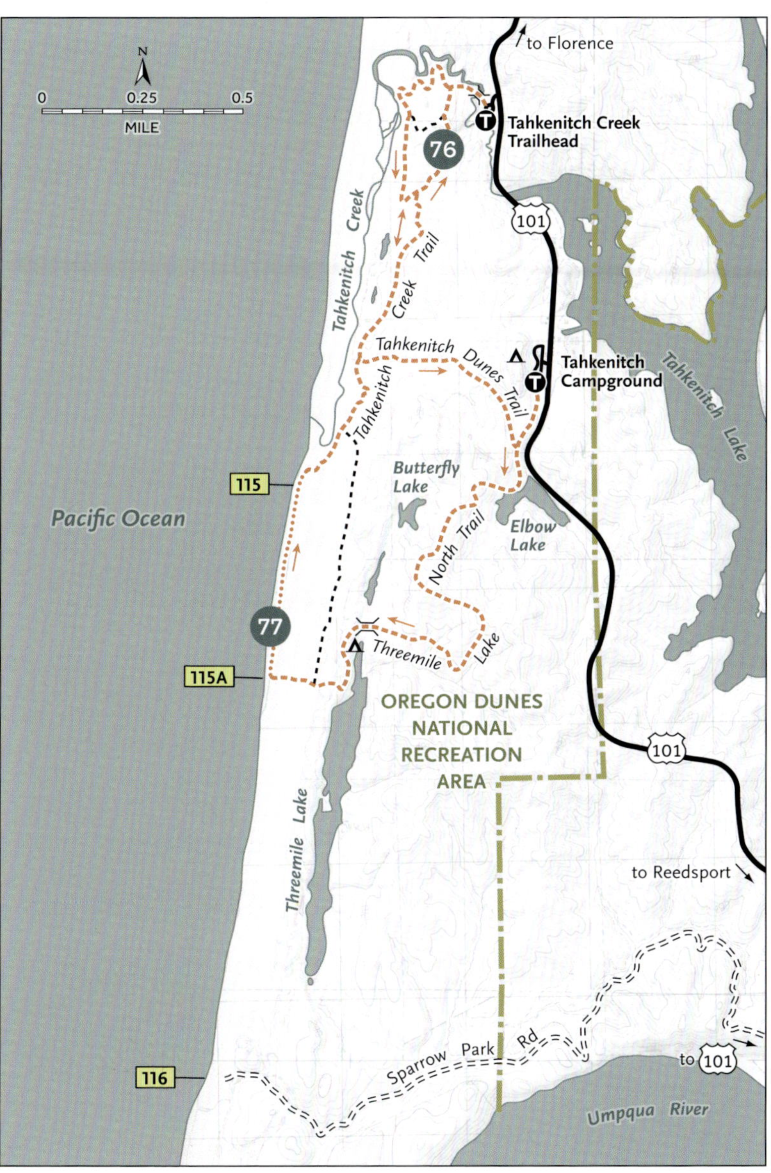
to Florence
N
0
0.25
0.5
MILE
Tahkenitch Creek Trailhead
76
101
Tahkenitch Creek
Tahkenitch Creek Trail
Tahkenitch Dunes Trail
Tahkenitch Campground
Tahkenitch Lake
Tahkenitch
Butterfly Lake
115
Pacific Ocean
North Trail
Elbow Lake
77
Threemile Lake
115A
OREGON DUNES NATIONAL RECREATION AREA
101
Threemile Lake
to Reedsport
Sparrow Park Rd
to 101
116
Umpqua River

you should see a sign pointing south to the beach. (Go left here for a 2.6-mile loop without the walk to the ocean shore). Heading south, enjoy a pleasant, shady 0.9 mile walk through the trees, then go right again to reach the beach in another 0.5 mile at Beach Access 115. To loop back, hike the trail north 1.4 miles to the "beach" sign, bear right, and bear right again in another 0.4 mile to return to the parking area.

## 77 Tahkenitch–Threemile Lake Loop

RATING/DIFFICULTY: ***/3
LOOP: 6.6 miles
ELEV GAIN: 600 feet

**Contact:** Oregon Dunes National Recreation Area, Siuslaw National Forest; **Notes:** USFS day-use fee. No dogs or kites on beach Mar 15–Sept 15. Toilets; **GPS:** 43.79518°, –124.14903°

**The trail to the north end of hidden Threemile Lake leads through gorgeous, lush second-growth forest. Flying squirrels inhabit the shrubby understory, and the creeks are reportedly home to eight different species of salamander. The full loop includes walks across open dunes and down nearly a mile of beach, making it one of the most varied and satisfying hikes on the Oregon coast. Backpackers can camp in the trees on the lake's northwest shore or on a high point along the trail just north of the lake. If you're hiking with a dog during snowy plover nesting season, substitute the beach walking portion with an inland walk on Tahkenitch Dunes Trail, but the trail is nearly all on soft sand and slow-going, so otherwise it is not recommended.**

### GETTING THERE

From US Highway 101 about 7 miles north of Reedsport (between mileposts 203 and 204), turn west at the sign to Tahkenitch Campground and signs to trailhead parking.

### ON THE TRAIL

For a clockwise loop, follow the trail uphill 0.25 mile to a junction with Tahkenitch Dunes

*The hike to this long freshwater lake includes a stretch of ocean beach and a gorgeous coastal forest.*

## SHARING THE BEACH WITH WESTERN SNOWY PLOVERS

*Western snowy plovers were in steep decline on the Oregon coast when conservation efforts began in the early 90s; their numbers have since rebounded by a factor of 10.* (Photo by Peter Pearsall/USFWS)

Spring through early fall you may see signage and orange plastic fencing in the dunes at certain trailheads letting you know that this is snowy plover nesting territory, and dogs are not allowed (even on-leash) spring and summer. What's that about? The western snowy plover, a small black-and-white shorebird, nests on flat, open sandy beaches just above the high tide line around active sand dunes, especially those with estuaries or ponds nearby. The introduction of nonnative beachgrass on the Oregon coast stabilized the dunes but diminished availability of open dunes, which sent this bird's population plummeting. Any disturbance—a passing vehicle, or dog, or human, or even kite in the sky—can flush an adult snowy plover from its nest, leaving eggs exposed on the sand and chicks (flightless in their first four weeks) vulnerable to predators such as raccoons and crows.

The population of snowy plovers in Oregon plunged to just twenty-eight breeding pairs in 1992, but a habitat conservation program put in place seems to be working. By 2022 biologists counted 483 birds on the Oregon coast. That program bans dogs (on- or off-leash), camping, beach fires, and even kite-flying from March 15 to September 15 in areas where plovers are found to be nesting. Those areas lie all along the coast, as far north as the mouth of the Columbia, but are mainly concentrated in Oregon Dunes National Recreation Area.

Trail on the right; bear left on Threemile Lake North Trail. From here the route mostly ascends for about 1.3 miles to a view of the ocean, then it gently descends through deep forest. Listen for the buzz of the rufous hummingbird flitting through the forest. In the early spring, bright yellow skunk cabbage blossoms fill lush creek beds.

Nearing Threemile Lake, the trail crosses a long footbridge and then ascends to a rise at the forest's edge, where there's a small campsite. Continue down the sandy trail a short distance, bearing left to see, and drop down steeply, to reach Threemile Lake at 3 miles.

To continue the loop, follow trail posts west across the dunes 0.5 mile (very steeply at first) to the beach (at Beach Access 115A). Hike north on the beach 0.9 mile and look for the Beach Access 115 and trail posts marking the southern end of Tahkenitch Creek Trail (if you reach the mouth of Tahkenitch Creek, you've gone too far). Follow the trail north and turn east on Tahkenitch Dunes Trail, and continue to the junction leading back to the trailhead at the campground.

## OREGON DUNES SOUTH

Off-highway vehicles (OHVs), such as dune buggies, are allowed on most of the dunes between the Umpqua River and the mouth of Coos Bay; they're also allowed on the beach between Tenmile Creek and Horsfall Beach Road (and south of here for a few miles in winter). Because of that, most self-propelled outdoorspeople avoid the beach south of the Umpqua. The good news is that Oregon Dunes National Recreation Area is designed to keep hikers and motorists from annoying one another. Also in most places OHVs aren't allowed on the beach itself and stick to the dunes instead.

Fortunately, there are plenty of appealing hikes on this part of the coast. There are short, easy trails encircling lakes at two campgrounds: Umpqua Lighthouse State Park (Lake Marie) and the US Forest Service's Bluebill Campground (Bluebill Lake, with a lovely boardwalk). The trail along part of the forested shoreline of Eel Lake, at William M. Tugman State Park, is a great out-and-back hike, particularly in winter (there's a nice campground here too). Just across US Highway 101 on Wildwood Drive lie a pair of small lakes—Hall and Schuttpelz—popular for paddleboarding; a 0.6-mile trail encircles Hall Lake and connects with another trail that leads most of the way around Schuttpelz Lake. More challenging and more fun, if you're game, is the John Dellenback Trail, which crosses the largest swath of open sand in the Oregon Dunes, with no OHVs allowed. It's beautiful and remote and a good choice for a fair-weather day (and there's a USFS campground next to the trailhead). Even more remote is the tip of Coos Bay North Spit. From March 15 to September 15, no vehicles are allowed in the dunes here, and hikers are restricted to the wet sand area to keep from disturbing the snowy plovers, which nest in the open dunes. Like the tips of many sand spits on the Oregon coast, it's not only remote and wild but often windy and exhilarating.

## 78 Beach Walk: Umpqua River to Tenmile Creek

ONE-WAY DISTANCE: 8.6 miles

This stretch of beach isn't much used by hikers; off-highway vehicles (OHVs) are allowed in—and thus dominate—the dunes here, giving hikes a noisy backdrop, especially on weekends, even though they're not allowed on the beach itself here. About the only other hikers you're likely to encounter are long-distance backpackers following the Oregon Coast Trail (or spouses of OHV enthusiasts walking the dog). Tenmile Creek defines the south end of this beach stretch; it is typically too high to cross in winter but can be waded at low tide in summer.

### BEACH ACCESS

BA 117, end of Triangle Road, off Salmon Harbor Road, Winchester Bay. Limited parking.

BA 118, Umpqua Beach Staging Area 1, off Salmon Harbor Road. Parking, vault toilet.

BA 119, Umpqua Beach Staging Area 2, off Salmon Harbor Road. Parking, vault toilet.

BA 120, Umpqua Beach Staging Area 3, off Salmon Harbor Road. Parking, restrooms (water not potable for drinking).

John Dellenback Trail (Hike 80).

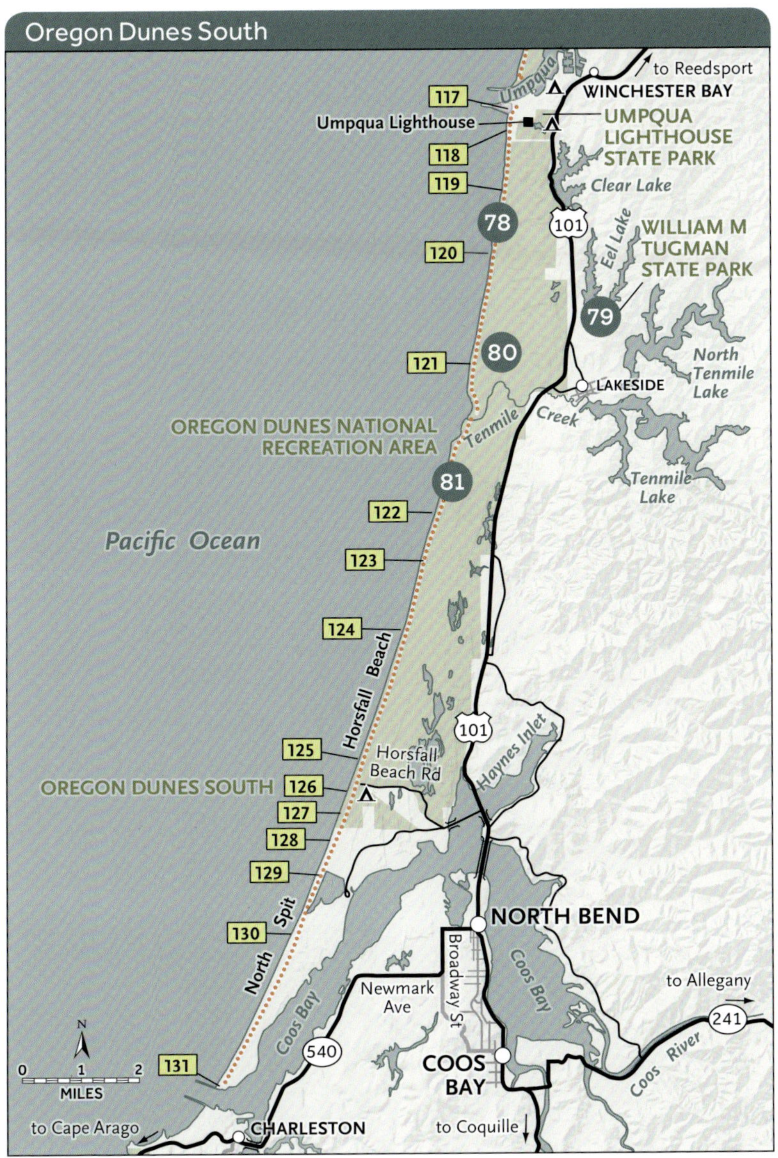
Oregon Dunes South
to Reedsport
WINCHESTER BAY
Umpqua
117
Umpqua Lighthouse
UMPQUA LIGHTHOUSE STATE PARK
118
119
Clear Lake
78
101
Eel Lake
WILLIAM M TUGMAN STATE PARK
120
79
80
121
North Tenmile Lake
LAKESIDE
Tenmile
Creek
OREGON DUNES NATIONAL RECREATION AREA
81
Tenmile Lake
122
Pacific Ocean
123
124
Horsfall Beach
101
Haynes Inlet
125
Horsfall Beach Rd
OREGON DUNES SOUTH
126
127
128
129
NORTH BEND
130
North Spit
Broadway St
Coos Bay
Newmark Ave
to Allegany
241
Coos Bay
540
Coos River
131
COOS BAY
MILES
to Cape Arago
CHARLESTON
to Coquille

*Among the few hikers who walk the beach south of the Umpqua are Oregon Coast Trail backpackers.*

## WHERE TO WALK

**Salmon Harbor Road.** Start at any of the beach parking areas along Salmon Harbor Road and head over the dunes to the beach. You may hear OHVs buzzing in the dunes, but they're not allowed on the beach itself any time of year. It's a good spot for dog-walking. Spring and fall, dogs are allowed as far south as about 2.8 miles north of the mouth of Tenmile Creek (watch for signage), where snowy plover restrictions are in effect March 15 to September 15.

**John Dellenback Trail.** A 2.7-mile trail leads out to the beach to 2 miles north of Tenmile Creek. That's the quickest and most enjoyable route to Tenmile Creek on foot (it's still 9.4 miles roundtrip). OHVs aren't allowed on either side of the creek, so unless you have a dog with you (not allowed March 15–September 15) the creek is a lovely, remote hiking destination.

# 79 Eel Lake

RATING/DIFFICULTY: **/2
ROUNDTRIP: 4 miles
ELEV GAIN: 350 feet

**Contact:** William M. Tugman State Park; **Notes:** Dogs on-leash. Toilets. **GPS:** 43.60247°, –124.17685°

**What makes this trail stand out among Oregon coast hikes? It's a hidden gem, not well known and never crowded. It's quiet. It's often calm here when the beach is windy. The grade is gentle, and the forest of large cedars, spruces, and hemlocks is gorgeous. In winter you may hear the lilting song of a Swainsons thrush—I once heard a loon on the lake—or see osprey and waterfowl. A 10 miles per hour speed limit for powerboats makes this lake**

**popular with kayakers. Note that there is no safe access to the water from the trail; do your lake dipping near the parking area at the trailhead.**

## GETTING THERE

Turn east off US Highway 101 at the sign to William M. Tugman State Park, 1 mile north of the town of Lakeside, and follow signs to the large lakeshore day-use parking area.

## ON THE TRAIL

No signs point to the trail from the parking area. From the restrooms, follow the paved path to the well-signed "fish trap," currently used to capture winter steelhead used as brood stock for hatcheries. (It's also been enhanced with a special ramp that allows native Pacific lamprey to climb around the fish ladder during their spring migration.) Follow the gravel path to the right and then left to a substantial wooden footbridge crossing Eel Creek—the start of the trail and site of the first trail signage. From here the trail rises gently and rolls through the forest above the south edge of the lake's eastern arm, crossing nearly a dozen footbridges and feeling more and more remote, especially in the quiet of winter. You'll have views of the lake most of the way except where the trail tucks briefly into deep woods. There's no real lake access; a couple of spurs lead that way but end with big drop-offs (nice for fishing or picnicking perhaps).

I suggest you turn around at 2 miles (there are mile markers along the trail). The trail continues for another 1.2 miles, but its condition deteriorates considerably. There are no footbridges past this point, just treacherous rotting logs spanning creek ravines. The path narrows and becomes overgrown, then returns to a wide footpath, then narrows again, continuing this back-and-forth until you reach the "end of trail" sign at 3.2 miles.

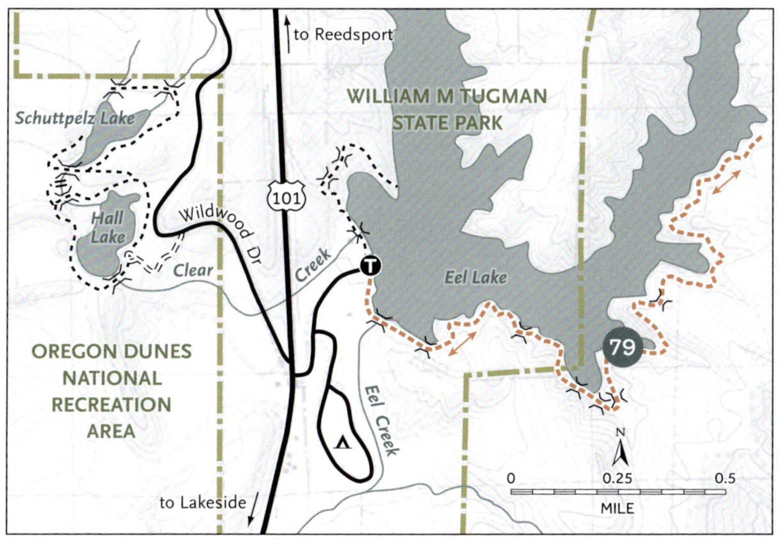

*With a speed limit for motorboats, Eel Lake is popular with kayakers as well as hikers.*

Especially if you have dogs or kids with you, skip this last 1.2 miles. Return as you came.

## EXTEND YOUR HIKE

A 0.5-mile lakeside trail also winds north from the end of the park access road. It crosses a couple of footbridges before ending at a little peninsula that anglers often use, but not swimmers; you could picnic here, but the drop-off is too steep for water access.

## 80 John Dellenback Dunes Trail

RATING/DIFFICULTY: ***/3

ROUNDTRIP: 5.2 miles

ELEV GAIN: approx. 100 feet

**Contact:** Oregon Dunes National Recreation Area, Siuslaw National Forest; **Notes:** USFS day-use fee. Not recommended for dogs. Toilets; **GPS:** 43.58410°, –124.18523°

**The exciting John Dellenback Dunes Trail across the Umpqua Dunes begins on a straightforward interpretive loop trail, with a spur to campsites at Eel Creek Campground. Then the trail ends, and the real adventure begins—crossing the widest swath of open dunes on the Oregon coast, with help navigating from a few widely scattered wooden posts. Hikers need to stay on their toes and do a little common-sense navigating to get back to where they started. The elevation figure listed above is approximate because it depends on the route you take from one post to the next, but it's not a big climb; the physical challenge comes from walking in soft sand much of the way. Pick a fair-weather day for this one—preferably a morning before the wind comes up. Dogs are allowed on the trail year-round but are banned from the beach March 15 to September 15 to protect nesting snowy plovers. Given the proximity of their noses to blowing sand, I recommend not bringing dogs on this hike.**

## GETTING THERE

The trailhead is 8 miles south of Reedsport and 12 miles north of North Bend, west off US Highway 101, just south of Eel Creek Campground.

## ON THE TRAIL

From the trailhead, a long footbridge immediately crosses Eel Creek and leads to a junction, the start of the 1-mile interpretive loop; either way will lead you through brushy coastal forest, up sandy paths, and around to the start of the dunes hike in 0.5 mile. The

*Be prepared to walk from post to post across open sand dunes on John Dellenback Dunes Trail.*

right-hand path crosses an Eel Creek Campground road before meeting the main trail to the beach.

Heading west across the open dunes, keep the big tree island on your left and follow the wooden posts, topped by a blue stripe. You can almost always see the next post from near the last one, and most are atop dune ridges, but a few are up to their necks in open sand. As you approach the forest at the end of the open sand (a scant 2 miles from the end of the interpretive loop), look for a sign pointing you north, along the forest's edge; in about 0.2 mile, signs will lead you to the start of the final 0.6-mile trail through the marshy forest to the beach. Thankfully a boardwalk

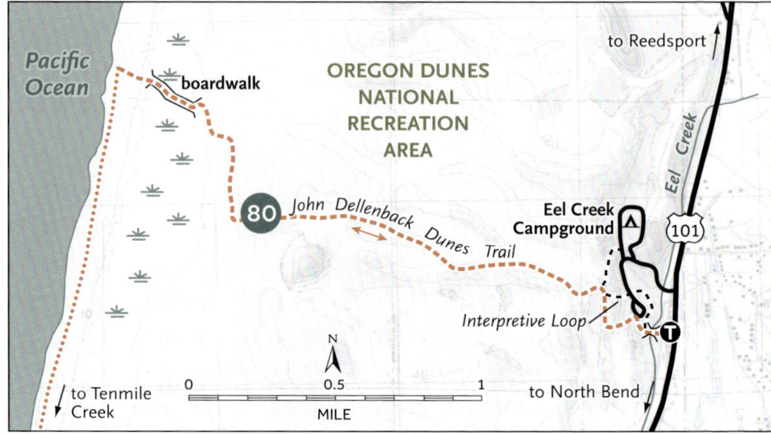


covers 0.2 mile of that walk, otherwise you'd be likely to get very wet feet much of the year.

Return as you came, watching the posts carefully to land you back on the interpretive trail leading back to the parking area.

## EXTEND YOUR HIKE

A roughly 2-mile beach walk south on the beach from trail's end at Beach Access 121 to the mouth of Tenmile Creek, a serene and remotely beautiful spot (though you might hear the distant roar of OHVs in the dunes to the east and south, you won't see them on the beach).

# 81 Beach Walk: Tenmile Creek to North Spit Coos Bay

ONE-WAY DISTANCE: 15.6 miles

Coos Bay was one of Oregon's earliest and most active commercial ports; it's still Oregon's busiest deepwater maritime port. This is a long but pretty inaccessible stretch of beach, reserved mainly for use by off-highway vehicles (OHVs) and used by them, making it less appealing than other beaches. The North Spit is where you can go for a long, lonely, wild walk.

## BEACH ACCESS

BA 126, Horsfall Beach day-use area, end of Horsfall Beach Road, north of North Bend. Parking, restrooms.

BA 128, Wetlands Trail, off Trans Pacific Lane, north of North Bend. Limited roadside parking.

BA 129, North Spit parking area, near the North Spit Boat Ramp off Trans Pacific Lane, 4.5 miles from US 101, north of North Bend. Parking.

## WHERE TO WALK

**To Tenmile Creek.** From Horsfall Campground (a big OHV parking lot), it's an 8.2-mile walk north to Tenmile Creek (no dogs or kites March 15 to September 15 starting at Beach Access 122, about 1.2 miles south of the creek). The creek can typically be waded at low tide in summer but not in

## BEACHGRASS: UNINTENDED CONSEQUENCES

*Native dune grass has given way to exotic beachgrass along most of the Oregon coast, changing the very nature of the dunes.*

Grasses help define the coastal dune ecosystem. American dune grass (*Leymus mollis*) is one of the most seaward native plants you'll find along the shoreline. As loose sand blows in from the beach, the grass's stems capture it, while its rhizomes—underground stems—hold the plants in place, stabilizing the sand and beginning the process of creating a sand dune. But early twentieth-century settlers on the Oregon coast wanted more control of those shifting dunes. A more aggressive variety of grass known as European beachgrass (*Ammophila arenaria*) was widely planted here to keep sand from drifting over roads and to better accommodate development, as well as to protect residents from storm surges and erosion. It worked, especially after a second nonnative species, American beachgrass (*A. breviligulata*), native to eastern North America, was introduced along the lower Columbia River. Now the two have largely displaced the native grass. The result: Foredunes are taller, and the once vast open dunes such as those at Oregon Dunes National Recreation Area are gradually becoming covered with vegetation, diminishing habitat for many native plant and animal species, notably the western snowy plover.

A new chapter in the Oregon beachgrass story opened in 2012 when scientists discovered the existence of a new hybrid of the two nonnative *Ammophilia* species on the north coast. They speculate that this hybrid will be even more invasive than its parent species, thus even more effective at building dunes and even more threatening to native dune flora and fauna.

winter. The beach access signs you'll see strung along the dune access OHV trails and a horse trail. OHVs are allowed on the beach as well as the dunes here (between signs 122 to 126), making it a less-than-ideal place to walk for the first 7 miles north of Horsfall Beach.

**To the North Spit.** It's very remote the farther you walk south toward the end of the spit. No OHVs are allowed on the beach south of Horsfall Beach (or in the adjacent dunes starting about 1 mile to the south)—only humans and other animals. From Horsfall Beach, it's a 7.5 one-way walk to the end

*Brushy wetlands alongside beach access trails for North Spit Coos Bay can offer good bird-watching.*

of the spit. Alternately walk west 0.6 mile on the Wetlands Trail (Beach Access 128), a gravel road; from here it's 5.3 miles to the end of the spit. Or walk the 0.9-mile sand road southwest from the North Spit parking area; from the end of that trail, it's 4.3 miles south to the end of the spit or 1.3 miles south to an FAA air traffic communication tower—a handy landmark, and the point beyond which dogs are not allowed spring and summer to protect snowy plover nesting sites. Humans on foot are asked to stick to the wet sand at this time to avoid disturbing the nesting plovers.

**OPPOSITE:** *Low tide is the time to visit South Cove at Cape Arago, for tidepool close-ups as well as distant views of the steep Seven Devils coastline.*

# THE SOUTH COAST

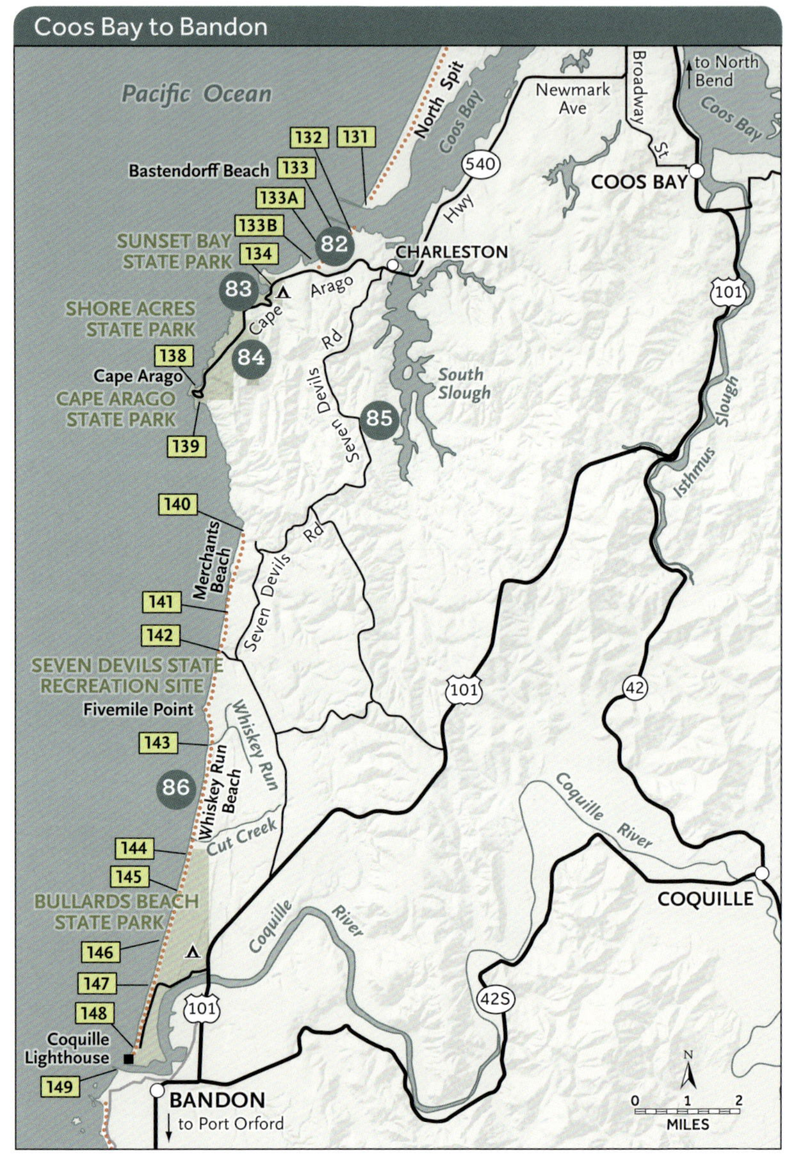
Coos Bay to Bandon
Pacific Ocean
North Spit
Coos Bay
Newmark Ave
Broadway St
to North Bend
Coos Bay
540
Hwy
COOS BAY
132
131
Bastendorff Beach
133
133A
133B
134
82
SUNSET BAY STATE PARK
83
CHARLESTON
Cape Arago
SHORE ACRES STATE PARK
84
138
Cape Arago
CAPE ARAGO STATE PARK
139
Seven Devils Rd
South Slough
85
101
Slough
Isthmus
140
Merchants Beach
141
142
Seven Devils Rd
SEVEN DEVILS STATE RECREATION SITE
Fivemile Point
143
Whiskey Run
Whiskey Run Beach
86
Cut Creek
101
42
Coquille River
144
145
BULLARDS BEACH STATE PARK
146
147
148
Coquille Lighthouse
149
Coquille River
COQUILLE
101
42S
BANDON
to Port Orford
N
0 1 2
MILES

FAR FROM INLAND POPULATION CENTERS, Oregon's south coast is remote, the beaches often unpeopled, the towns small, the views big. A prime example is Cape Arago, where the Shoreline Trail links three stunning state parks. The beach stretches for miles north and south of the Coquille River at Bandon. A network of trails at Blacklock Point—the site of Floras Lake State Natural Area, an entirely undeveloped state park—includes a scenic shoreline route linking Floras Lake with the beach north of Cape Blanco, the westernmost point in Oregon. Two big headlands—Humbug Mountain and Cape Sebastian—offer two very different hiking experiences. Short trails in Sam Boardman State Scenic Corridor lead to a gorgeous rocky coastline you can't see from the car on US Highway 101; string a few of these trails together, as hikes described in this section do, for a satisfying day hike.

## COOS BAY TO BANDON

The southern terminus of the Oregon Dunes is at fishhook-shaped Coos Bay, the second-largest estuary in Oregon, smaller only than the Columbia River's mouth. Much of the salt marsh that used to surround the bay has been altered to serve agricultural or industrial interests, but the bay's many sloughs and inlets still provide important habitat for a variety of plants, fish, birds, and mammals. The cities of North Bend and Coos Bay form one metro area and offer travelers a lot of lodging and the Oregon coast's only commercial airport. In the middle of North Bend lies John Topits Park, with 5.5 miles of trails winding through the forest and along the shores of freshwater Upper and Lower Empire Lakes; with no gas-powered motors allowed on the lakes, it's a good choice for a swim or some kayaking or paddleboarding. In Coos Bay you can get a taste of the native vegetation and seasonal rhythms at Millicoma Marsh, a 1-mile loop trail that starts at Millicoma Middle School in Coos Bay. And check out the Sawmill and Tribal Trail (coasttrails.org/sawmilltribaltrail.html) cutting through town from one arm of the bay to another, honoring tribal and early settlers' history.

Charleston, located just inside the mouth of Coos Bay and a short drive off US 101, has a mini-aquarium—Charleston Marine Life Center—the public outreach venue for the Oregon Institute of Marine Biology across the road. It's geared for kids; consider a visit if it's open when you're in town (hours are limited). From here it's a short drive to South Slough National Estuarine Research Reserve, where trails and boardwalks lead down and out into a stunningly beautiful salt marsh. Take a turn through the small interpretive center here too if it's open when you visit.

Charleston is also the gateway to one of the most dramatic stretches of the Oregon coast. Cape Arago Highway leads to off-the-beaten-path Bastendorff Beach, views of a lighthouse-topped island, an idyllic crescent-shaped bay, a formal public garden, and views of a nearshore island and reef that host species ranging from elephant seals to double-crested cormorants, plus upland and shoreline trails creating loop options of varying length. A few hike options are included here; the trails down to the north and south coves at the end of Cape Arago Highway are not long hikes but are well worth walking. It's 0.1 mile down to the shore on the North Cape Arago Cove Trail (Beach Access 138); visit at low tide or there might be no beach to visit. The South Cape Arago Cove Trail (Beach

Access 139) leads a scant 0.2 mile and 100 feet down to a slightly larger beach with extensive tidepools and a spectacular view to the south; it's also best at low tide.

From Cape Arago the beach stretches south to the Coquille River: It is very remote at the north end just below the cape and not remote at all as it approaches Bullards Beach State Park and the town of Bandon, a lovely tourist town with a lively bayfront. Three miles north of town lies Bandon Dunes Golf Resort, one of country's top-rated golf venues; the public is welcome to walk its modest network of trails that wind among its six courses (and ten dining establishments). Pick up a map at the front desk or print it from the website, and don't miss the labyrinth, off the Woodland Trail. (The website says no dogs allowed, but signage on site says to keep dogs leashed at all times.)

## 82 Beach Walk: Bastendorff

**ONE-WAY DISTANCE:** 1 mile

Bastendorff Beach seems to be a best-kept secret among locals; though short, it's lovely and remote. It ends at Yoakam Point to the south and runs north to the south jetty at the entrance to Coos Bay (beach access parking here as well). Until the south jetty at the mouth of Coos Bay was built in 1924, there was no beach here at all—just steep cliffs to the sea. The jetty caused sand to accumulate. You can still see (and step inside) the tunnel at the north end of the beach, built for the

*Bastendorff Beach stretches from the mouth of Coos Bay to Yoakam Point, with several beach access points between.*

rail line that delivered the rock to build the south jetty.

## BEACH ACCESS

BA 132, Bastendorff Beach Jetty, end of Coos Head Road, Charleston. Parking.

BA 133, Bastendorff Beach North, off Bastendorff Beach Road, Charleston. Parking.

BA 133A, Bastendorff Beach Middle, off Bastendorff Beach Road, Charleston. Parking, vault toilet.

BA 133B, Bastendorff Beach South, off Bastendorff Beach Road, Charleston. Parking.

BA 134, Yoakam Point, off Cape Arago Highway. Small pullout for at most a half-dozen vehicles.

## WHERE TO WALK

**Long.** Start at Coos Bay South Jetty (Beach Access 132) and walk south to where the beach ends at a minor headland just north of Yoakam Point. A creek splits the beach, but it's usually small enough to step over.

**Short.** Shorten your walk by starting at one of the beach access points in the middle.

Note: Lighthouse Beach (0.5 mile long) is just on the other side (west) of Yoakam Point from Bastendorff Beach. It's popular with surfers and is a favorite gathering spot for locals, who fought to maintain legal access to the beach off Lighthouse Way, but there is limited street parking.

# 83 Sunset Bay to Simpson Reef Overlook

RATING/DIFFICULTY: **/3
ROUNDTRIP: 6.6 miles
ELEV GAIN: 1,300 feet

**Contact:** Sunset Bay State Park; **Notes:** OPRD day-use fee. Dogs on-leash (see below). Toilets; **GPS:** 43.3316°, –124.37302°

**What's also called Cape Arago Shoreline Trail begins at Sunset Bay and ends at Cape Arago, providing views of offshore rocks and reefs that you can't get from a car. Along the way you pass by (or through) a formal botanical garden brimming with exotic plants. The gardens were originally part of the estate of Louis J. Simpson, a lumber baron who had a summer home built here in 1906. The long growing season makes a visit interesting any time of year, even in midwinter; at Christmastime the local Friends of Shore Acres group holds an open house and decorates the gardens with about a quarter-million tiny lights. Whale Watch volunteers are posted at Shore Acres during Whale Watch Weeks.**

**This hike turns around at the Shell Island and Simpson Reef Overlook, where in spring and early summer with binoculars you may see a variety of nesting seabirds and even (rare in Oregon) elephant seals, as well as seals and sea lions year-round. But you needn't walk the whole trail; turn around where you like. There's little elevation gain, but the trail can be muddy in places.**

**Note to dog owners: This trail goes through three adjacent state parks, with most of it within Shore Acres State Park. Dogs are not allowed in Shore Acres, but that applies only to the developed areas; if you start hiking at either Sunset Bay or the Simpson Reef Overlook and stay on the main trail as it winds through Shore Acres, you're OK (as long as your dog stays on-leash).**

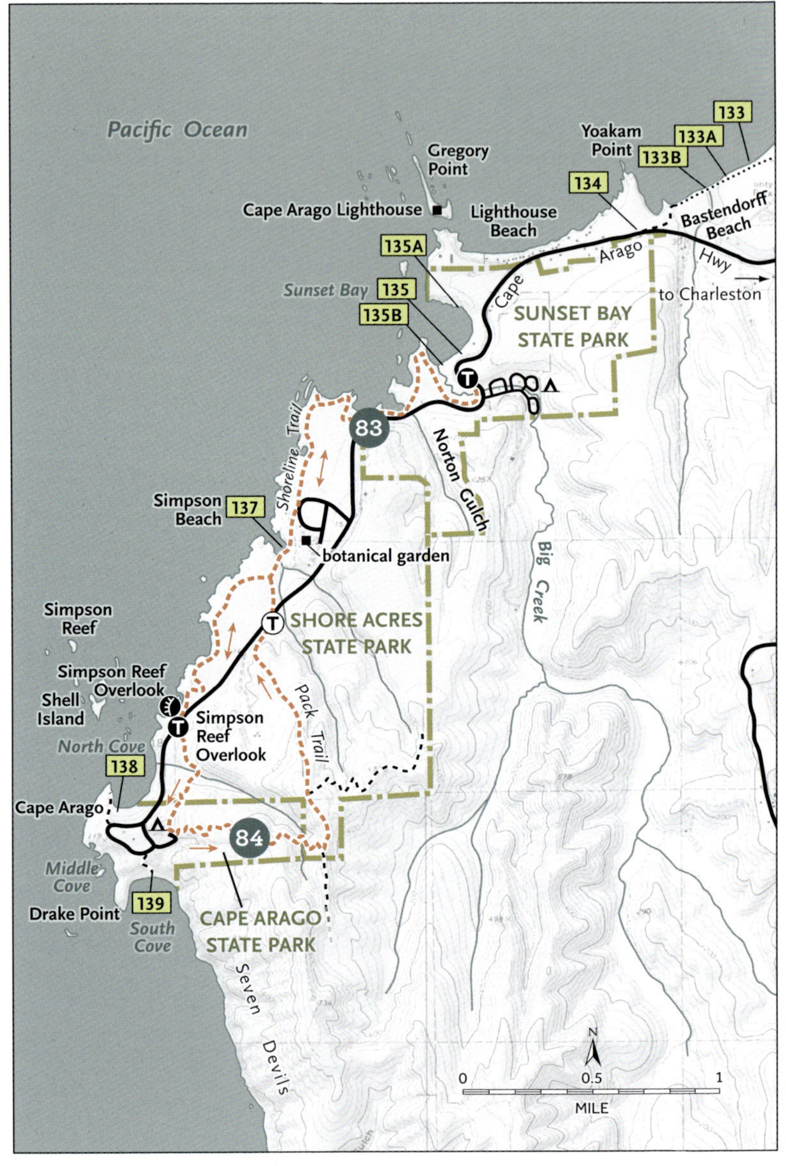
Pacific Ocean
Gregory Point
Cape Arago Lighthouse
Lighthouse Beach
Yoakam Point
133
133A
133B
134
Bastendorff Beach
Cape Arago Hwy
to Charleston
135A
Sunset Bay
135
135B
SUNSET BAY STATE PARK
83
Shoreline Trail
Norton Gulch
Big Creek
Simpson Beach
137
botanical garden
Simpson Reef
SHORE ACRES STATE PARK
Simpson Reef Overlook
Shell Island
Simpson Reef Overlook
Pack Trail
North Cove
138
Cape Arago
84
Middle Cove
Drake Point
139
South Cove
CAPE ARAGO STATE PARK
Seven Devils
0
0.5
1
MILE
N

*Shallow, enclosed Sunset Bay has some of the warmest water you'll find on the Oregon coast. It's the starting point for the trail walk to an overlook at Cape Arago.*

## GETTING THERE

From US Highway 101 at Coos Bay or North Bend, follow signs about 8 miles west and south to Charleston. Continue south on Cape Arago Highway about 3 miles to Sunset Bay State Park. (For a one-way hike, park a second car at the Simpson Reef Overlook 0.5 mile from the road's end.)

## ON THE TRAIL

Look for a trail post near the restrooms at the south end of the Sunset Bay State Park parking area. On the trail, cross Big Creek, ascend the headland, and bear right around a big, mowed meadow (Norton Gulch Group Camp), with a spur trail out to a viewpoint. At 0.7 mile the trail leads back to Cape Arago Highway; follow the highway south a short distance and return to the trail on the other side of the guardrail. The route continues through woods to a junction; veer north and west out to the bluff, where you get views of Cape Arago Lighthouse to the north and rocks to the south (or continue south for a shortcut through the forest to Shore Acres State Park).

Approaching Shore Acres gardens, just shy of 2 miles, bear right at any junction to stay on the shoreline trail (or detour into the gardens if you don't have a dog, exiting through the open gate at the back of the gardens, where you can pick up the trail again). Continuing past the gardens, the trail leads down to the intimate Simpson Beach at 2.4 miles, then into woods and then back up onto a bluff. At the next junction bear right (a left leads up to the highway). Continue on the main trail another 0.6 mile until you reach Cape Arago Highway at 3.3 miles; the Simpson Reef Overlook parking area is just ahead. Return as you came, unless you're making a one-way hike with a shuttle car.

## EXTEND YOUR HIKE

Continue (on foot, or drive) 0.5 mile on to Cape Arago, where the North Cove (Beach Access 138) and South Cove (Beach Access 139) Trails, each about 0.2 mile, lead down to pocket beaches and spectacular tidepools. They're best visited at low tide.

# 84 Cape Arago Pack Trail Loop

RATING/DIFFICULTY: **/2
LOOP: 3.6 miles
ELEV GAIN: 640 feet

**Contact:** Sunset Bay State Park; **Notes:** OPRD day-use fee. Dogs on-leash. Toilets at Sunset Bay State Park; **GPS:** 43.31261°, –124.39571°

**Meandering through old-growth forest east of Cape Arago, the Pack Trail follows an old wagon road that once led down to Whiskey Run Beach and Bandon. It was revived during World War II as an access route to hidden mountainside bunkers and, in our era, as a forest trail option for hikers at Cape Arago. Link up with the Cape Arago Shoreline Trail for a loop hike.**

## GETTING THERE

From US Highway 101 in North Bend or Coos Bay, follow signs about 8 miles west and south to Charleston. Continue south on Cape Arago Highway for 5 miles to the Simpson Reef Overlook 0.5 mile before the end of the road at Cape Arago. Or pick up the trail at the signed parking area along the highway 1.4 miles past the Sunset Bay Campground entrance, with room for about four vehicles (GPS: 43.31863°, –124.38801°).

## ON THE TRAIL

From Simpson Reef Overlook, cross the highway to pick up the trail. It climbs above the road then contours above it to Cape Arago Group Camp at 0.6 mile. Pick up the

*Dense coastal vegetation turns the Pack Trail into a tunnel much of the way.*

old roadbed leading up the hill, ascending steadily. The old road turns to a footpath and descends briefly to cross a creek, then resumes the ascent, switchbacking up steadily to reach the ridgetop at 1.7 miles. Here the trail turns sharply left, descending steadily on an old roadbed. (A right turn leads you out of the park and into privately owned timberland.) In 0.25, you'll pass a trail junction with the East Trail (not yet fully developed), and in another 0.5 mile, the old cement bunkers (now graffiti-covered), before reaching Cape Arago Highway at 2.7 miles near an alternative trailhead parking area. Cross the road and pick up a short spur trail leading to Cape Arago Shoreline Trail; go left and follow the Shoreline Trail 0.75 mile back southwest to your starting point.

*The view from the long footbridge across Rhodes Marsh is captivating at any tide.*

## 85 Coos Bay South Slough Loop

RATING/DIFFICULTY: ***/2

LOOP: 3 miles

ELEV GAIN: 640 feet

**Contact:** South Slough National Estuarine Research Reserve, Oregon Department of State Lands; **Notes:** Dogs on-leash. Toilets; **GPS:** 43.29582°, –124.33502°

**Hiking in an estuary is, by definition, problematic. Estuaries are defined by water: They are the places where freshwater and saltwater mix, where tides rise and fall, where shorelines shift up and down, where boot-sucking mudflats appear and disappear, and where beavers and bald eagles, otters and herons—and not so much humans—are at home. This is why hiking trails at the edge of estuaries can be iffy.**

**But South Slough National Estuarine Research Reserve, on a remote arm of Coos Bay on the southern Oregon coast, has made it work. Here the remains of dikes built by farmers long ago have been linked with boardwalks and upland trails, allowing visitors to immerse themselves in this lush, wild coastal environment without losing their boots. South Slough is a finger of Coos Bay stretching south from Charleston. Considered by scientists to be a relatively complete estuarine system, it was the country's first federally designated national estuarine research reserve. The hiking here is exceedingly scenic and varied; loop trails lead down to the edge of the salt marsh and out onto old dikes that are slowly being reclaimed by the tides, offering many options for hikes**

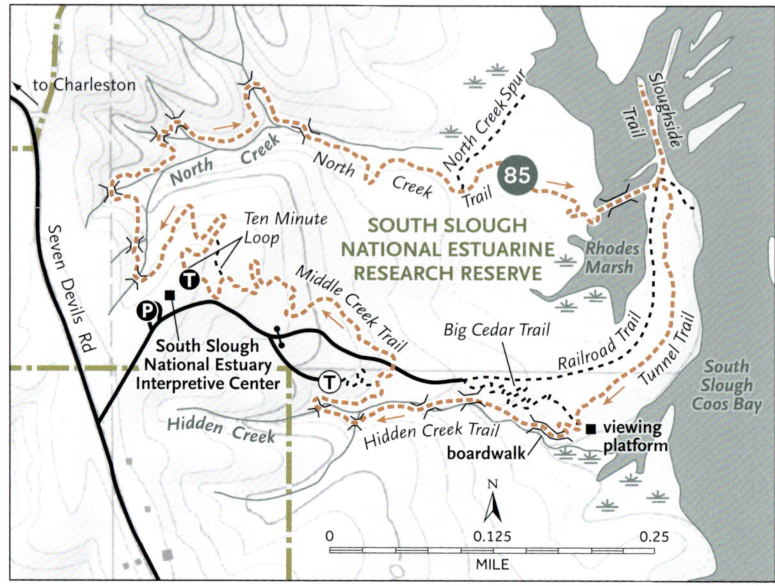


**of varying lengths. High points include Hidden Creek Trail, leading through a variety of ecosystems ranging from Douglas-fir forest to skunk cabbage bog accessed by boardwalk, and the old dikes and footbridges leading across Rhodes Marsh from North Creek Trail; this loop includes both. A small interpretive center near the entrance to the reserve presents the complex interactions of estuarine ecology in terms kids can relate to.**

## GETTING THERE

From US Highway 101 in North Bend, follow signs west and south about 8 miles to Charleston. Turn left at the sign to South Slough and follow Seven Devils Road south 4.3 miles to the signed entrance to the research reserve and its interpretive center on the left.

## ON THE TRAIL

From the interpretive center, take the Ten Minute Loop to the left and bear left at a junction to connect with the North Creek Trail, which gently descends to the salt marsh, following the contours of the hillside in and out of creek ravines crossed by numerous footbridges and passing a 0.1-mile spur trail to North Creek Spur that ends with a view of the marsh. At 1.4 miles the trail reaches Rhodes Marsh, crossing it on a long footbridge. At the junction just past the end of the bridge, bear left to reach the 0.1-mile Sloughside Trail spur by following a very narrow levee—a great spot for bird-watching or just slough-watching at any tide. Walk it out and back to the junction, then bear left onto the Tunnel Trail, which leads to a large, elevated viewing platform at 2.1 miles. (If you accidentally ended up on the Railroad Trail

## SKUNK CABBAGE

*Start looking for skunk cabbage's bright yellow blooms in almost any coastal wetland as early as February.*

Skunk cabbage (*Lysichition americanum*) is an iconic harbinger of early spring in coastal wetlands, well deserving of its much-less-common name, the swamp lantern. The musty odor of the plant draws its prime pollinators, beetles and flies, which then go forth and spread pollen to other plants in the bog. According to Mountaineers Books' *Cascadia Field Guide* (a fabulous reference guide for art and science lovers), it was one of the first flowering plants to evolve: "Skunk Cabbage was on Earth before Bee and birds and other sweet-lured, nectar-loving pollinators." It's the leaves that give the plant a bad rap for its odor, but bend down and stick your nose up close; its tiny flowers, arrayed on a stalk and enclosed in a bright yellow leaf-like sheath, smell quite sweet. You can see the bright yellow blooms from almost any Oregon coast trail bordering a wetland as early as February. Among the stand-outs: Hidden Creek Trail at South Slough National Estuarine Research Reserve (Hike 85).

instead of the Tunnel Trail, no worries; watch for the Big Cedar Boardwalk on your left to lead you back down to the Tunnel Trail just before reaching the viewing platform.)

A zigzag trail leads from the viewing platform and onto the Hidden Creek Trail boardwalk, which leads away from the water's edge and into a gorgeous marsh crowded, at the freshwater upper end, with skunk cabbage blooming in early spring. It becomes a footpath as it winds up the hillside, crossing and recrossing the musical creek. At 2.5 miles the trail crosses a road; continue up to a junction with the Ten Minute Loop at 2.9 miles. Bear left to get back to where you started.

### EXTEND YOUR HIKE

Hop back in the car and drive south 1 mile on Seven Devils Road, then left on Hinch Road. Turn right at the junction and continue 0.2 mile to a parking area where a roughly 1-mile loop trail winds through an old farm that's being returned to the wild. Head right on an all-access trail that leads to a boardwalk and juts into the restored marsh at Wasson Creek. Return as you came, or—to walk the whole loop—bear right back at the start of the boardwalk (not all-access past here) and follow the trail along Wasson Marsh and to Fredrickson Marsh, through the forest, and back to the trailhead.

*You can generally get around Fivemile Point at low to mid-tide. Then you'll have to negotiate a field of small boulders to go farther south on the beach.*

## 86 Beach Walk: Seven Devils to Coquille Spit

ONE-WAY DISTANCE: 10.5 miles

This long stretch of sand is a beautiful, remote beach with good hard-sand walking. The most remote part is that north of Seven Devils State Recreation Site, accessible only at lower tides. You'll see more people (but no issues with tide) in the vicinity of Bullards Beach.

### BEACH ACCESS

BA 142, Seven Devils State Recreation Site, off Seven Devils Road north of Bandon. Parking, vault toilet.

BA 143, Whiskey Run Beach, end of Whiskey Run Road, north of Bandon. Limited parking along road.

BA 147, Bullards Beach State Park day-use area, north of Bandon. OPRD day-use fee. Parking, restrooms.

BA 148, Coquille Lighthouse, south end of Coquille Spit, Bullards Beach State Park. OPRD day-use fee. Limited parking.

### WHERE TO WALK

**North of Seven Devils State Recreation Site.** This is a beautiful 2.4-mile stretch of beach, granting views of Cape Arago from the south. A couple of headlands, the first at not quite 0.9 mile and one 1.6 miles from the state recreation area, limit walks here to low or possibly mid-tide. You'll see a few homes and pass two access signs here, but the beach is not otherwise accessible; the only way to enjoy this beach is to walk up from the south.

**South of Seven Devils State Recreation Site.** It's a 2.4-mile roundtrip walk from here south to Fivemile Point, which typically can be rounded only at mid-tide or below. (If you do make it past Fivemile Point, there's nothing blocking you from walking all the way to the end of Coquille Spit.) At low tide the rocks and tidepools at the point are fun to explore.

**South of Whiskey Run Beach.** Walk north about 0.5 mile to Fivemile Point, or south as far as Coquille Spit.

**Bullards Beach Loop north.** From the park's day-use area, walk the beach north to Beach Access 146 and turn inland on Pearl's Trail on a combination of footpaths and long boardwalks, 0.8 mile to the park's campground, then follow campground roads and the paved bike path south and west back to day-use area for a 3.2-mile loop.

**To the lighthouse.** Coquille Lighthouse is 1.5 miles south of the Bullards Beach day-use area; you can drive there or walk there via the beach.

## BANDON TO FLORAS LAKE

South of the Coquille River, the Coast Range gives way to the far more ancient Klamath Mountains. You'll see the difference in the sand, in the multicolored tumble of rocks on the beach, and in the imposing headlands. The beach stretching south from Bandon begins in a field of scenic sea stacks on a broad, fine-grained sandy beach, but it becomes lonelier and tougher to walk as you head south. South of Bandon State Natural Area, the New River runs south to north just one foredune away from the beach, effectively cutting off beach access from inland. The beach walking in this vicinity is particularly steep, narrow, and gravelly, making for difficult walking exacerbated by the sometimes-fierce winds in summer. You'll encounter creeks that can typically be waded in summer but not in winter, and New River can be crossed only at its mouth and only at low tide (unless the river has breached its sand banks in a second or even third location, as sometimes happens, splitting the flow).

How new is the New River? About a century old, according to local lore. The flood of 1890 apparently created a new northbound channel for Floras Lake. Today the New River flows about 10 miles north from Floras Lake before it turns to meet the ocean. Wild chinook salmon run up the river, and thousands of Aleutian Canada geese use the river every spring to rest and forage before heading out over the ocean toward nesting sites on the Aleutian Islands, stopping again in November on their southward migration.

The biodiversity here led the Bureau of Land Management to designate four tracts of land along the New River as a collective Area of Critical Environmental Concern. One of those areas, Storm Ranch, has a modest visitor center and a 2.3-mile system of short trails to explore. It's at the end of Croft Lake Lane, about 8 miles south of Bandon.

## 87 Beach Walk: Bandon to Floras Lake

ONE-WAY DISTANCE: 17.5 miles

Only the northern 4 miles or so of Oregon's longest continuous beach are well known to visitors (and even locals); here, large rocks stud the beach and there are a lot of access points. The farther south you go, the less accessible the beach is, to the point where you are unlikely to see anyone except an Oregon Coast Trail thru hiker. The sand west of the New River tends to be soft and unpleasant for walking. Not until you approach Floras Lake does it harden and become more pleasant underfoot. Most of the beach is off-limits to dogs March 15 to September 15; only north of China Creek and south of Floras Lake are they allowed due to snowy plover protections.

### BEACH ACCESS

BA 149, Bandon South Jetty Park, three blocks past end of Jetty Road SW, Bandon. Parking, restrooms.

BA 150A, Coquille Point North, end of 8th Street SW, Bandon. Parking.

BA 150, Coquille Point, end of 11th Street SW, Bandon. Parking.

BA 151, Face Rock State Scenic Viewpoint, near end of Face Rock Drive, Bandon. OPRD day-use fee.

BA 154, Devils Kitchen, Bandon State Natural Area, off Beach Loop Road, Bandon. Parking, restrooms.

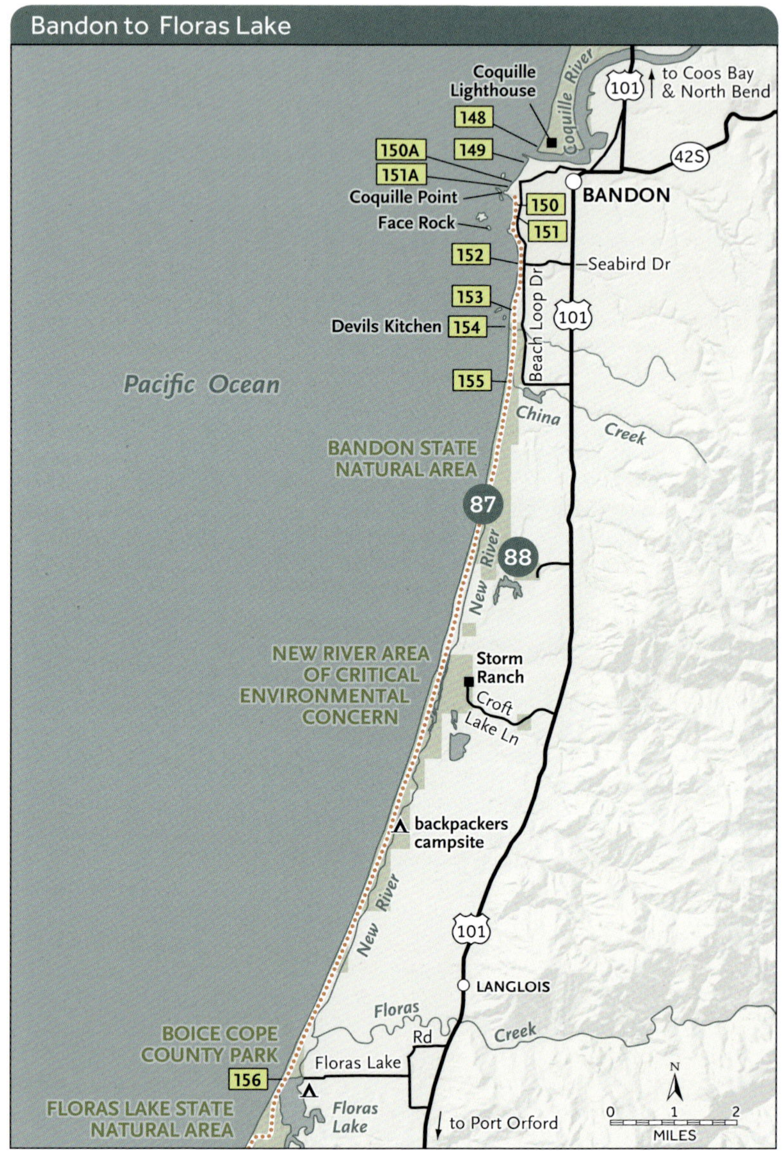
Bandon to Floras Lake
Coquille Lighthouse
Coquille River
101
to Coos Bay & North Bend
148
150A
149
151A
42S
BANDON
Coquille Point
150
Face Rock
151
152
Seabird Dr
Beach Loop Dr
153
101
Devils Kitchen
154
155
Pacific Ocean
China Creek
BANDON STATE NATURAL AREA
87
88
New River
NEW RIVER AREA OF CRITICAL ENVIRONMENTAL CONCERN
Storm Ranch
Croft Lake Ln
backpackers campsite
New River
101
LANGLOIS
Floras Creek
Rd
BOICE COPE COUNTY PARK
Floras Lake
156
FLORAS LAKE STATE NATURAL AREA
Floras Lake
to Port Orford
N
0 1 2
MILES

*Huge monoliths characterize the north end of the beach at Bandon.*

BA 155, China Creek Beach, Bandon State Natural Area, off Beach Loop Road, Bandon. Parking.

BA 156, Boice Cope County Park at Floras Lake, end of Floras Lake Road, Langlois. Day-use parking (fee) next to boat ramp. Restrooms at adjacent campground.

## WHERE TO WALK

**Picture perfect.** The northern 2 miles or so of the beach, between the south jetty and around Face Rock State Scenic Viewpoint, is the Bandon Beach most often pictured in postcards and photographs, with its monolithic rocks and headlands. Start a walk at either end or walk down the stairs from the top of either Coquille Point access. Face Rock is in the ocean just offshore from the viewpoint; look to see if you can see a face in the rock, peering upward toward the North Star. Local volunteers draw labyrinths in the sand here at low tide late in April through late August, usually four mornings per month; visit sandypathbandon.com for the schedule. There's good tidepooling here too.

**Bandon State Natural Area.** Get away from the crowds by starting at Devils Kitchen or China Creek Beach, in Bandon State Natural Area, the last beach access points north of Floras Lake (that don't require crossing New River from the west). If you walk south very far from here, you can count on crossing one or more creeks or rivers, depending on the movement of sand and water year to year and even within one season. Twomile Creek and New River are generally not crossable in winter but are at low tide in summer.

**North from Floras Lake.** The walking can be tiresome here, with coarse sand and a narrow, relatively steep beach, but 4.2 miles north of the beach access at Floras Lake is a primitive campground in the dunes between the beach and New River; it has room for a few tents but no water or toilet.

**South from Floras Lake.** The beach runs out in about 1.5 miles, at the base of the cliffs leading to Blacklock Point. To continue south from here, see Hikes 89 and 90.

## SHARKS, ON AND OFF THE BEACH

*This juvenile salmon shark washed up on the beach at Arch Cape in September 2021.* (Photo by Tiffany Boothe/Seaside Aquarium)

If you stumble across what looks like a small dead or dying shark on the beach—not uncommon on the Oregon coast from July to December—it's probably a young salmon shark, born in the spring in the ocean between British Columbia and central California. Like great white and mako sharks (but more so), salmon sharks are homeothermic (warm-blooded), which allows them to maintain body temperature even in the cold waters off Alaska and Canada. Scientists believe that this ability to thermoregulate may develop only after the shark matures and may be a factor in young salmon shark mortality.

Salmon sharks are one of fifteen shark species found in the ocean off Oregon, from massive but harmless basking sharks to brown cat sharks barely two feet long. Most feared are great white sharks, for their large size and rapid attack style. According to marine scientists, every recorded encounter with a great white shark in Oregon has been an unprovoked, nonlethal attack on a surfer, likely because the shark mistook the surfer for one of its prey species such as a seal or sea lion.

## 88 Lost Lake

RATING/DIFFICULTY: */2
ROUNDTRIP: 2.6 miles
ELEV GAIN: 170 feet

**Contact:** New River Area of Critical Environmental Concern, Bureau of Land Management Coos Bay District; **Notes:** Dogs on-leash; **GPS:** 43.02334°, –124.42932°

**The hike past Lost Lake to the New River begins in a lush forest of cedars and rhododendrons, which slowly gives way to pines and eventually no trees at all as you wind into open dunes. It ends about 1 mile south of the mouth of New River, unless the mouth has changed locations, as it tends to do. Even if you could wade the river in late summer, people aren't allowed on the dunes west of New River during snowy plover nesting season (March 15 to September 15). With much of the trail on soft sand, it's more of a workout than distance alone would suggest.**

### GETTING THERE

South of Bandon, between mileposts 280 and 281 on US Highway 101, turn west on McTimmons Lane. Drive 0.6 mile, turn right on Woods Way, and continue 0.2 mile to the trailhead.

## ON THE TRAIL

The dirt trail starts off flat, skirting the edge of Lost Lake. Watch for a little spur trail to the lake's edge at about 0.25 mile to see a dense bog of *Darlingtonia* (the carnivorous pitcher plant) that appear to be floating in the middle of the lake but are actually growing on a floating mat of woody debris. Walk through a tunnel of rhododendrons before dropping down to a plank footbridge across the neck of the lake and climbing back up to a sand bowl; look for a trail marker to stay on the route. From here you'll be walking mostly on soft sand, initially past another arm of the lake on your left. Past 0.5 mile, the trail is at times crowded by prickly gorse (at one point you walk through a virtual tunnel of gorse) before it emerges at the edge of the New River. The river is likely to be too high to ford fall through spring (when the snowy plovers have finished nesting and access to the foredune is allowed). Return as you came.

*Stop and scrutinize Lost Lake from the trail: you may see carnivorous* darlingtonia *growing on mats of vegetation floating in the lake.*

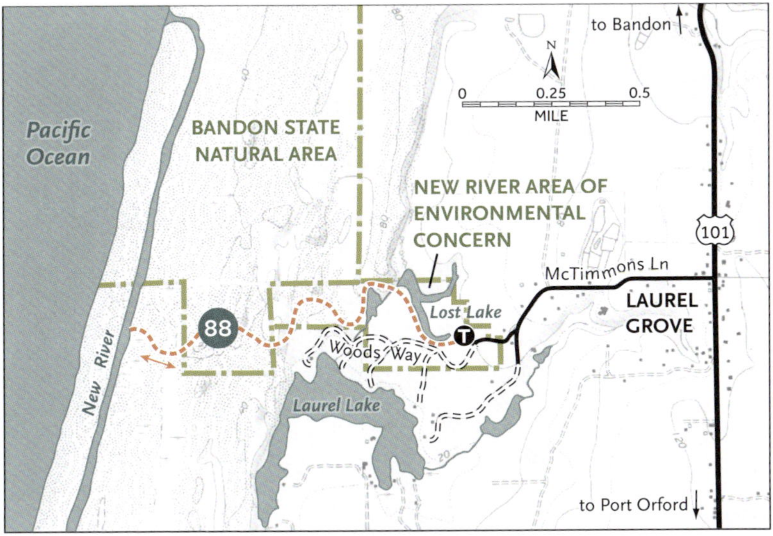

## FLORAS LAKE TO HUMBUG MOUNTAIN

The area of cliffs and cape between Floras Lake and the beach north of Cape Blanco, state park land officially designated Floras Lake State Natural Area, is entirely undeveloped but for an extensive network of trails, including at Blacklock Point, the first big headland south of Bandon. The trails here wind through a dense forest of shore pines and lead out to some spectacular shoreline views. Signage is a little spotty, and some trails are pocked with large potholes that can be wet even in midsummer. The park land is adjacent to Cape Blanco State Airport, built during World War II as part of West Coast defense efforts and still in use by private pilots. The north end of the trail system, where it links with trails and the beach at Floras Lake, is especially confusing; a GPS device might be handy.

Cape Blanco State Park is on a windswept promontory, site of the westernmost lighthouse in the forty-eight contiguous states. Fortunately the park's campground is sheltered in a grove of trees. The park occupies much of the nearly 2000-acre former Hughes family ranch, established in the late 1800s, and its trails wend through meadows, trees, and beach to create many loop options. From here the beach stretches south several miles to Port Orford Heads, former site of the Port Orford Lifeboat Station, offering a grand view south to Humbug Mountain. Humbug is the site of more trails; the summit hike is highly recommended. In Port Orford check out the unusual fishing port with its dry-dock marina; rather than docking in slips, boats are lifted out of the water at high tide by cranes and kept high and dry between trips.

In addition to Humbug Mountain State Park, there are public campgrounds at Floras Lake (Boice Cope County Park), mainly catering to kiteboarders, and at Cape Blanco State Park.

## 89 Floras Lake and Blacklock Point Loop

RATING/DIFFICULTY: **/3
LOOP: 7.3 to 8.5 miles
ELEV GAIN: 390 feet

**Contact:** Boice Cope County Park, Curry County Parks and Recreation, or Cape Blanco State Park; **Notes:** Curry County day-use fee. Trails open to bikes. Toilets available in campground; **GPS:** 42.90316°, –124.50188°

**This loop utilizes the wealth of (poorly maintained and sometimes confusing) trails between Floras Lake and Blacklock Point. Yes, it's not fancy, but it's also relatively little used, requires little elevation gain, and offers some great views. This route is described starting at Floras Lake, but you could also pick it up from the north (see map, plus directions in Hike 90).**

### GETTING THERE

About 14 miles south of Bandon, just south of milepost 289 on US Highway 101, turn west at the sign to Boice Cope County Park and follow signs about 3 miles to park in the boat ramp area.

### ON THE TRAIL

From the boat ramp parking area, cross the footbridge over the lake's outlet (the start of the New River) and begin following the path west. Quickly the trail forks; veer south

into the dunes west of the shore of Floras Lake, following little trail stakes. At 0.7 mile the trail splits, with one fork headed over the foredune to the beach (signed as the Oregon Coast Trail [OCT] route); follow where it leads up onto a sandstone plateau and

*Native iris borders parts of the trail between Floras Lake and Blacklock Point in spring.*

between two boulders just before entering the forest. Instead go straight, climbing onto a sandstone clearing that leads straight to a trailhead entering thick vegetation. Continue 0.1 mile and squeeze between two boulders. Continue straight for 0.4 mile to another junction. Bear right here, following the route of the OCT. The trail leads down to a creek, which may or may not have a footbridge to help you cross, then back out and up to the main trail leading along the ocean cliffs. If the signage is confusing, note that right turns usually lead to viewpoints and lefts usually keep you on the main trail.

You'll meet the top of the Connector Trail at 2.3 miles; from here you're basically following Hike 90 but backward. Meaning, bear right to stay along the cliffs (and visit the waterfall), then the main trail south. Study the map and read about Hike 90 to detour 1.2 additional miles roundtrip to the tip of Blacklock Point or follow the main trail back to the spur that leads to the top of the runway. Here's your express route back to where you started: Cross the top of the runway and pick up the Airport Trail leading an uninspiring 2.2 miles north to the junction with the OCT. From here retrace your steps back to Floras Lake.

## 90 Blacklock Point Loop

RATING/DIFFICULTY: **/2

LOOP: 4 to 5.2 miles

ELEV GAIN: 240 feet

**Contact:** Cape Blanco State Park; **Notes:** Open to bikes; **GPS:** 42.85679°, –124.51973°

**A remote shoreline bluff with solitude, spectacular ocean vistas, a waterfall plunging into the ocean: Blacklock Point**

is a find. But first you have to find it. It's part of undeveloped Floras Lake State Natural Area; the network of trails here are minimally maintained (winter storms destroy portions of the trail from time to time). Note that some of the trails at Blacklock Point are old roads with massive potholes. Detours with little boardwalks keep you out of the water in many places, but waterproof sandals are a good choice of footwear here much of the year. This is one option for a scenic loop hike (Hike 89 is another) or pick your own route among the many choices between the Sixes River to the south and Floras Lake to the north.

*Detour off the main trail to reach stunning clifftop viewpoints approaching Blacklock Point.* (Photo by Terrie Pigeon)

## GETTING THERE

Turn west off US Highway 101 between mileposts 293 and 294 at the Airport Road sign; follow it west 2.8 miles to Cape Blanco State Airport and park along the fence at the road's end. (There's also a gravel parking area, but it's somewhat secluded and has had vandalism problems, so I'd stick to roadside parking.)

## ON THE TRAIL

Follow signs to the start of the trail heading northwest. Follow it north as it parallels the airport runway on your right (glimpse it through the trees here and there). At 0.7 mile go straight (spur on the right leads back to the end of the runway), then (for a clockwise loop) immediately bear left where the Connector Trail takes off to the right. The next junction is in 0.5 mile; go right here. (If you'd like to visit the tip of Blacklock Point, highly recommended, go left here, then right, out to a grand viewpoint; it's a 1.2-mile addition to your loop hike.)

Skipping Blacklock Point, your route veers right (north); continue not quite 0.5 mile to an opening to the west; follow it out to the bluffs and around to the north, where a creek winds out of the pine woods and pours into a hole in the sandstone, spills out, drops onto a rock pile, and ends on the beach just north of the point. When the wind is strong, the modest cataract seems to flow up, not down. The bluffs here are stunning and dramatically sculpted by storms, but be careful walking at the edge of the sometimes-undercut cliffs.

Return to the main trail and continue to the northeast about 0.6 mile more to another bluff-top viewpoint and an even better look back to the falls. In about 0.1 mile you'll reach a junction with the other end of the Connector Trail; take it to the right as it leads south 1.8 miles through the forest on an old road (no views) to rejoin the main Blacklock Point Trail alongside the airport runway and return to the trailhead.

## 91 Beach Walk: North of Cape Blanco

ONE-WAY DISTANCE: 2.8 miles

It's often windy and wild on the beach on either side of Cape Blanco, and there are rivers blocking beach walkers' ways, unless it's summer and you hit it at low tide. The Sixes River in particular is very variable, ranging from a rushing torrent to an underground stream seeping unseen through the sand. If it's flowing and you do cross, keep the tides in mind for your return.

### BEACH ACCESS

BA 158, Sixes River trailhead, Cape Blanco State Park, at end of road to the historic Hughes House. Parking.

Gate near end of Cape Blanco Road leading to lighthouse, Cape Blanco State Park. Roadside parking. Vault toilet at lighthouse, 0.3 mile farther. Restrooms in nearby campground.

### WHERE TO WALK

**Sixes River adventure.** Park at the parking area for Beach Access 158, next to the Sixes River, then walk through the gate and follow the trail across the cow pasture—complete with grazing cows, or sometimes sheep—0.6 mile to the beach. From here you can walk north to the river—even cross it if conditions permit—or south to the foot of the cape. The pasture is part of the original Hughes family ranch established here in the late 1800s; by leasing the land to neighboring farmers for grazing, the state park is continuing a historical practice while helping to limit the spread of invasive plant species.

**From the lighthouse.** This is the most straightforward way to reach this beach: A 0.2-mile trail takes you down the hillside from the road leading to Cape Blanco Lighthouse; the Sixes River is 1.6 miles up the beach. Sixes River can be waded at low tide in summer, giving you access to more beach walking to the base of Blacklock Point.

## 92 Beach Walk: Cape Blanco to Port Orford Heads

ONE-WAY DISTANCE: 7 miles

The beach south of Cape Blanco is wide and walkable except for one river that stops you in winter but can be waded in the right conditions in summer.

*You may find yourself among grazing cattle or sheep if you follow the beach access trail along the Sixes River.*

*Port Orford Heads is the backdrop when you take a walk northbound from Tseriadun State Recreation Site. Vehicles are allowed on parts of this beach.*

## BEACH ACCESS

BA 159, south end of Cape Blanco Beach Road, Cape Blanco State Park. Parking, restrooms in nearby campground.

BA 160, Paradise Point State Recreation Site, end of Paradise Point Road, Port Orford. Parking.

BA 161, Tseriadun State Recreation Site, end of Agate Beach Road, Port Orford. Parking, restrooms.

## WHERE TO WALK

**South from Cape Blanco.** The Elk River is roughly 0.9 mile ahead; turn around here, or in summer at low to mid tide, wade it and continue on. Return before the incoming tide raises the river too high to wade.

**From Paradise Point State Recreation Site.** A trail leads a short distance downhill to the beach, allowing you to stroll north or south.

**From Tseriadun State Recreation Site.** This day-use area (pronounced *serry-AH-dune*) is named for the people who lived at this site for thousands of years until they were forcibly removed in 1856; many of their descendants are today part of the Confederated Tribes of Siletz Indians. What is now called Port Orford Heads looms to the south; walk north (typically into the wind in summer) until you're ready to turn around; the mouth of the Elk River is about 4.7 miles away.

## 93 Port Orford Heads

RATING/DIFFICULTY: **/1

ROUNDTRIP: 1.2 miles

ELEV GAIN: 280 feet

**Contact:** Port Orford Heads State Park; **Notes:** Dogs on-leash; **GPS:** 42.73929°, –124.51084°

**This short trail network is well worth a visit, both for the stunning vistas and for the history. The buildings at Port Orford Heads State Park were originally built for Port Orford Lifeboat Station, whose staff of "surfmen" kept watch over 40 miles of coastline from Cape Blanco to Cape Sebastian between 1934 and 1970. The station was decommissioned after more sophisticated search-and-rescue methods**

**made it obsolete. Walk the trails, lined in spring with wild purple iris, to dazzling viewpoints and you'll understand why this was such a valuable lookout site. The former crew quarters now house the Port Orford Lifeboat Station Museum (check for current hours). The station's legendary 36-foot unsinkable motor lifeboat is on display, covered, outside.**

## GETTING THERE

From the town of Port Orford on US Highway 101, turn west on 9th Street (north of milepost 301), then left on Coast Guard Hill Road and follow signs to Port Orford Heads State Park. Park at the small parking area at the top of the head, west of the old barracks and tennis court.

## ON THE TRAIL

A network network of short trails begins outside the museum and interpretive center. Three trailheads begin on the south side on the lawn; take the one on the left (Cove Trail) to a viewpoint where you can see Nellies Cove, site of the boathouse (destroyed by fire in 1970) where surfmen would launch their boats after descending 280 feet on a 500-step staircase. At 0.4 mile the trail reaches another viewpoint at the site of the station's observation tower (removed in 1970), where if weather permits you'll get a good view of

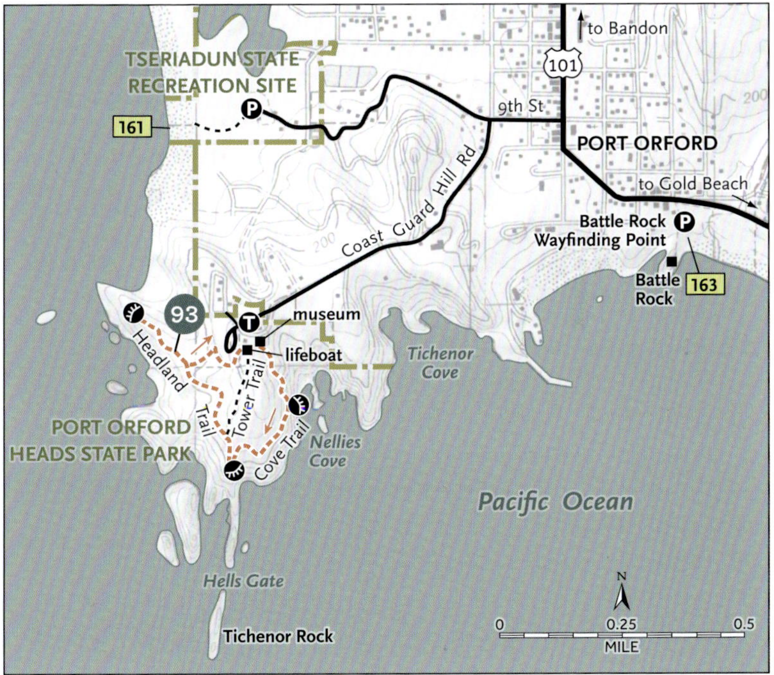

*Nellies Cove, where surfmen stationed at Port Orford Heads once launched their lifeboats, takes on an aquamarine hue on sunny days.*

Humbug Mountain. Head north on the paved Tower Trail a short distance to a junction and bear left (straight leads 0.3 mile back on the Tower Trail to the trailhead), then left again at the next junction to take the Headland Trail 0.2 mile to the park's westernmost viewpoint. To complete the loop, backtrack out to the main trail, turn left, and walk the last 0.2 mile back to the parking area.

## 94 Beach Walk: Port Orford to Rocky Point

ONE-WAY DISTANCE: 2.4 miles

Battle Rock, marking the north end of the beach at Port Orford, takes its name from a multiday fight between the local Quatomah people and white settlers arriving by steamer in 1851. There was a minor gold rush, and apparently the Quatomah had had enough of newcomers. They set upon the settlers, who used a small cannon to fire on the locals, killing seventeen of them. The settlers eventually crept off the rock and made their way up the coast. For the rest of the story, read about the Rogue River Wars. The wayside here commemorates that violent episode from early in the settlement era. The bluff provides access to the beach, which stretches south to Humbug Mountain, interrupted by one minor headland.

### BEACH ACCESS

BA 163, Battle Rock Wayfinding Point, off US 101 just south of downtown Port Orford. Parking, restrooms.

BA 164, Hubbard Creek, wide gravel pullout on east side of US 101, 1 mile south of Battle Rock Wayside, Port Orford.

## WHERE TO WALK

**Battle Rock to Rocky Point.** The wayside at Battle Rock is the main access to the beach south of Port Orford, though there are other places where you can pull off US 101 and scramble down to the beach, including at Hubbard Creek. How far south you can walk depends on the tide, but unless the tide is very high, you should be able to walk nearly to Rocky Point, a 4.8-mile roundtrip from Battle Rock. Even at a very low tide, you cannot safely walk around Rocky Point; it's a field of very slippery boulders down to the sea. But you could arrange a one-way walk south nearly to Rocky Point, leaving the beach at an unmarked (but for a small Oregon Coast Trail [OCT] trail marker and a line of rocks) trailhead 1 mile south of Hubbard Creek; it's not built as a parking area (narrow, with a drop-off), but you could pull over and pick up hikers. On the beach, look for an OCT trail post and path leading up the hillside about 0.5 mile before the end of Rocky Point.

# 95 Humbug Old Highway 101 Loop

RATING/DIFFICULTY: */2
LOOP: 1.7 miles
ELEV GAIN: 582 feet

**Contact:** Humbug Mountain State Park; **Notes:** Dogs on-leash. Toilets and water available in campground only; **GPS:** Northern trailhead 42.70684°, –124.45726°; southern (Humbug Mountain) trailhead 42.68792°, –124.43924°

**The main users of this trail are Oregon Coast Trail hikers; after them it's campers at Humbug Mountain State Park. For day visitors not quite up to summiting Humbug Mountain (Hike 96), this hike is a pleasant, vigorous, and shorter alternative.**

*Humbug Mountain dominates the horizon on a southbound walk from Port Orford.*

*Paintbrush blooms on dry hillsides along the Old Highway 101 Scenic Trail at Humbug Mountain State Park.* (Photo by Vickie Skellcerf)

## GETTING THERE

From US Highway 101 about 3.5 miles south of Port Orford, turn east just past the sign for Humbug Mountain State Park and follow the road as it curves right for 0.1 mile; bear right and park at the gate.

## ON THE TRAIL

From the gate, walk the road west into the campground and take the trail that heads uphill between campsites 34 and 51. If you're camping here, just walk the campground road to the trail. (Alternately, park at the parking area for Hike 96 and cross a pedestrian tunnel under US 101 to the campground road.) Follow the trail past the amphitheater and continue up 0.4 mile. Turn right and follow the old road around the hillside, over a bridge, and down to a junction with the campground entrance road. The deteriorating asphalt road can be

## DEAD SEABIRDS TELL TALES

It's not unusual to find dead seabirds on the beach, though you may not notice them among the seaweed and driftwood. It doesn't take long for a dead gull or murre or fulmar to be consumed by other creatures, its feathers and bones spread on the beach and buried in the sand. If you find one in good shape, take a moment to study its feet, the shape of its beak, its feathers: You'll never get close enough to a live seabird to see such details. Scientists have begun tracking patterns of bird die-offs, seeking correlations with changing conditions in the marine environment. They are helped by a citizen science project called Coastal Observation and Seabird Survey Team; learn more at coasst.org. They welcome new volunteers, on the Oregon coast as well as California, Washington, and Alaska.

*Young common murres are often seen washed up on Oregon beaches June through November, especially when certain ocean conditions make food scarce.*

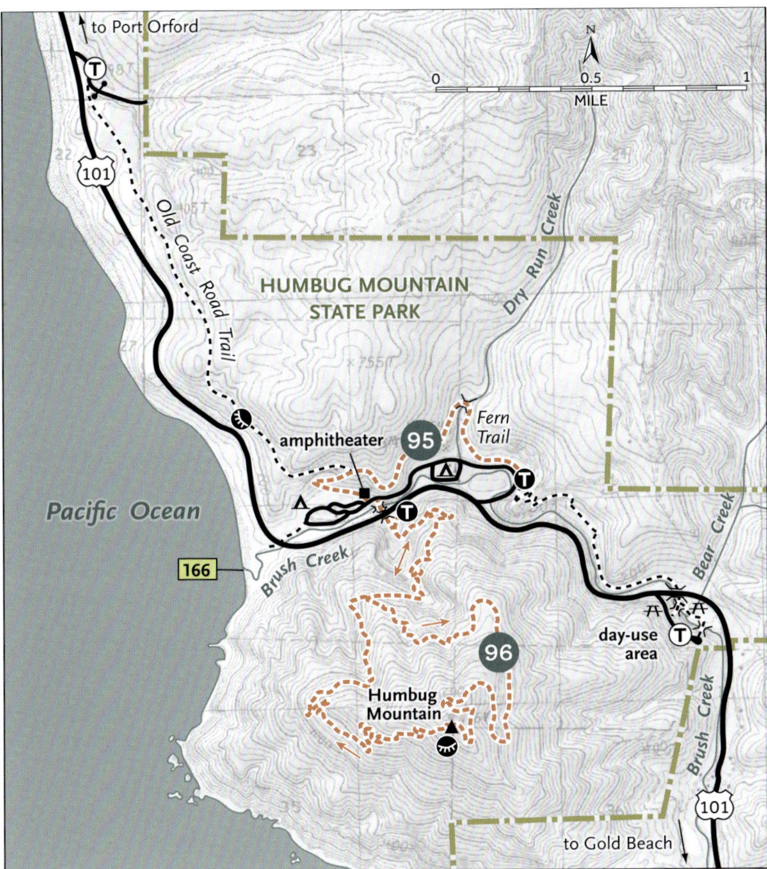


slippery when wet due to the lichens and mosses growing on it. A sign identifies this trail section as the Fern Trail for the varieties of ferns growing trailside. But keep an eye out for poison oak too, also found along the trail.

The loop hike ends where the trail meets the campground road.

## EXTEND YOUR HIKE

Rather than (or in addition to) turning right on the Old Coast Road Trail, turn left; it's 1.7 miles to the north trailhead, off US 101. The route rises gently for about 0.8 mile, then slowly descends to the trailhead, providing ocean views above the highway along the way. Alternately, instead of bearing right to complete the loop when you hit the campground

*The route to the summit of Humbug Mountain starts as a gentle incline in a quiet glade but quickly starts to climb.*

road, turn left onto the footpath heading east. This 0.9-mile addition starts by switchbacking up a steep hillside, then—in 0.5 mile—tops a ridge before beginning a gradual descent. Reaching Brush Creek, it follows the creek upstream, crosses a tributary (Bear Creek) on a footbridge, then ducks under US 101 to the park's day-use picnic area (toilets, no water). Watch for poison oak on this trail stretch too. Return as you came.

## 96 Humbug Mountain

RATING/DIFFICULTY: ***/3
ROUNDTRIP: 5.3 miles
ELEV GAIN: 3,500 feet

**Contact:** Humbug Mountain State Park; **Notes:** Dogs on-leash. Toilets available in campground; **GPS:** 42.68792°, –124.43924°

**This is one of the south coast's biggest and most rewarding hikes. In spring, wildflowers brighten the trailside and the creeks are raucous. In autumn, fallen bay leaves crunch underfoot, sending their spicy fragrance into the air. There's no season when the hike up Humbug Mountain isn't appealing. But don't expect good whale-watching from the top; you'll be much too high to see any detail in the ocean vista spread below you from the 1,761-foot summit meadow.**

### GETTING THERE

Look for the trailhead parking area on the south side of US Highway 101 about 6 miles south of Port Orford, 0.3 mile west of the entrance to Humbug Mountain State Park campground. Campground campers can take a short access trail from the campground road near Loop B, over Brush Creek, and under the highway to the trailhead parking area.

### ON THE TRAIL

The trail immediately crosses a small creek and begins climbing through an airy forest of Douglas-fir, rhododendrons, and bay trees; it continues up at a moderately steep grade. Just past a 1-mile marker, the trail splits. Bear left on the eastern route for a more moderate climb of not-quite 2 miles more to a junction just below the summit; follow the spur trail a few paces to the summit at 2.8 miles, where you can drink in the view to the south from a small, grassy clearing. To return, bear left at the summit junction to descend via the scenic 1.6-mile western route with its views of the ocean and Port Orford. At the junction with the eastern route, go left to return to the trailhead.

## HUMBUG MOUNTAIN TO GOLD BEACH

For several miles south of Humbug Mountain, the shoreline is steep and rocky and inaccessible until you reach Arizona Beach, a sweet pocket of sand backed by a day-use state recreation area. The land adjacent to both Arizona Beach and Sisters Rocks has been acquired by Oregon Parks and Recreation Department; Arizona Beach has toilets and water, but Sisters Rocks State Natural Area remains undeveloped.

Past another minor headland is long Nesika Beach, which ends at a residential community also called Nesika Beach. Past a couple more headlands is Bailey Beach, which stretches south to the Rogue River. Get to the beach from the trail down the bluff at Otter Point State Recreation Site or from the Rogue's north jetty. There are no public campgrounds between Humbug Mountain and Gold Beach, but there are a couple of private campgrounds with lovely tent camping areas. Indian Creek RV Park, at the north end of Gold Beach, offers a quiet creekside tent camping area beyond the RV park. Honey Bear by the Sea RV Resort and Campground also has a few tent sites arranged around a large meadow out of sight of the RV area; it's expensive but quite exceptional.

## 97 Beach Walk: Arizona Beach to Sisters Rocks

ONE-WAY DISTANCE: 1.8 miles

Sisters Rocks refers to three large rocks, two "twins" accessible from shore and a third sister in the nearshore ocean. During summer low tides, you can walk the beach south from Arizona Beach, round a point, and visit the near-magical Sisters Rocks area, with its sea stacks and arch rocks and sea

*It's not easy, but it's possible, to reach the caves and coves on the beach at Sisters Rocks; you'll see more if you can get there at low tide.*

Humbug Mountain to Gold Beach
166
to Port Orford
HUMBUG MOUNTAIN STATE PARK
Humbug Mountain
ROGUE RIVER–SISKIYOU NATIONAL FOREST
101
ARIZONA BEACH STATE RECREATION SITE
167
Mussel Creek
97
168
Sisters Rocks
Euchre Creek
OPHIR
Pacific Ocean
169
OPHIR WAYSIDE
170
98
171
Nesika Beach
NESIKA BEACH
Rogue River
101
545
OTTER POINT STATE RECREATION SITE
595
99
173
Bailey Beach
Rogue River
174
175
176
GOLD BEACH
to Brookings
N
0 1 2
MILES

*From Ophir, the beach stretches 3 miles south to the bluffs at Nesika Beach.*

caves. (The nearest-to-shore Sisters Rocks are also accessible with a scramble down from US 101.) In the nineteenth century this area served as a minor seaport known as Frankport. Look around and you might see evidence of an old narrow-gauge railroad and rock quarrying operations conducted here decades ago.

### BEACH ACCESS

BA 167, Arizona Beach State Recreation Site, south of Port Orford at US 101 milepost 313. Parking, vault toilets.

BA 168, Sisters Rocks, south of Port Orford between US 101 mileposts 314 and 315. Unsigned pullout on west side of highway.

### WHERE TO WALK

**From the north.** In winter, follow Mussel Creek as it flows north, then bends south, giving you access to about 0.3 mile of beach. In summer, hop the creek and head south; if it's low tide to mid-tide, round the point about 0.4 mile south to get access to the beach at Sisters Rocks. There's a big boulder pile ahead; if the tide's low enough you may be able to walk around it, otherwise scramble carefully over it.

**From the south.** Near the Beach Access 168 sign just off the highway, look for a trail leading down the rocky hillside to the beach. After another stretch of open sand, you'll reach Sisters Rocks: one big seaward knob (North Sister), a lesser landward bump, and an offshore island. There's plenty to explore here, especially at low tide, or walk north on the beach as far as the tide allows.

## 98 Beach Walk: Ophir to Nesika Beach

ONE-WAY DISTANCE: 5.8 miles

US Highway 101 follows close by the beach here, except at the very north and south ends. Note that the only legal beach access in the community of Nesika Beach is at Beach Access 171; south of that point the beachfront property is all privately owned, and the residents don't like trespassers.

### BEACH ACCESS

BA 170, Ophir Wayside, at US Highway 101 milepost 319 about 3 miles north of Nesika Beach. Parking, restrooms.

## SO MUCH SAND, ALWAYS ON THE MOVE

*Oregon Dunes National Recreation Area has the coast's largest expanse of open sand.*

Where'd all that sand come from? Basically from the mountains that back the beach, though in fact much of the Coast Range and foothills is built of sedimentary rock that itself began as sand sixty million years ago, compacted into rock when most of Oregon was underwater. The movement of tectonic plates thrust that rock upward to create a mountain range. Rain and rivers eroded it and neighboring rock, carrying it out to sea and creating a huge reservoir of sand lying on the continental shelf.

Waves move the sand toward the shore, and wind blows it farther inland except where its movement is blocked by tall foredunes or by headlands composed of harder volcanic rock. South of the Coquille River at Bandon, the beaches are primarily made of decomposed metamorphosed rock from the ancient Klamath Mountains; north of Tillamook Head most of the sand came down the Columbia River.

It may look solid, but every beach is constantly moving—shifting north to south in summer and back north in winter, growing and shrinking with the seasons. Every winter the beach is cut back by high waves that push the sand into deeper waters, where it accumulates in offshore bars and creates two lines of breakers in winter. Come summer, low waves move the sand back on shore. The size of the sand grains on a particular beach determines the steepness of its slope: Very fine sand creates almost-level Cannon Beach, for example, while the gravelly beach at the end of Yaquina Head has a relatively steep slope. Most beaches in Oregon are light tan in color because most are composed mainly of quartz and feldspar grains. In some places, black-sand placer deposits create dark patches on the beach.

Though broken into pocket beaches by dozens of headlands, Oregon's nearly 400-mile coastline includes a total of 262 miles of sandy beach. The longest stretch of beach uninterrupted by headlands is the 52 miles of beach running from Heceta Head to the mouth of Coos Bay, much of which lies within Oregon Dunes National Recreation Area.

BA 171, Nesika Beach, off the north end of Nesika Beach Road. Roadside parking.

### WHERE TO WALK

**North from Ophir Wayside.** The beach runs out at Devils Backbone (2.9 miles one way). Greggs Creek crosses the beach at about 0.8 mile and Euchre Creek 0.3 mile beyond that; neither may be wadeable in winter.

**South from Ophir Wayside.** It's 1.6 miles of creek-free walking between the two beach access points; you can continue south 1.3 miles more, but there is no beach access south of BA 171 so plan to backtrack.

## 99 Beach Walk: Otter Point to the Rogue River

ONE-WAY DISTANCE: 3 miles

A wide beach stretches between the Rogue River's north jetty and Otter Point to the north. Pick any access point and walk as far as you like. Otter Point is the farthest north and the most remote, but the other access points get you to the beach (and back up) with less effort.

### BEACH ACCESS

Otter Point State Recreation Site, 0.4 mile west of US 101 south of milepost 324. Parking. A trail leads 0.5 mile to the beach.

BA 173, Bailey Beach, Old Coast Road 1 mile north of Bailey Beach South, north of Gold Beach. Gravel turnout with room for about six vehicles. Short trail leads to the beach.

BA 174, Bailey Beach South, Old Coast Road across from Knox Lane, north of Gold Beach. Park along tangle of dirt roads west of the Old Coast Road.

BA 175, Rogue River North Jetty, off Wedderburn Loop, north of Gold Beach. Parking on gravel roads alongside jetty.

### WHERE TO WALK

**From Otter Point.** At the south end of the parking lot, go through a break in the pole fence and immediately veer left at the Oregon Coast Trail post (a right turn takes you out on the point, a worthwhile detour to a sheer cliff and spectacular views). Follow a tunnel of salal and evergreen huckleberry as the trail heads south along the bluff for about 0.4 mile, nearly touching the road before turning to descend steeply 110 feet down the hillside to reach Bailey Beach at the mouth of a creek. The base of Otter Point is a scant 0.2 mile to the north; look for the sea cave in the rock. Most summer days you can get a break from the wind at the base of the cliffs here or walk south as far as the Rogue River.

**From beach access points on Old Coast Road.** Parking is scant here; these short access trails are mostly used by locals.

**From the Rogue River north jetty.** No formal parking area here; just drive out the jetty until you can't drive anymore and walk down to the beach, then walk to Otter Point (or someplace along the way) and turn around.

*Bailey Beach follows a wide curve in the shoreline from Otter Point at its north end to the mouth of the Rogue River.*

## GOLD BEACH TO CROOK POINT

Gold Beach, named for the mineral discovered in the sands here in the early 1850s, is perched at the mouth of the Rogue River, a federally designated wild and scenic river notable for its rugged beauty, salmon and steelhead fishing, and stellar whitewater rafting. A 40-mile national recreational trail follows the river through the heart of its lower canyon; camp along the way or stay in secluded guest lodges. Access the trail by road or via a jet-powered tour boat from Gold Beach.

South of town, the shore is easily accessible from US Highway 101 as far south as Buena Vista Ocean Wayside, at which point the highway veers inland to start its climb up 700-foot-tall Cape Sebastian; south of here the beach is quiet and remote to its termination at the base of the headland. Most of Cape Sebastian—cloaked in a dark forest of Sitka spruce—is conserved as a state park. A well-established trail leads from the top of the cape down the south side of the headland to Hunters Cove; with both ends of the trail accessible by car, locals often hike it one way. A less well-established trail also ascends the north side of the cape from the beach; it serves mainly as a link in the Oregon Coast Trail.

South of Pistol River lies a remote stretch of beach ending near Crook Point, a rocky promontory and one of just two (with Coquille Point at Bandon) mainland sections of the Oregon Islands National Wildlife Refuge. That vast refuge includes every rock, reef, and island immediately off the Oregon coast; it protects the million-plus seabirds that nest along the coast as well as the marine mammals that haul out on the rocks. Crook Point itself and its adjacent rocks and islands host a huge concentration of nesting seabirds—typically more than 200,000—from April to September. Tidepools form at the base of the point at low tide, native cutthroat trout live in Sand Creek (emptying into the ocean north of the point), sea lions and seals lounge on rocky shelves, and rare native plants grow on the uplands. Bring binoculars to catch the action, but humans must stay off the rocks.

There are no public campgrounds in this section; the closest (at Harris Beach State Park) is in Brookings.

## 100 Beach Walk: Gold Beach

ONE-WAY DISTANCE: 5.5 miles

There's plenty of beach to walk here, and a lot of access points. Note that you can't reach the beach between the Rogue River's south jetty and 5th Place; the municipal airport lies between downtown and the shore.

### BEACH ACCESS

BA 176, Rogue River South Jetty, off Oceanside Drive. Parking on gravel roads alongside jetty.

5th Street access, end of 5th Street, Gold Beach. Roadside parking.

BA 177, fairgrounds access, end of 10th Street, Gold Beach. Roadside parking.

BA 178, Gold Beach Visitor's Center access, end of Shirley Lane, Gold Beach. Roadside parking, restrooms in visitor center (open daily 9 a.m. to 3 p.m.).

BA 179, Kissing Rock, off US 101 south of downtown Gold Beach at US 101 milepost 331. Parking.

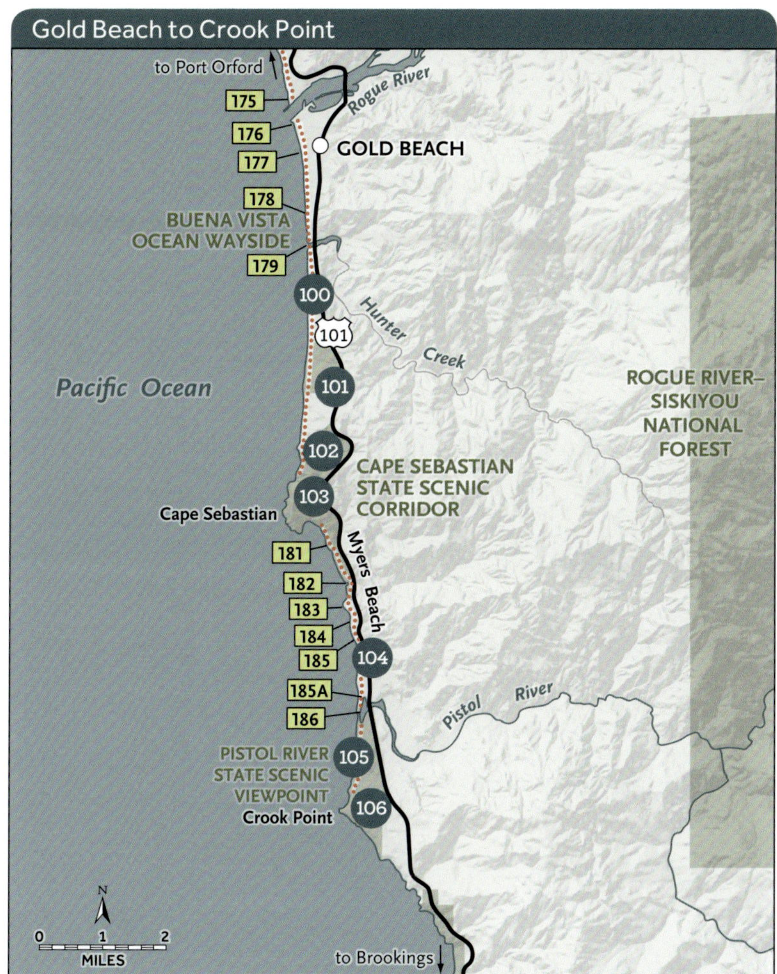


## WHERE TO WALK

**Near town.** Pick any access point and start walking.

**Kissing Rock.** South from this wayside US 101 rises and pulls away from the shoreline, which makes for a quiet, remote stretch of beach for southbound beach walkers. From the beach you can also connect with the 333 Trail or the Oregon Coast Trail leading to the top of Cape Sebastian (see Hike 101). Or just

*Early morning sun brings out the color in the rocks at Kissing Rock, south of Gold Beach.*

stay on the sand as far as the base of Cape Sebastian and enjoy this secluded gem of a beach, returning as you came. Northbound from Kissing Rock you will soon encounter the mouth of Hunter Creek, which (in summer) often seeps through the sand, with no wading or leaping required.

## 101 Cape Sebastian 333 Trail Loop

RATING/DIFFICULTY: **/2
LOOP: 4.2 miles
ELEV GAIN: 580 feet

**Contact:** Cape Sebastian State Scenic Corridor; **Notes:** Dogs on-leash; **GPS:** 42.35365°, –124.41326°

**There are many ways to hike Cape Sebastian, the headland south of Gold Beach. Most day hikers walk the main southbound trail from the top of the cape down to Meyers Beach (Hike 103). Here's another option: Link up the 333 Trail—named for the milepost where you access it—with a portion of the Oregon Coast Trail (OCT) and a lovely, quiet stretch of beach on the cape's north side. It's easy to do, but the signage can be confusing and the trail steep, rough, and overgrown in places. Follow these directions and watch your step. Avoid hitting the beach at high tide, especially in winter.**

### GETTING THERE

South of Gold Beach (but north of the access to Cape Sebastian State Scenic

Corridor), pull into a wide gravel turnout on the west side of US Highway 101 just north of milepost 333 and across the highway from Eighty Acres Road.

## ON THE TRAIL

Just south of the informal parking area is a trail leading into the woods and marked by an OCT signpost (confusion point no. 1: This is not actually part of the OCT). In a very short distance you'll reach a junction—the start of the loop hike. I suggest going right, or north, which will make your return (uphill) hike more pleasant. You're now on the 333 Trail. Follow it as it descends through the forest for 1.2 miles, crossing a handful of little streams on wooden bridges, to end at a tidal inlet next to a huge boulder on the beach. At this point you're 2.4 miles south of the closest beach access on US 101 (Beach Access 179, an alternate starting point that would add 4.8 miles to the loop's total distance).

Head south down the beach for 0.9 mile, toward where the cape juts into the sea. Watch on your left for what looks like a grassy ramp angling gradually up the hillside: That's your return trail. As you near the bottom of the "ramp" after cutting across the dunes, you'll see OCT signage: This, indeed, is a section of the Oregon Coast Trail.

Follow the OCT for 1 mile of gradual ascent to a gate (walk around it) and a trail junction. Here OCT southbound hikers go right, but you'll go left 0.2 mile to another junction. Turn left, over a stream, and follow the trail right and up as it steepens briefly, swings west along a ridge, and then bends back to return you—0.8 mile from that last trail junction—to where your loop started near highway milepost 333.

*The Cape Sebastian 333 Trail can be brushy and overgrown, but it's full of interest, from the trailside vegetation to the large boulders where the trail joins the Oregon Coast Trail.*

to Gold Beach
179
Pacific Ocean
101
Hunter Creek Rd
Hunter Creek
101
CAPE SEBASTIAN
STATE SCENIC
CORRIDOR
333 Trail
Eighty Acres Rd
Oregon
Coast
102
Trail
103
Cape
Sebastian
Trail
Cape
Sebastian
101
Myers
Beach
181
0
0.5
1
MILE
Hunters
Island
Hunters
Cove
to Brookings

# 102 Cape Sebastian Waterfall Trail

RATING/DIFFICULTY: **/2

ROUNDTRIP: 3.8 miles

ELEV GAIN: 1,300 feet

**Contact:** Cape Sebastian State Scenic Corridor; **Notes:** Dogs on-leash; **GPS:** 42.32908°, –124.42588°

**Most hikers on Cape Sebastian take the trail that leads south of the south parking area and down to the beach (Hike 103). But a trail also leads north from here. It's part of the Oregon Coast Trail, used mainly by thru hikers, and it's less well-maintained than the southbound trail. Give it a try if you want to change things up; this route leads to the top of a waterfall plunging onto the beach. (The last bit of trail to the top of the waterfall requires a scramble on large boulders; not a great idea with kids or dogs.)**

## GETTING THERE

Turn west off US Highway 101, 5 miles south of Gold Beach and just north of milepost 335 at the sign to Cape Sebastian State Scenic Corridor; bear left and park in the south (main) parking lot.

## ON THE TRAIL

Head north out of the parking area across, in summer, a field of wildflowers, before plunging into the Sitka spruce forest. The trail ascends for a bit, then descends—eventually on stairs—to 0.8 mile, where a short spur leads to viewpoint. Continuing, the main trail rises gently, crossing a creek, to another

*The walk to the Cape Sebastian waterfall is its own reward; you may want to turn around before you get to the large, slippery boulders at the top of the waterfall itself.*

junction at 1.5 miles; here's where you turn left to reach the waterfall. This final 0.4 mile is a gentle descent. The trail ends at a tumble of boulders that are tricky to negotiate if you want to reach the tip-top of the waterfall; depending on your party's abilities, this might be the place to turn around. Return as you came.

## 103 Cape Sebastian

RATING/DIFFICULTY: **/2
ROUNDTRIP: 3.4 miles
ELEV GAIN: 1,360 feet

**Contact:** Cape Sebastian State Scenic Corridor; **Notes:** Dogs on-leash; **GPS:** 42.32908°, –124.42588°

**It's a more than 1300-foot elevation gain if you descend, and then ascend, scenic Cape Sebastian on an out-and-back hike. If you have the option, consider leaving a shuttle car at Meyers Beach North Wayside and make a (nearly) all-downhill glide through towering forest on this steep cape. The beach at the cape's base is a good spot to escape the north wind on an otherwise warm day. The trail ends with a precipitous drop to the beach; make sure your party is up for that challenge.**

*The view stretches north for miles from the top of the Cape Sebastian Trail.*

### GETTING THERE

Turn west off US Highway 101, 5 miles south of Gold Beach and just north of milepost 335 at the sign to Cape Sebastian State Scenic Corridor; bear left and park in the south (main) parking lot. The trail hits the beach a scant 1 mile north of Meyers Beach North Wayside (Beach Access 181), an alternate starting point (making it a 5.2-mile loop).

### ON THE TRAIL

From the south (main) parking lot, follow the asphalt path west as it drops and then ascends past a bank of fragrant ceanothus, heads into a grove of trees, and at 0.2 mile reaches a view north to Gold Beach and Humbug Mountain. The trail then curves south, switchbacking down through a Sitka spruce forest. Nearing the end, the trail rises slightly and crosses two small creeks. At about 1.5 miles it emerges from the forest onto a rock bench above the bedrock at the base of the cape, curving west with the contour of the mountain and angling down the hillside to the beach. Hang on to the rope installed to get hikers down to the beach safely (if its anchors haven't eroded away) and watch for poison oak at the trailside. Explore the beach and return as you came. Alternately, walk south on the beach 0.9 mile to Meyers Beach North Wayside (Beach

Access 181, north of milepost 337) if you've arranged a shuttle car for a one-way hike.

If you're making a roundtrip hike in reverse to the top of the cape and back, the bottom of the trail can be a little tricky to spot the first time. Approaching from the south via the beach, cross several small creeks; pass a big, stratified rock face; cross another little creek, and walk onto the boulders where the beach runs out. Look up to catch a remnant of trail; it may require a bit of a scramble to get up to it.

## 104 Beach Walk: Cape Sebastian to Pistol River

ONE-WAY DISTANCE: 2.2 miles

Were it closer to a tourist town, and not so close to US Highway 101, Meyers Beach would rival Bandon Beach for popularity. Rocks the size of multi-story buildings are scattered on a wide expanse of sand, leaving plenty of room to walk among them. It's a fun place to play, with easy access from the road. During some parts of some summers, the Pistol River can be waded; most times it forms a barrier to farther southbound beach travel.

### BEACH ACCESS

Cape Sebastian Trail (see Hike 103).
BA 181, Meyers Beach North.
BA 182, Meyers Beach Middle.
BA 183, Meyers Beach South.
BA 184, Pistol River North.
BA 185, Pistol River Middle.
BA 185A, Pistol River Beach: off US 101 south of Cape Sebastian. Limited parking in highway pullouts.

### WHERE TO WALK

**Meyers Beach.** Park at any of the Meyers Beach or Pistol River beach access points, except 185A, and start walking north or south.

*House-size rocks stud the wide beach south of Cape Sebastian.* (Photo by Donna Scurlock)

Access 185A may be cut off from the beach to the north by the lagoon that forms at the mouth of Pistol River. Instead start at Beach Access 185 (next to a house-sized rock) for a long walk north or a short walk south to the river's mouth.

## 105 Beach Walk: Pistol River to Crook Point

ONE-WAY DISTANCE: 2.3 miles

This quiet beach, mostly out of sight of the highway, is easy to reach and combines nicely with an upland hike for satisfying beach-trail loop.

### BEACH ACCESS

BA 186, Pistol River State Scenic Viewpoint, just south of Pistol River Bridge on US 101. Parking.

Lola Lake Loop (Hike 106).

### WHERE TO WALK

**From Pistol River State Scenic Viewpoint.** Park in the large gravel parking area, then cross the lagoon (dry in summer) and climb over the foredune to reach the beach. A spit stretches north about 0.8 mile to the mouth of Pistol River. Or you can walk south 1.5 miles to the base of Crook Point. Bring binoculars and look, don't touch; the point is part of Oregon Islands National Wildlife Refuge and off-limits to humans.

**To Lola Lake.** See Hike 106.

## 106 Lola Lake Loop

RATING/DIFFICULTY: **/3

ROUNDTRIP: 5.8 miles

ELEV GAIN: 360 feet

**Contact:** Harris Beach State Park; **Notes:** Dogs on-leash; **GPS:** Pistol River State Scenic Viewpoint 42.27545°, –124.40496°; southern trail access 42.25344°, –124.39627°

*Sand Creek trickles through a pile of driftwood where the beach ends approaching Crook Point.*

## SEALS AND SEA LIONS: THEY DON'T NEED OUR HELP

Hike enough on Oregon's beaches and you can't help but see harbor seals—popping up a sleek, dark head in the surf or lounging on offshore rocks or sand spits. They are distinguished from sea lions—which you may see lounging at marinas or on shoreline rocks—not only by their size (sea lions are much larger) but by the arrangement of their hind limbs. True seals' rear flippers point permanently backward; they wriggle awkwardly on land. Sea lions, on the other hand, can rotate their rear flippers to walk on all four limbs.

*Harbor seals lounge on the rocks at Quarry Cove, within Yaquina Head Outstanding Natural Area north of Newport.*

If you're walking on the beach in spring, you might come across a baby seal crying like a kitten—or an adult seal or sea lion in apparent distress. Your instinct may be to offer help, but don't. The adult is probably molting—an unpleasant process for the animal, especially for elephant seals (who undergo what scientists call a "catastrophic molt"). They get over it. Baby seals may be left on the beach alone for hours by their mother while she hunts for food; the baby seal will be fine as long as we don't interfere.

**The most enjoyable route to Lola Lake—more of a wetland in winter and a swath of yellow grass in summer—is via the secluded beach from the north. A lagoon might block your way between parking lot and beach in the winter, however. In that case approach it from the tiny trailhead at the south end, just off US 101. Crook Point is only the second mainland site to be added to Oregon Islands National Wildlife Refuge, the vast complex of islands and offshore reefs all along the Oregon coast. The rocks off the headland have the second-highest density of nesting seabirds on the Oregon coast; the grassy headland itself, with its unusual geological formations, is home to rare plant species. This route stays within the adjacent state park and off the refuge land (where people aren't allowed).**

### GETTING THERE

Immediately south of the Pistol River Bridge (south of milepost 339, US Highway 101), turn west into the Pistol River State Scenic Viewpoint parking area. Alternately use the south trailhead, a tiny pullout on the west side of US 101 just north of milepost 341. It is best approached from the north; watch for it carefully on the right just past where the guardrail ends. (If you approached from the south, you would have to cross two lanes of fast traffic to tuck in.) You know you're at the right spot if you see a small blue, black, and

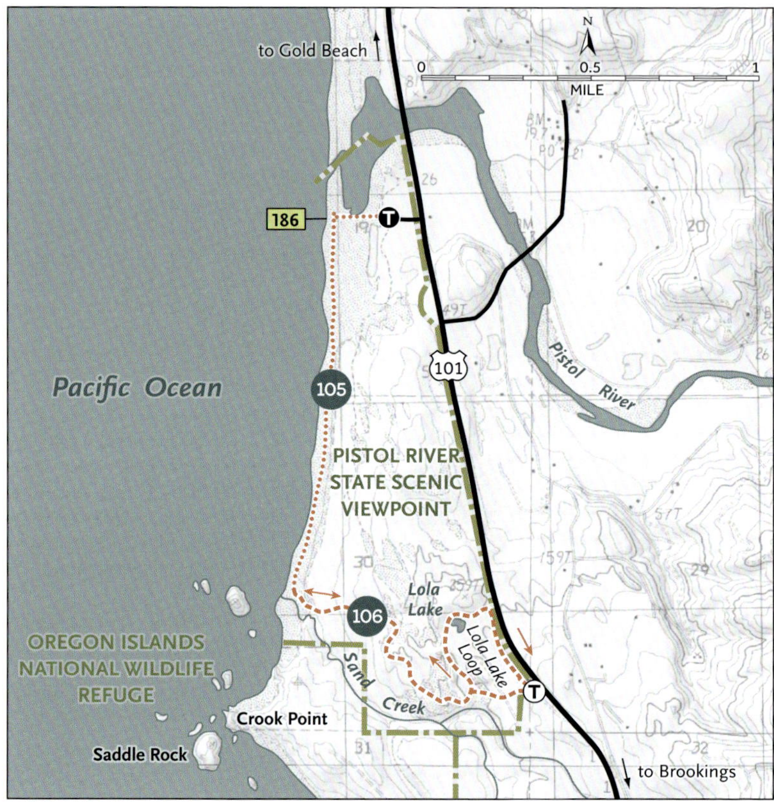


white Oregon Coast Trail (OCT) sign and a path leading into the woods.

## ON THE TRAIL

From the Pistol River State Scenic Viewpoint parking area, cross the (dry) lagoon, climb over the foredune, and head south on the beach for 1.3 miles, to the mouth of little Sand Creek, about 0.2 mile north of the end of the beach and the start of Crook Point. Scramble across the driftwood pile at the bottom of the creek to find and follow an OCT trail-marker post across the dunes. Overhanging beachgrass partially obscures the route; just follow your feet and a few white-topped trail posts painted with black U-shaped symbols (representing horseshoes; the trail is also used by horseback riders). At 0.3 mile from the beach, enter an open bowl of sand; cross it and rejoin the trail at the wooden "coast trail" sign. From here the trail climbs and contours around hillside ravines, mostly on soft sands, in and out of cool spruce forest and open piney dunes. At 0.75 mile from the

*Among the mixture of wayfinding signs between Lola Lake Loop and the ocean is one that apparently points the way for equestrians (as well as hikers).*

beach you'll reach a junction with Lola Lake Loop. Bear left here, then take a sharp right, ascending to a narrow dune ridge through the forest and, ultimately, above the edge of Lola Lake. From a viewpoint at the end of the lake, the trail descends and runs parallel to US 101 to rejoin the main trail about 0.6 mile from where you left it, just short of the trailhead off US 101. Bear right to follow the main trail back to the start of the loop and back to the beach. Retrace your beach walk back to the parking area south of the Pistol River. The lake's name commemorates Lola Gardner, a naturalist and longtime resident of Pistol River. The trails here were apparently built (and signed) by local volunteers, perhaps led by trails enthusiast and former state legislator Walt Schroeder; Oregon State Parks managers take no credit for them (nor blame for the narrow trails and lack of signage).

If you start at the south end of the route, you'll connect with the loop trail just a few steps from where you hit the main trail. Either go left to head to the beach first or do a counterclockwise walk on the loop and then head to the beach. You could, of course, shorten the hike to just the 1-mile loop, but what would be the fun in that?

## BOARDMAN TO THE BORDER

Samuel H. Boardman State Scenic Corridor winds along 12 miles of US Highway 101, but the spectacular, rocky shoreline it protects isn't visible from a car window. You need to stop and walk on parts of the park's 20 miles of hiking trails to see the natural bridges, arch rocks, and pocket beaches that characterize this coast. The long, narrow park offers many options for day hikes from very short to a dozen or more miles; this guide suggests a few hikes among many, and each can be lengthened if you find yourself feeling ambitious. With many unsigned spur trails, it's easy to get temporarily confused, but not actually lost. Be aware that the trail is constantly going up or down, there are vault toilets at only three sites (Arch Rock, Whaleshead Beach, and Lone Ranch Beach Picnic Areas), and no drinking water (or camping) anywhere. The closest public campground is at Harris Beach State Park, on the northern fringe of Brookings. A few miles out of town there's more camping along the Chetco River at Alfred A. Loeb State Park.

Brookings and Harbor are the commercial anchors of the south coast; they function as one town separated by the Chetco River. You can't see the ocean as you travel through on US 101, but if you know where to go you can enjoy spectacular coastline vistas and short walks just blocks from the highway. Consider a walk out Chetco Point (Beach Access 194), a dramatic headland just west of the city's clifftop water treatment facility; a short asphalt path leads down to the shoreline and back up before crossing a narrow gap on a footbridge and ending at a plateau with nearly 360 degrees of ocean views (0.8 mile roundtrip, less than 100 feet elevation gain). Not too far out of town are a couple hikes through the world's northernmost coast redwood groves.

## 107 Secret Beach

RATING/DIFFICULTY: ***/1–2
ROUNDTRIP: 1 to 2.9 miles
ELEV GAIN: 100 to 900 feet

**Contact:** Samuel H. Boardman State Scenic Corridor; **Notes:** Dogs on-leash. Closest toilets are at Arch Rock Picnic Area; **GPS:** Arch Rock Picnic Area 42.20488°, –124.37349°

**Secret Beach feels like a little piece of tropical paradise wedged into a niche on the southern Oregon coast, with hidden coves, blue-green water, and a waterfall spilling onto the sand. A visit at low tide allows you to sneak down the coast as far as the rocks allow—which isn't very far. There is a very quick way to get there, down a short, steep, unsigned social trail straight down from the highway, but there's little parking and it can be slippery. Instead make a hike out of it by starting at one of these three trailheads. The longer hike you take, the more you'll experience Boardman's charms—forested cliffs, arch rocks, and offshore islands. You'll need to do some careful scrambling down a rock face to get to the beach itself. To the north is a little cove, and to the left a waterfall where Miner Creek drops to the beach. If the tide is very low, you may be able to explore a little farther to the south.**

### GETTING THERE

Arch Rock Picnic Area, in Boardman State Scenic Corridor (SSC), is off US Highway 101 just north of milepost 345. Spruce

Island Viewpoint trailhead in Boardman SCC is at a gravel pullout along US 101 at milepost 345. Thunder Rock Cove trailhead, in Boardman SCC, is at a gravel pullout along US 101 just north of milepost 346.

*Scramble down from trail to rock to reach tiny Secret Beach; go at low tide to reach a little more beach to the north and south.*

## ON THE TRAIL

Here are three suggestions for reaching Secret Beach on foot.

**1 mile roundtrip.** From Thunder Rock Cove trailhead, pick up the trail heading north. The trail descends 0.5 mile, crosses Miner Creek on a footbridge, and curves around to a view of Secret Beach about 25 feet below. Return as you came.

**2.2 miles roundtrip.** From Spruce Island Viewpoint trailhead, look for the trail leading south from the south end of the parking area. Entering the woods, the trail climbs quickly, then begins to descend Deer Point through a ghostly spruce forest to a dramatic view of flatiron-shaped Spruce Island. The route continues no more than a spruce's width from the cliff's edge, rounding a steep-walled cove. It switchbacks up almost to the highway, runs alongside it for a short stretch, then veers west and descends to, at 1.1 miles, the viewpoint just above Secret Beach. Return as you came.

**2.9 miles roundtrip.** From Arch Rock Picnic Area, look for the trail leading south from the upper corner of the parking area. The trail climbs a bit, then rolls along the hillside to Spruce Island Viewpoint; walk through the parking pullout and pick up the trail at the south end, then follow the description above. Return as you came. Consider a short side trip to a view of Arch Rock before leaving the picnic area.

## 108 China Beach

RATING/DIFFICULTY: ***/1

ROUNDTRIP: 1.5 miles

ELEV GAIN: 430 feet

**Contact:** Samuel H. Boardman State Scenic Corridor; **Notes:** Dogs on-leash; **GPS:** 42.20488°, –124.37349°

**An easy trail leads to the lovely China Beach, the most remote beach in**

to Gold Beach
Arch Rock
Arch Rock Picnic Area
Spruce Island Viewpoint trailhead
Spruce Island
107
Miner Creek
Deer Point
Thunder Rock Cove trailhead
Secret Beach
Wridge Creek
Natural Bridges Viewpoint trailhead
Dunning Creek
Natural Bridges
Horse Prairie Creek
Pacific Ocean
108
SAMUEL H BOARDMAN STATE SCENIC CORRIDOR
Spruce Creek
China Beach
101
China Creek
North Island Viewpoint trailhead
Thomas Creek
Thomas Creek Bridge
0
0.5
1
MILE
to Brookings

*China Beach, in Boardman State Scenic Corridor, is accessible by trail from the north or south; if it's high tide, approach from the north to avoid getting stuck behind a minor headland.*

Boardman State Scenic Corridor. Trails approach it from the north and south, but a headland blocks access to the beach from the north at high tide; this approach gets you onto the beach regardless of tide. You'll want to explore the 0.8-mile-long beach too (or 0.6 mile if you have to stay north of the point due to tide). If

**tide allows, consider extending your hike north on the Oregon Coast Trail (OCT), but only at low to mid-tide or you'll get stuck on the beach north of the point and need to hike back up the OCT to the next highway parking area and walk back on the highway shoulder.**

### GETTING THERE

In Boardman State Scenic Corridor, park at North Island Viewpoint trailhead, 0.4 mile north of Thomas Creek Bridge between US Highway 101 mileposts 347 and 348.

### ON THE TRAIL

The trail leading out of the gravel parking area immediately splits; bear right and begin a slow descent to the beach. (Ignore the social trail that veers west and continue hiking northwest.) Approaching the beach, the trail steepens, and you'll need to climb over cobbles and driftwood to get to the sandy shore. After exploring the beach, look for the bottom of the trail where a creek trickles into the beach, and return as you came.

### EXTEND YOUR HIKE

If tide allows, consider picking up the OCT heading up the hillside just north of the headland that splits the beach and follow it northbound to enjoy more of Boardman State Scenic Corridor.

## 109 Indian Sands

RATING/DIFFICULTY: **/2
ROUNDTRIP: 2.5 miles
ELEV GAIN: 1,080 feet

**Contact:** Samuel H. Boardman State Scenic Corridor; **Notes:** Dogs on-leash; **GPS:** 42.16278°, –124.35840°

**People have been visiting Indian Sands for a long time—at least 12,000 years, in fact. It's the oldest archaeological site on the Oregon**

*Rising mist softens the landscape at Indian Sands, in Boardman State Scenic Corridor.*

coast. But it's the beauty of this sandy landscape perched high above the ocean that draws hikers. Alongside broad, open sand dunes, wind and water have carved ocher sandstone cliffs into fantastic shapes. The color of the rock is particularly striking late in the afternoon. This route gives you a satisfying short hike, but there's a much shorter route to Indian Sands if you're in a hurry; a 0.2-mile trail begins at the large Indian Sands trailhead parking area just south of US 101 milepost 348.

## GETTING THERE

Drive to just north of milepost 348 on US Highway 101 and pull off at the large parking area south of Thomas Creek Bridge.

## ON THE TRAIL

From the parking area, bear left to follow the trail down a draw, into a forest, and across a hillside, then back nearly to US 101 at 0.5 mile. Follow the trail just below the highway guardrail a short distance and continue as it heads west to a broad viewpoint northward, then descends along the contour of a steep draw, climbs over a saddle, and leads onto the dunes at Indian Sands at 1.2 miles. Continue through the open dunes a short distance (you'll see signs for Beach Access 188, but there is no actual beach access) and return as you came.

## EXTEND YOUR HIKE

Consider following the Oregon Coast Trail (OCT) another 0.9 mile south (bypassing the spur to the Indian Sands parking area) to the top of the Whaleshead Beach access road and continuing down to the beach (see Hike 110), unless you set up a one-way hike with a shuttle car.

# 110 Whaleshead Beach Loop

RATING/DIFFICULTY: **/2

LOOP: 3.6 miles

ELEV GAIN: 850 feet

**Contact:** Samuel H. Boardman State Scenic Corridor; **Notes:** Dogs on-leash. Vault toilets along trail at Whaleshead Beach (Beach Access 189); **GPS:** 42.14705°, –124.35538°

*Whaleshead Beach is easier to reach than other beaches in Boardman State Scenic Corridor, with the option of a loop hike.* (Photo by Donna Scurlock)

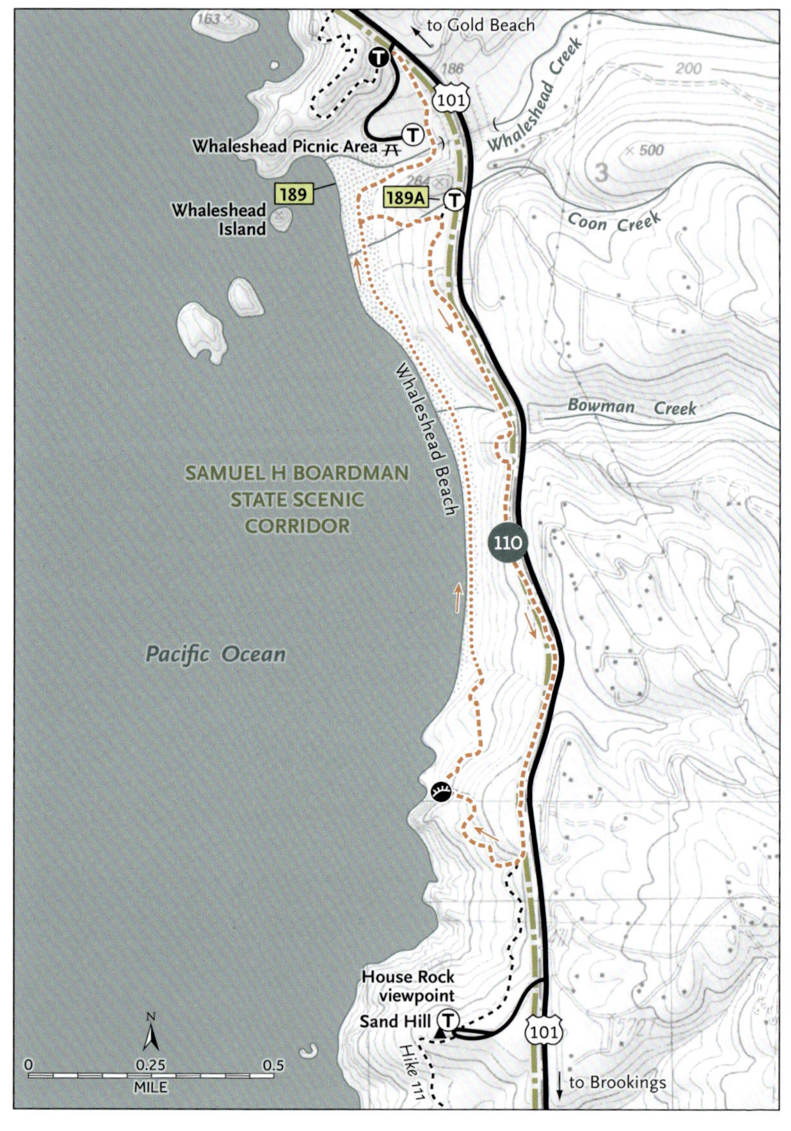

to Gold Beach
101
Whaleshead Creek
200
186
163
Whaleshead Picnic Area
189
189A
Whaleshead Island
500
3
Coon Creek
Whaleshead Beach
Bowman Creek
SAMUEL H BOARDMAN
STATE SCENIC
CORRIDOR
110
Pacific Ocean
House Rock
viewpoint
Sand Hill
101
Hike 111
to Brookings
0
0.25
0.5
MILE
N

**The headland at the north end of this beach bears a resemblance to a certain marine mammal, which gave the headland, the beach, and the creek at the beach's north end its name. It's a sweet beach for an out-and back walk if your vehicle can handle the access road to the lower parking area. Alternately, if your party is nimble and up for an adventure, try this loop involving beach and upland trail. They're both alternate routes on the Oregon Coast Trail (OCT), but that doesn't mean they're easy; you will need to do a steep scramble up or down at either end of the beach to complete the loop. Avoid this hike if it's been rainy and trails are muddy.**

## GETTING THERE

Turn west off US Highway 101 at the sign to Whaleshead Beach, just south of milepost 349, and immediately pull into the gravel parking area on your right. The trail description starts here (in part because the road down to the beach is rough and recommended for four-wheel-drive vehicles only). Alternately you can join this loop at the end of the beach road (at Beach Access 189) or at a gravel parking area off US 101 about 0.5 mile to the south. You can also start at House Rock Viewpoint at the top of Sand Hill, just south of milepost 351; look for the trail leading north out of the parking area's west end. It joins the loop trail in 0.8 miles, making this a longer (5.2-mile) lollipop trail.

## ON THE TRAIL

From the parking area at the top of Whaleshead Beach Road, peer across the road and look carefully for an OCT marker in the shrubbery at the end of the highway guardrail. Follow this narrow trail down the hill; it could be very overgrown, especially near the top. At 0.25 mile you'll pass the park's vault toilets and parking area; continue on the trail, crossing a footbridge and following Whaleshead Creek until the trail ends at the beach at 0.4 mile. In a scant 0.2 mile look for a scramble trail leading about 200 feet up the steep hillside; climb up it with care and top out at the gravel parking for Beach Access 189A.

Now look for the trail (possibly signed "Oregon Coast Trail" or "Coast Trail") heading south near the middle of the parking area. It quickly becomes a fairly level path through the forest above the beach. About 0.5 mile from the parking area there's a spur to the right; it's just a viewpoint loop that immediately rejoins the main trail. At the next junction, 0.7 mile farther, turn right to the beach to loop back. Things get tricky as you approach the bottom of this trail, where the trail has essentially slid away; take great care descending here. Complete the loop by walking the beach north 0.9 mile to the Beach Access 189 parking area and reconnecting with the OCT behind the vault toilets; a left leads up the brushy trail and back to where you started.

# 111 House Rock Viewpoint to Lone Ranch Beach

RATING/DIFFICULTY: ***/3
ROUNDTRIP: 4 miles
ELEV GAIN: 990 feet

**Contact:** Samuel H. Boardman State Scenic Corridor; **Notes:** Dogs on-leash. Vault toilets at Lone Ranch Beach; **GPS:** 42.11810°, –124.35235°

**This section of the Oregon Coast Trail (OCT) leads through deep forest to grassy, windy Cape Ferrelo—not the tallest cape on the coast, but one with outstanding**

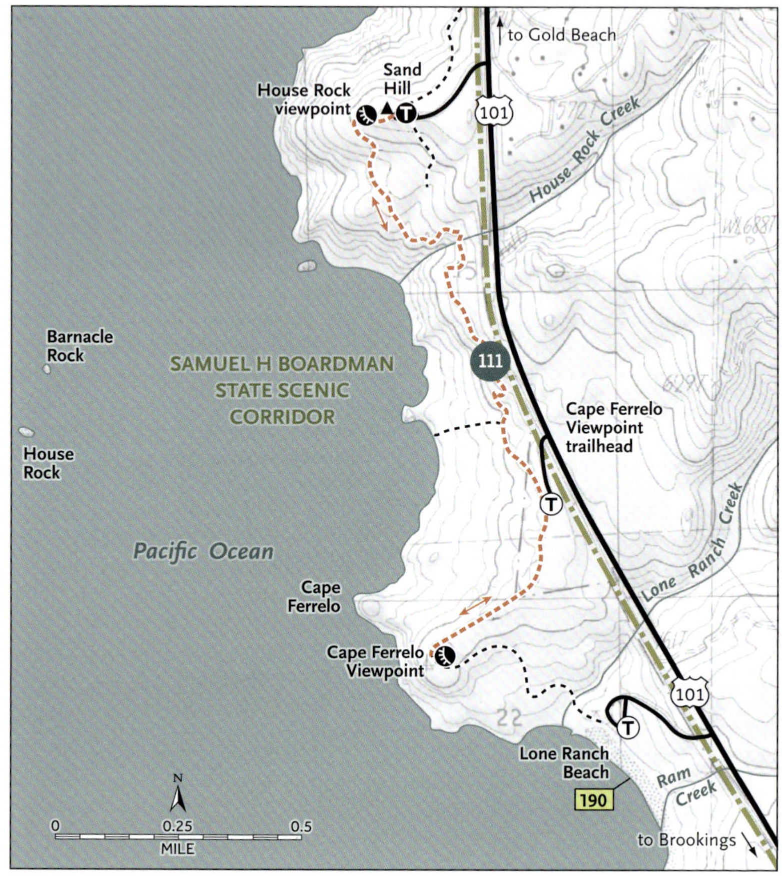


views nonetheless. Turn around there for a 3.6-mile roundtrip hike, or continue on to Lone Ranch Beach just 1 mile farther and the southern end of Samuel H. Boardman State Scenic Corridor. At low tide, scattered rocks form tide pools at the end of the beach. Cape Ferrelo is a good south coast whale-watching spot, particularly in winter and spring.

## GETTING THERE

Southbound on US Highway 101 past milepost 351, turn west into the parking area for House Rock Viewpoint.

*The trail south from House Rock Viewpoint leads to Lone Ranch Beach.*

## ON THE TRAIL

Look for an OCT post off the parking area's southwest corner heading west. (There's another trail starting just to the left of this one; don't take it.) The trail heads south, mostly descending through the woods, to emerge at about 1 mile onto open grassy slopes approaching Cape Ferrelo. At 1.3 miles a spur leads west to a tiny beach, reportedly known to locals as a nude beach. Continue on the main trail to the parking area at Cape Ferrelo Viewpoint and look for OCT posts leading southwest 0.2 mile to a hilltop junction. From here the tip of the cape is just 0.25 mile west; definitely check it out. From the tip of the cape the trail continues down the hillside, but it gets very overgrown; instead, return to the junction and return as you came for a 3.5-mile roundtrip. Otherwise continue south on the main trail for a gentle descent to the north end of Lone Ranch Beach. Return as you came, unless you have a shuttle car and can make a one-way, 2-mile hike (southern access is at Lone Ranch Picnic Area, Beach Access 190, off US 101 south of milepost 352).

## 112 Beach Walks: Brookings Beaches

The coastline at the towns of Brookings and Harbor is rocky and mostly inaccessible, but among the rocky headlands are some sweet, short beaches and, at Chetco Point, a tall footbridge to a broad ocean view (details in

## THE ENDANGERED DRIFT LOG

*A tangle of roots from a big tree washed onto the sand north of Cannon Beach—and parked itself.*

Oregon's ocean beaches used to be piled high with drift logs. They haven't been declared an endangered species, but as critical as their role is in ocean, seashore, and estuarine ecology, perhaps they should be. Drift logs block windblown sand, helping to build beaches and stabilize dunes. They batter rocky shorelines and open up attachment sites for less dominant intertidal species. In estuaries, drift logs serve many purposes, providing nurseries for spruce seedlings and cover for salmon and steelhead smolts. In the open ocean, drifting logs provide food and habitat for species ranging from tiny ocean strider insects to schools of tuna. So leave that log on the beach. And don't build a fire against a log or in a pile of driftwood (it's against the law in Oregon).

Boardman to the Border). Beach access isn't obvious from US 101, so here's a guide to getting on the beach at Brookings–Harbor.

**Harris Beach Day Use**

ONE-WAY DISTANCE: 0.4 mile

**Easy-to-access beach offers views of Goat Island and smaller offshore rocks.**

### Beach Access

BA 191, in Harris Beach State Park; bear left where a right turn leads to the campground. Restrooms. OPRD day-use fee.

**Harris Beach South**

ONE-WAY DISTANCE: 0.4 mile

**A bumpy and somewhat steep asphalt trail leads to the beach.**

### Beach Access

BA 192, in Harris Beach State Park; park just inside park entrance. OPRD day-use fee.

**Mill Beach**

ONE-WAY DISTANCE: 0.4 mile

**The beach curves past Table Rock and grants views of Chetco Point.**

### Beach Access

BA 193: From US 101 in Brookings, turn south onto Mill Beach Road, then in 0.4 mile left on Macklyn Cove Drive and left again where the road splits; there are four parking spots just below and four more at the road's end.

*The northern of two beaches at Harris Beach State Park invites short walks with views of the region's garden of offshore rocks.*

**Sports Haven Beach**

ONE-WAY DISTANCE: 0.8 mile

**Popular dog-walking beach stretches from the Chetco River south jetty to cliffs and offshore rocks perched to the south.**

### Beach Access

BA 195, in Harbor, off Boat Basin Road via Lower Harbor Road; park between beach and RV park. Also accessible via 0.2-mile walk on south jetty from the end of Boat Basin Road.

## 113 Beach Walk: McVay Beach to Winchuck River

ONE-WAY DISTANCE: 2.5 miles

South of the craggy coastline at Brookings–Harbor lies a stretch of sand known mostly to locals. McVay Rock State Recreation Site sits among the commercial lily fields north of the Winchuck River. A big grass field invites kite-flying, Frisbee-tossing, or playing with the family dog. To the west lies the beach and, just offshore, a collection of rock monoliths, though the park is named for a nearby on-shore monolith commemorating an early nineteenth-century settler. The beach itself is steep and narrow, the sand is coarse, and it's not remote; houses are scattered along the shore. But the joy of this beach includes broad tidepools to explore at low tide and rocks to appreciate at any tide. There are offshore sea stacks with caves and arches, onshore boulders, and multicolored gravels—and in places, large cobbles—from the Klamath Mountains, stones in hues of gray and green and crimson and ocher and white, smoothed by the intertidal tumbler.

### BEACH ACCESS

BA 196, McVay Rock State Recreation Site, off Oceanview Drive, south of Brookings–Harbor. Parking.

*Headlands shorten the walkable beach near McVay Rock; visit at low tide.*

BA 197, Winchuck North Access, immediately north of Winchuck River Bridge, off US 101 south of Brookings–Harbor. Parking.

### WHERE TO WALK

**From McVay Rock State Recreation Site.** A short trail leads from the southwest corner of the lawn and down to the beach. The beach stretches north about 1 mile to a rocky point and south 1.5 miles to the Winchuck River, though a rock outcrop 0.4 mile south of McVay Rock access can be rounded only at low tide. In summer you may be able to wade the Winchuck River mouth at low tide; conditions vary considerably.

**From Winchuck River access.** Only at low tide can you hope to get much of a beach walk from here, and generally only in summer; otherwise the river stops you southbound and the headland stops you northbound.

## 114 Oregon Redwoods Trail

RATING/DIFFICULTY: **/2

LOOP: 2.2 miles

ELEV GAIN: 350 feet

**Contact:** USFS Gold Beach Ranger District; **Notes:** Dogs on-leash. Vault toilet; **GPS:** 42.00839°, –124.14720°

**This loop hike takes you into one of the northernmost groves of coast redwoods in the world. While not as impressive as some of the old-growth redwoods in California's national and state parks across the border, there are some big trees on this loop, and this mixed**

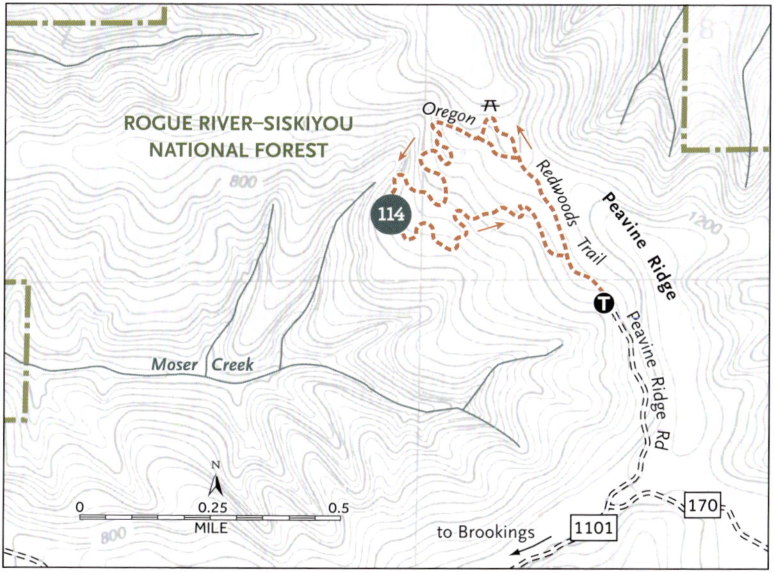

*Oregon's northernmost redwood groves tend to be found mixed with other tree species such as Douglas-fir and hemlock.*

coastal forest has its own charms, with Douglas-fir and hemlocks among the redwoods and an airy understory of evergreen huckleberry, rhododendrons, and ferns. It's similar to but longer than Redwood Nature Trail at Alfred Loeb State Park, on the Chetco River northeast of Brookings.

## GETTING THERE

From US Highway 101 south of Brookings south of milepost 362, turn east onto

Winchuck River Road and drive 1.6 miles, then turn right across the Winchuck River onto gravel Peavine Ridge Road and continue 4 miles to the trailhead at the road's end. (Road is slow and bumpy but passable for passenger cars.)

## ON THE TRAIL

From the trailhead kiosk, walk 0.1 mile and bear right at the junction, then right again at 0.4 mile, passing tall, straight redwoods and equally majestic snags of older trees. Past a picnic table you'll soon reach another junction. For a short walk on this wide and nearly level trail, bear left here to return to the trailhead for an easy 0.7-mile loop. Otherwise turn right and begin to plunge down the hillside, winding in and out of ravines. At about 1.4 miles the trail begins to ascend, ultimately rejoining the easier loop path at that first junction and leading back to the trailhead.

## 115 Beach Walk: Winchuck River to Pelican State Beach

ONE-WAY DISTANCE: 0.7 mile

The short beach here is Oregon's southernmost. Crissey Field State Recreation Site houses a welcome center for travelers, with interpretive exhibits and advice for motorists, and serves as the official end of the Oregon Coast Trail (OCT) for thru-hikers. It's also a model of sustainable construction. Solar panels heat the building's water and provide power to Coos-Curry Electric Co-op, and the earth warms the building in the winter and cools it in the summer.

*Driftwood tends to accumulate between the beach and the visitor center at Crissey Field.*

## BEACH ACCESS

BA 198, Crissey Field State Recreation Site, off US 101 just north of the California border and milepost 363. Parking. Restrooms open 8 a.m. to dusk in summer; hours limited in winter.

Pelican State Beach, south of the California border off US 101. Dogs not allowed on beach. Parking.

## WHERE TO WALK

**From the Winchuck.** From the river's south bank (or the beach in front of the welcome center), it's about 0.3 mile to the (invisible) border with California, and another 0.4 mile to beach access at California State Parks' Pelican State Beach. The beach runs out at a headland 0.2 mile farther.

# Acknowledgments

A broad thank you to the friends and family who have accompanied me on many of these hikes, and for letting me pick the day's trail. I am especially grateful to my longtime friend Betsy Ayres, who has welcomed me to stay in "Bonnie's apartment" on the north coast these many years. Ditto to Donna Scurlock and her "annex" on the central coast.

I want to thank all those who support two organizations that work hard to protect the Oregon coast for people and other animals. North Coast Land Conservancy (nclctrust.org) connects and conserves wild lands from the Columbia River to Siletz Bay in perpetuity. Next time you're in Cannon Beach, look south to the jagged horizon, home to plants and animals found nowhere else on Earth: These mountains will never again be logged, thanks to NCLC. Trailkeepers of Oregon (trailkeepersoforegon.org) helps make it possible for us to hike the coast by marshaling volunteers to maintain existing trails, some of which are nearly a century old and take a lot of pounding from the weather and our own footfalls. TKO is also leading efforts to maintain and expand the Oregon Coast Trail.

It is a privilege to work with the editors at Mountaineers Books, whose high standards ensure that all their guidebooks are accurate (and attractive). Thanks for supporting this independent, nonprofit book publisher.

# Land Managers

**City of Cannon Beach**
www.ci.cannon-beach.or.us
**City of Lincoln City**
www.lincolncity.org
**City of Warrenton**
www.ci.warrenton.or.us
**City of Yachats**
www.yachatsoregon.org
**Curry County**
www.co.curry.or.us
**Lewis and Clark National Historical Park**
www.nps.gov/lewi
**Nestucca Bay National Wildlife Refuge**
www.fws.gov/refuge/nestucca-bay
**New River Area of Critical Environmental Concern, Bureau of Land Management**
www.blm.gov/visit/new-river-area-critical-environmental-concern
**North Coast Land Conservancy**
www.nclctrust.org
**Oregon Islands National Wildlife Refuge**
www.fws.gov/refuge/oregon-islands
**Oregon Parks and Recreation Department**
www.oregonstateparks.org
**Siuslaw National Forest**
www.fs.usda.gov/detail/siuslaw/about-forest/offices
**South Slough National Estuarine Research Reserve**
www.oregon.gov/dsl/ss/pages/default.aspx
**The Nature Conservancy in Oregon**
www.nature.org/en-us/about-us/where-we-work/united-states/oregon
**Tillamook County Parks**
www.tillamookcounty.gov/parks
**Washington State Parks**
www.parks.wa.gov

**OPPOSITE:** *Tillamook Head looms to the south beyond grassy dunes at Seaside (Beach Walk 9).*

# Resources for Hikers

**Author's website**
www.bonniehendersonwrites.com
**Oregon Coast Visitors Association**
www.visittheoregoncoast.com
**Trailkeepers of Oregon**
www.trailkeepersoforegon.org

## NORTH COAST

**Astoria/Warrenton Area Chamber of Commerce**
www.oldoregon.com
**Cannon Beach Chamber of Commerce**
www.cannonbeach.org
**Depoe Bay Chamber of Commerce**
www.discoverdepoebay.org
**Greater Newport Chamber of Commerce**
www.newportchamber.org
**Hatfield Visitor Center**
seagrant.oregonstate.edu/visitor-center
**Jetty Fishery (Nehalem Bay)**
www.jettyfishery.com
**Lincoln City Visitors & Convention Bureau**
www.explorelincolncity.com
**Oregon Coast Aquarium**
www.aquarium.org
**Pacific City–Nestucca Valley Chamber of Commerce**
www.pcnvchamber.org
**Rockaway Beach Chamber of Commerce**
www.rockawaybeach.net
**Seaside Chamber of Commerce and Visitors' Bureau**
www.seasideor.com
**Tillamook Chamber of Commerce**
www.tillamookchamber.org

## CENTRAL COAST

**Florence Area Chamber of Commerce**
www.florencechamber.com
**Reedsport/Winchester Bay Chamber of Commerce**
www.reedsportcc.org
**Waldport Chamber of Commerce**
www.findyourselfinwaldport.com
**Yachats Area Chamber of Commerce**
www.yachats.org

## SOUTH COAST

**Bandon Chamber of Commerce**
www.bandon.com
**Bandon Dunes Golf Resort**
www.bandondunesgolf.com
**Bay Area Chamber of Commerce (Coos Bay–North Bend)**
www.oregonsbayareachamber.com
**Brookings Visitor Center**
www.brookings.or.us/9/Visiting
**Gold Beach Visitor Center**
www.visitgoldbeach.com

**OPPOSITE:** *The trail over Tillamook Head grants occasional glimpses of steep seaward cliffs (Hike 12).*

# Index



**OPPOSITE:** *Boardwalks keep your feet dry on South Slough Trail at Fort Clatsop (Hike 7).*

# 1% for Trails

Where would we be without trails? Not very far into the wilderness. That's why Mountaineers Books designates 1 percent of sales of select guidebooks in our Day Hiking series toward trail maintenance. Since launching this program, we've contributed more than $39,000 toward improving trails.

For this book, our 1 percent of sales is going to Trailkeepers of Oregon (TKO). Founded in 2007, TKO protects and enhances the Oregon hiking experience through stewardship, advocacy, outreach, and education. Each year, more than three thousand TKO volunteers help design new trails, restore damaged trails, clear fallen logs, and support safe and welcoming experiences on urban and wilderness trails--from the Columbia River Gorge to the Oregon coast and beyond.

Mountaineers Books donates many books to nonprofit recreation and conservation organizations. Our 1% for Trails campaign is one more way we help fellow nonprofit organizations as we work together to get people outside, to both enjoy and protect our wild public lands.

If you'd like to support Mountaineers Books and our nonprofit partnership programs, please visit our website to learn more or contact mbooks@mountaineersbooks.org.

**OPPOSITE:** *Unless there's a surfing competition under way, the beach south of Yaquina Head is quiet (Beach Walk 50).*

# About the Author

Journalist Bonnie Henderson is author of the critically acclaimed *The Next Tsunami: Living on a Restless Coast* and *Strand: An Odyssey of Pacific Ocean Debris*, which was listed as a Best Book of 2008 by the *Seattle Times* and was a finalist for the 2009 Oregon Book Awards. She is also the author of two popular hiking guidebooks, *Hiking the Oregon Coast Trail* and (with co-author Zach Urness) *Best Hikes with Kids: Oregon*. She lives in Eugene, Oregon, and can be found online at bonniehendersonwrites.com.

recreation • lifestyle • conservation

**MOUNTAINEERS BOOKS**, including its two imprints, Skipstone and Braided River, is a leading publisher of quality outdoor recreation, sustainability, and conservation titles. As a 501(c)(3) nonprofit, we are committed to supporting the environmental and educational goals of our organization by providing expert information on human-powered adventure, sustainable practices at home and on the trail, and preservation of wilderness.

Our publications are made possible through the generosity of donors, and through sales of 700 titles on outdoor recreation, sustainable lifestyle, and conservation. To donate, purchase books, or learn more, visit us online:

**MOUNTAINEERS BOOKS**
1001 SW Klickitat Way, Suite 201 • Seattle, WA 98134
800-553-4453 • mbooks@mountaineersbooks.org • www.mountaineersbooks.org

*An independent nonprofit publisher since 1960*

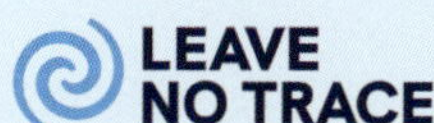


Mountaineers Books is proud to support the Leave No Trace Center for Outdoor Ethics, whose mission is to use the power of science, education, and stewardship to ensure a sustainable future for the outdoors and the planet. The Leave No Trace program is focused specifically on human-powered (nonmotorized) recreation. For more information, visit www.lnt.org.

**YOU MAY ALSO LIKE:**

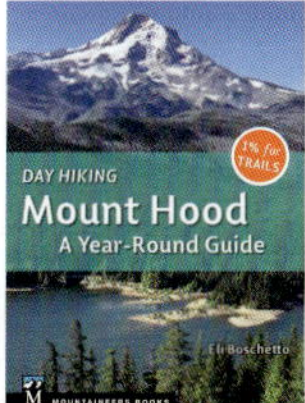